THE ANATOMY OF MANCHESTER UNITED

By Jonathan Wilson

Behind the Curtain: Travels in Eastern European Football
Sunderland: A Club Transformed
Inverting the Pyramid
The Anatomy of England
Brian Clough: Nobody Ever Says Thank You
The Outsider: A History of the Goalkeeper
The Anatomy of Liverpool
Angels with Dirty Faces: The Footballing History of Argentina
The Anatomy of Manchester United

THE ANATOMY OF MANCHESTER UNITED

A History in Ten Matches

JONATHAN WILSON

WEIDENFELD & NICOLSON

First published in Great Britain in 2017 by Orion Books
an imprint of The Orion Publishing Group Ltd
Carmelite House, 50 Victoria Embankment
London EC4Y 0DZ

An Hachette UK Company

1 3 5 7 9 10 8 6 4 2

A CIP catalogue record for this book is
available from the British Library.

ISBN 978-1-4091-4445-8

Typeset by Input Data Services Ltd, Somerset

Printed and bound by CPI Group (UK) Ltd, Croydon, CR0 4YY

www.orionbooks.co.uk

CONTENTS

LIST OF ILLUSTRATIONS

Section One

1. Billy Meredith (Getty).
2. Ernest Mangnall (PA Images).
3. Sandy Turnbull and Knocker West (Getty).
4. More than 71,000 packed in to Crystal Palace for the 1909 FA Cup final (Getty/Bob Thomas/Popperfoto).
5. Sandy Turnbull beats Harry Clay (Getty/Bob Thomas/Popperfoto).
6. Jack Rowley (Getty/Popperfoto).
7. United's captain Johnny Carey (Getty/William Vanderson).
8. Matt Busby (Getty).
9. Roger Byrne (Getty).
10. Duncan Edwards (Getty).
11. Bobby Charlton (Getty/Bob Thomas/Popperfoto).
12. The horror of the crash (PA Images).
13. Brian Kidd (Topfoto).
14. An exhausted Bobby Charlton (Getty/Popperfoto).
15. A 17-year-old George Best (Getty).
16. Frank O'Farrell with Ted MacDougall (PA Images).

Section Two

17. Martin Buchan (Getty/Popperfoto).
18. Wyn 'the Leap' Davies (Getty).
19. Ron Atkinson completes the £1.5 million signing of Bryan Robson (Getty).
20. Bryan Robson puts United 1–0 (Getty).

ACKNOWLEDGEMENTS

Nobody ever writes a non-fiction book alone. This could not have come about without the assistance, advice and generosity of a huge number of people, and thanks are due particularly to all those who offered their time to be interviewed, whether on or off the record.

Thanks to my agent David Luxton, my editor Paul Murphy, my copy-editor John English and all at Orion.

Thanks, as ever, to Kat Petersen for performing her usual miracles with the manuscript and especially for her surprising expertise in the Berlin football clubs of the late 1960s.

Thanks to the staff at the British Library at St Pancras, particularly whoever it was who decided to move the newspaper section from Colindale, sparing me hours on the Northern Line.

And thanks also to John Brewin, Miguel Delaney, Richard Jolly, Andy Mitten, Vladimir Novak, Jack Pitt-Brooke and Rob Smyth for help, suggestions and stimulation.

INTRODUCTION

The first time I was allowed to sit up for *Match of the Day* I was eight. It was November 1984 and because my parents were away I was staying at my gran's. She lived about 200 yards from Roker Park and on that Saturday afternoon we sat in the front room watching *Grandstand*, listening to the roars drifting over the rooftops. Sunderland went 2–0 down to goals from Bryan Robson and Mark Hughes inside quarter of an hour. Clive Walker pulled one back within six seconds of the restart, Dave Hodgson and Hughes were then sent off for some mild fisticuffs and, before half-time, two Walker penalties had Sunderland 3–2 up.

My gran would probably have let me stay up even if I hadn't brazenly claimed that, 'Oh yes, Dad always lets me watch it.' It wasn't just that Sunderland were on television, and had won, both rare enough in what turned out to be a relegation season. It was that this was a win over Manchester United and, even then, even seventeen years after their last league title, that was significant. There was a lustre to their name that seemed out of keeping with their week-to-week performances. I suspect most people of my generation went through a similar process of struggling to reconcile the image of the club with the reality.

My recollection of much of the sport I watched in the mid-eighties is far sharper than of games I watched a week or two ago. I suspect this is just how memory works, that what your brain deems important when you're eight is imprinted there for ever, while even big matches blur and merge when you're watching a dozen games a week. Looking back, I was clear that the second game on *Match of the Day* that week was Oxford United coming from 2–0 down to beat Leeds 5–2 and that Peter Lorimer was sent off for the crime of being punched, but I thought, just as an experiment, it was worth digging out the footage of that Sunderland v United game on YouTube. The goalscorers and the sendings off I remembered clearly enough, and my sense of it having been a windy day, the pitch dry and a little awkward, was accurate. But other aspects I'd misremembered completely. I'd totally forgotten, for instance, Norman Whiteside hitting the bar early on, and the delicious ball inside the full-back and the Jesper Olsen cross that led to that. I'd thought the two dismissals were at 1–0 rather than 2–1, although I was right about the punctiliousness of the referee, John Key, a prime example of the balding, side-burned portly Yorkshire type, and the harshness of the decision (he also penalised Gary Bailey for time wasting and gave an indirect free-kick in the box – in the first minute). And Ron Atkinson's Gestapo-style black leather overcoat had slipped from my memory completely.

But more significant was my failure to recall quite important detail. In my head, Walker's first was a neat goal after a darting dribble. In fact, it was awful United defending. Tapped kick-off, rolled back, knocked out to Colin West on the left, header on for Walker through the middle, Bailey slow to come out and the ball lofted over him. Perhaps the wind made the flight of the ball hard to judge, but it looked like a failure of concentration from United – the sort of laxity that, in hindsight, was why that team never quite achieved what it perhaps should have done.

The first penalty, I knew, was for a clumsy foul by Bailey on Gary Bennett, although the question of what Sunderland's centre-back should be doing in the opposition box had never occurred to me. Watching it again, I still can't work it out, but what I'd forgotten was that Key was about sixty yards away, dealing with the aftermath of a late challenge by Olsen on Howard Gayle; Gayle's retaliatory kick at the Dane was arguably worse than anything Hughes or Hodgson had done. Similarly the detail of Mike Duxbury, playing at left-back that day, hopelessly misjudging an attempted clearing header, had faded, as had the ridiculousness of Bailey's challenge. This was defending of the most shambolic kind. Bailey's shuffling on his line, feigning one way then the other as Walker approached the ball, seemed very of its era.

I'd been able to recall little of the build-up to the second penalty, but Sunderland's football was excellent – far better than I'd imagined them capable of that season – as Stan Cummins, Peter Daniel and West put together a string of sharp passes, ending with Cummins receiving the return, bursting into the box and being hacked down by a reckless challenge from Gordon McQueen. Why was he lunging in? This was a defence whose mind seemed collectively scrambled; little wonder United also let slip a two-goal lead at Nottingham Forest a fortnight later.

That's the benefit of rewatching old footage. Some aspects that seemed natural now stand out as quirks of the period. With the full knowledge of context, patterns emerge, incidents that lead to future events or that confirm patterns of behaviour become clear. And, most valuable of all, there is detail that adds a richness to interpretation.

'I've seen the first editions,' Sir Alex Ferguson used to like to remind journalists, referring specifically to those from 27 May 1999, the morning after Manchester United completed the Treble by winning the Champions League. In the running copy they'd filed on the final whistle, journalists had written of Bayern's domination, of United's subdued display, of the failure of the rejigged midfield in the absence of Paul Scholes and Roy Keane. Until injury-time, it had seemed like another tale of United underperformance in Europe and the pieces reflected that, with a top and a tail hastily thrown on to describe the astonishing late drama, United yet again, in that season of seasons, conjuring a victory from a game that seemed lost. By the time of the rewrites, written an hour or so later with time for reflection and with the addition of quotes, the tone was very different, glorying in United's success.

Yet it had been the first editions that had more accurately reflected what had happened in the match, before knowledge of the outcome had coloured the perception. Or at least it more accurately reflected how people had felt the game was going at the time – but perhaps they too were influenced by the scoreline. Ferguson himself, in his autobiography, trenchantly argues that David Beckham was 'the most effective midfielder on the park' and that the runs of Ryan Giggs on the right had left the Bayern full-back Michael Tarnat constantly calling for cover, gradually wearing down the defence until they were rendered too exhausted properly to defend those two decisive late corners. Perhaps Ferguson too is guilty of filtering history through his knowledge of what subsequently happened.

'You can't validate the process through the results,' as the Spanish coach Juanma Lillo told Sid Lowe in Issue One of *The Blizzard*. 'Human beings tend to venerate what finished well, not what was done well. We attack what ended up badly, not what was done badly ... Bayern Munich are a great team in the ninetieth minute when they are winning the Champions League and in the ninety-second minute they're rubbish. How can that be? ... The thing is, *después del visto todo el mundo es listo*: everyone's a genius after the event. I call them prophets of the past. And yet they are wrong even to evaluate the process in the light solely of how it came out in the end.'

The quest for an explicatory narrative does more than that: it also destroys nuance. No game follows a simple path. It is almost never a case of one team being better and so winning. There are always ebbs and flows, moments when the match threatens to tip one way and then goes the other. Football is not always fair. Myths build up around games, individual moments are hailed as decisive. When Brian Clough didn't talk to his players between the end of normal time and the beginning of extra-time in the 1991 FA Cup final, it was seen as a decisive failure in Nottingham Forest's defeat; when, as Derby

County manager, he had done the same in a League Cup tie away to Tottenham two decades earlier, it had been hailed as an act of genius because Derby went on to win. Victory is the great validator.

That's why, if we are really to understand football's past and draw meaningful lessons from it, there is need to go back to the sources, the games themselves, and to subject them to forensic examination. This book provides close readings of ten key games in the history of Manchester United, from their first FA Cup success in 1909 through to the strangely consolatory success in the FA Cup final of 2016. For the first game no video footage exists and for the second two there are only brief highlights (it's one of the great losses of English football history that all that remains of the 1948 FA Cup final, reputedly one of the greatest finals there has been, is the Pathé news footage). The descriptions of those games have had to be compiled from old match reports and interviews, a process that reveals both the fallibility of memory and the difficulty of writing copy without the benefit of press-box replays: one man's routine save is another's incredible parry, crosses are put in and blocks made by a variety of possible players, chances that are key in one paper pass without mention in another. But on the other hand, match reports in those days tended to be relayed as the match was going on and so are less prone to be influenced by knowledge of the result; as a consequence they offer a more accurate sense of the feel of the game even if specifics at times get lost. Compiling a coherent narrative is an act of consensus.

For the other seven games, I've been through the video again and again, looking for patterns, trying to carve through the thickets of a sport that continues to confound easy analysis to find the pathways that explain the game. There must also be, though, a sense of context. Each game is part of a sequence, whether good or bad, and it will always be influenced by personnel and the prevailing ideology. Circumstances, equally, play their part, whether sporting or to do with the wider world. The ten games discussed here have been selected not because they are necessarily the best games Manchester United have been involved in, or even the most important in terms of happening in the latter stages of competitions, but because they highlight wider trends, or because they lie on the fault lines of history, marking the end of one era or the beginning of the next.

And because this is United, there is perhaps additional resonance. From the completion of Old Trafford in 1910, United have had a significant financial advantage. Yet their history has not been one of sustained success. They may be the most successful club in English league history but their story could also be seen as one of protracted failure alleviated only by three great managers. Only under the second of them, Matt Busby, did United become the most glamorous team in England, a status grimly underpinned by the tragedy of Munich. Since then, though, even in the fallow years between Busby and Ferguson, United have been consistently the biggest team in the country. As such their history is also, to an extent, a history of English football and the possibilities and frustrations it offered its elite.

This is a book that tries to be about football as it was played on the field. It tries to re-evaluate and reassess, to go beyond the white noise of banal player quotes and instant judgements to discover why what happened happened. Of course external events impinge, for at a certain level everything is connected, but it is, as far as possible, a football history.

CHAPTER I

FA Cup final, Crystal Palace, London, 24 April 1909

Bristol City **0–1** **Manchester United**

S Turnbull 22

Bristol City	Manchester United
Harry Clay	Harry Moger
Archie Annan	George Stacey
Joe Cottle	Vince Hayes
Pat Hanlin	Dick Duckworth
Billy Wedlock	Charlie Roberts
Arthur Spear	Alex Bell
Fred Staniforth	Billy Meredith
Bob Hardy	Harold Halse
Sam Gilligan	Jimmy Turnbull
Andy Burton	Sandy Turnbull
Frank Hilton	George Wall
Harry Thickett	Ernest Mangnall

Ref: Jim Mason
Bkd:
Att: 71,401

'**IT WAS VERY EVIDENT TO** the Londoner when he turned out this morning to perform his usual daily duties that it was cup day – or "coop" day as he prefers to call it in ridicule of the northern accent,' reported the London Correspondent of the *Manchester Evening News* on 24 April 1909. Around 60,000 fans made the journey from Manchester, most of them arriving between three and seven in the morning. As some waited at the station for the heavy rain to ease, others took advantage of the offer of shopkeepers on Euston Road for a 'wash and a brush up' for 2d. Numerous restaurants opened at 5 a.m. to provide breakfast for the early arrivals.

A photograph in the *Manchester Evening News* shows a group of fans in matching red-and-white-striped bonnets, glumly looking out at a wet street. One wears a striped suit, and another holds an umbrella bearing the legend 'Rocca's Brigade'. Uncertain as they appear, the general mood before the final against Bristol City was one of excitement and optimism: Manchester United had won the league the previous season, but this was their chance to win the FA Cup for the first time, the primary competition of the age, and so cement the club's position among the elite.

United's title defence had begun to come apart in the October with a run of four games without a victory and by January had collapsed entirely. But as their league form deteriorated, the Cup offered solace. Brighton and Everton were both beaten 1–0 at home, and then Blackburn Rovers were hammered 6–1 to set up a home quarter-final against Burnley.

On an icy pitch and amid heavy snow, United were trailing

1–0 with eighteen minutes remaining when the referee, Herbert Bamlett, decided to abandon the game. So exhausted was he that United's centre-half Charlie Roberts had to blow the final whistle for him. Or at least that was the story that later became accepted as fact. The contemporaneous *Athletic News* report described Bamlett blowing the whistle himself, then consulting his linesmen and the respective club secretaries. 'It is said,' the *Athletic News*'s correspondent noted, 'that Mr Bamlett ought never to have commenced the match, but I will not go so far, as while during the whole of the first half the small snow was blowing with great force into the faces of the United players, the conditions were altogether different in the second half. Football is a winter game and I believe that referees should not abandon matches until absolutely compelled to do so; but after the interval the flakes of real snow were so thick and blinding that, in my opinion, Mr Bamlett was quite justified.'

United won the rearranged game 3–2.

There was bad weather for the semi-final as well, at Bramall Lane against Newcastle United, who were on their way to the league title despite suffering that season what remains the record home defeat in the English top flight, going down 9–1 to Sunderland. Heavy rain made good football all but impossible: 'There was no denying the fact that Manchester were the better team, and they have well-earned the chance of making their first appearance in the final tie,' the *Manchester Evening News* reported. 'The standard of play was not so high as the League records of the clubs led the onlookers to anticipate, but it was a rare struggle for the ninety minutes, and it was only the rare determination of the Manchester side that pulled them through.'

The only goal came from the inside-forward Harold Halse, who would become the first man to play in Cup finals for three different sides. 'A long lob by the half-backs enabled [George] Wall to turn the ball in front of goal,' the *Athletic News* reported. 'Three Manchester men played it – or tried to play it – on the six-yard line. Alec [better known as Sandy] Turnbull fell in the effort and James Turnbull only scraped the ball and while all this was happening, Halse rushed up at full speed and with a fast rocket shot forced the ball up to the roof of the goal.' It was, the *MEN* suggested, 'a shot that [the Newcastle keeper Jimmy] Lawrence probably never saw'.

'Manchester United, with valiant half-backs and a forward line which is distinguished by cleverness and dash, never looked like losing,' said *Athletic News*. 'Just when a drawn game was becoming probable, Halse saved his comrades from another ordeal.'

As United focused increasingly on the Cup, their league form worsened and they won only one of their final fifteen games of the season to finish thirteenth, a run that included a draw and a defeat to Bristol City. A change of kit was required and, with Bristol City opting for blue, United turned out in white with a red V, the shirts bought from Billy Meredith's sports shop and presented to the squad by the music-hall star George Robey.

For fans just as much as the club, the Cup outweighed all else and thousands flocked to London to be roundly patronised by the southern media. 'They bring stone jars of strong ale and sandwiches an inch thick packed in little wicker baskets which can also be used for conveying carrier pigeons,' *The Times* reported.

For Mancunians, the Cup final wasn't just about the match: it was a day out and a chance to see London. As the rain eased, fans began to take brakes around the city on sightseeing tours. 'The fashion in caps in the provinces is evidently not that in London,' the *MEN*'s London correspondent noted. 'I have never seen such pronounced unanimity in colouring as this year. Nearly every cap one sees – and they are largely new for the occasion – is of some shade of green . . . Green has not become at all pronounced even in the suburbs of London for holiday purposes as it is among the visitors today.'

The clash of cultures was a habitual feature of early

newspaper coverage of FA Cup finals. United fans, if the MEN's London man is to be believed, were startled by the market at Covent Garden, where they watched the 'noisy scenes attendant upon the selling of fruit and flowers . . . with interest and not a little amazement.'

A porter outside the Cecil Hotel on the Strand 'caused considerable amusement' by 'drunkenly dancing to a northern concertina'. Other fans played trumpets but, by and large, the MEN correspondent was relieved by the restraint of United fans. 'The demeanour of the people shows generally a great improvement on that of the crowds which have visited us on previous occasions,' he wrote. 'It may please the temperance man to know that less than half the accommodation usually required for the storage of intoxicating liquor was needed this morning.'

The United team stayed at Chingford, their approach to Crystal Palace by coach delayed by vast crowds, many of them apparently fascinated by the three-card sharpers who plied their con on the pavements outside the stadium. Everything seemed exotic. 'With more than superstition,' the MEN reported, 'they regarded as a good omen the dusky figure of an oriental child in a white turban, with blood-coloured flowing robes, which flitted among the crowds.'

But alongside the familiar tropes of excitable aliens abroad in the big city (as though Manchester were some backwater), there was a sense that the final didn't quite live up to those of previous years. 'London was not excited,' said the *Daily Mirror*, taking an admirably equal-opportunities approach to patronising fans. 'The Cockney element did not go to see the game in its usual numbers, with the result that the army of spectators lacked that leaven of hilarity which the light-hearted Londoner imparts to most sporting functions in the Metropolis . . . Then too we lacked the Northumberland element, which had been present in recent years when Newcastle were fighting in the final battle – and we all know the light-heartedness of the Geordie . . .

'Another thing which tended to make the crowd a drab one was the fact that the teams were not playing in their accustomed colours and as all white does not lend itself to spectacular effect the United's supporters could not paint the town with a splash of red, although they did wear red favours and geraniums in their buttonholes. Bristol's partisans wore blue ribbons and violets, but they were never very conspicuous. There were few, if any, flags, decorated toppers, or suits. One man certainly came from Manchester dressed as a footballer, but what is one among many?'

United had the bulk of the support and were widely regarded as favourites, especially given injury had denied City the half-back Reuben Marr, a key figure in the side that had finished runners-up in the league in 1907, and the centre-forward Willis Rippon.

For United, Sandy Turnbull had been a fitness concern until an hour or so before the game when Charlie Roberts, the captain, urged the manager Ernest Mangnall to 'let him play. He might get a goal and if he does, we can afford a passenger.'

Roberts won the toss and, according to the *MEN*, 'decided to play with the wind behind his team', the sort of detail that featured heavily in early match reports, often, it seemed less for any impact it had on the game than through force of habit. Here, though, the wind does seem to have been strong enough to make a difference. 'Bristol City found it necessary to put forth every effort to check their heavier rivals who naturally found some assistance,' reported the *Leeds Mercury*. 'In defence, the Manchester halves and backs could always play coolly, knowing that the breeze would not cause them trouble.'

The *Mercury*'s reporter was generally unimpressed. 'As a display of football, and even as a great struggle, the match proved somewhat disappointing,' he wrote. 'Manchester United played well in the first half and Bristol City, by their sound defence and neatness in combination, did so well that there was every expectation of a thoroughly interesting and high-class game all through. But the form was not maintained, the pace slackened, and at times the play lacked life, while much of the football was scrappy and uncertain.'

The game began at a frenetic tempo, with play seemingly fractured and neither side able to take control. 'Before such a throng and in such conditions, one could excuse the early uncertainty and the opening slips,' said the reporter for the *Lincolnshire Echo*, who seemed generally to have been more enthused than his peers.

'[Billy] Wedlock and Roberts had a tussle in the first minute,' the *MEN* reported and '[Archie] Annan sent the Bristol left away, but [Vince] Hayes kicked clear for [Billy] Meredith to dash off. He dropped the ball on the head of Sandy Turnbull, but [Joe] Cottle met it and kicked clear. The United then took a free-kick, which Cottle kicked away, but [Alex] Bell and [George] Stacey returned the ball, Sandy Turnbull putting round the post.

'When Bristol made their first effort [Bob] Hardy and [Fred] Staniforth showed some really clever play, but when the outside-right centred [Sam] Gilligan put the ball just past the post.'

Or did he? Early match reports, with details scribbled down and then relayed down a phone line, are always heavily focused on the opening minutes and often contradict each other. 'Gilligan was the first to infuse the real Cup-tie fire into the battle,' reported the excitable man from the *Lincolnshire Echo*. 'He had a great run and his first drive at goal shook the United post.

'Then followed a bout between Wedlock and Turnbull in which the brainy Bristol player came out with flying colours but in the next moment the Manchester front rank made a magnificent onslaught on City's citadel. Meredith had a terrific shot, which staggered the Bristol custodian and then Wall, from the other side, sent in a shot like a cannon-ball.'

In that, there is at least corroboration. 'It was a grand, high drive to the far corner,' said the *MEN*, 'but [Harry] Clay made a glorious save, and when the ball was returned into the goal-mouth by Duckworth, Annan headed away.

'Some clever footwork by Roberts saw Manchester make another raid, and after Annan had once beaten him, Wall got the ball across the goal. The wind, however, carried it out.

'From a centre by Meredith, Clay made a poor save as James Turnbull dashed into line, and in clearing Annan was slightly damaged. He, however, soon recovered and, Manchester keeping play at the Bristol end, Meredith forced the first corner. He placed the ball badly, but he did much better with a second one in the next minute, from which Roberts headed into touch.'

Gradually, United began to assert themselves. 'The United,' the *MEN* went on, 'were certainly making the most of a promising start, and a third corner came as the result of clever play by Halse. From this another inch better direction from the head of James Turnbull would have given Manchester a goal, Clay being helpless.

'Then by way of variety Wall took a couple of corners and from the second a terrific drive by Duckworth missed the mark by inches only. Thanks to Wedlock, Bristol at length got away and Hardy put a warm shot into the hands of [Harry] Moger, who pulled the ball round and then punted away.'

The opener finally arrived after twenty-one minutes and justified Mangnall's selection gamble. 'Meredith almost lifted the crossbar off,' reported the *Lincolnshire Echo*, 'and then on the rebound A. Turnbull sent the leather home. Thus was the first goal scored and if ever a goal in a football match had been earned it was this one.'

The *Leeds Mercury* agreed: 'Long before the one goal was scored Bristol City were obviously engaged in a stubborn hustle against a superior side . . . Try as they would, Bristol City could not break away during long periods, and in the course of fully ten minutes they only once passed the centre line.'

Having fallen behind, though, 'gradually Bristol had more of the play and Hardy began one of the best passing movements of the day,' the *Mercury* reported, 'while a little later

Burton was cleverly making a way through when fouled by Hayes. Wedlock's free-kick lifted the ball over the bar.'

'Just before the half-time whistle sounded, Bristol City had another excellent chance,' said the *Daily Mail*, 'but the inside man instead of shooting when in a good position hesitated and passed out to Staniforth, who again shot wide.'

There was a feeling that with the wind in the second half, City would come back into the game. 'The opinion would have been a correct one,' the *Mirror* said, 'but for the feeble display given by the Bristol forwards in the subsequent exchanges. They had many glorious opportunities, and in a League match would have taken them. But they were obsessed with final flurry, and they missed them . . .'

'There was not much to choose between the teams in the early play after the change of ends,' the *Mercury* reported, 'but Manchester's defence still controlled the game to a large extent, and Meredith and Wall were again the most trouble-some men in attack. From a centre by Hilton, Gilligan shot low, Moger only just turning the ball away by falling full-length on the turf, but Bristol City's goal had an equally narrow escape.'

Again, the *Lincolnshire Echo* version was more colourful: 'Hardy ripped in a stinger and Gilligan shook up the giant Moger as he had never been hustled in the initial moiety.'

'Less than ten minutes had elapsed after the change of ends,' the *Leeds Mercury* continued, 'when Hayes had to retire hurt and it says much for the versatility of Duckworth and Halse that they should have made Manchester's defence sufficiently strong to withstand all attacks and even keep the play level. For the course the game took, the side were much indebted to Meredith who by timely passes to his half made matters easy and often carried on attacks unaided. Gilligan caused some excitement by dashing through the backs but Moger came out and cleared, and then James Turnbull missed what looked like the simplest of chances, his kick when close in sending the ball over the bar.'

'Once Gilligan got right through,' the *Mirror* went on, 'but

Moger ran out and, throwing his 6ft 2½in at full length, literally scooped the ball off his toes. Another time Hilton had the goal absolutely at his mercy, and shot wildly and wide.'

As Bristol City became increasingly desperate, the game became more physical. 'Tempers were lost,' the *Mirror* reported, 'and J. Turnbull was lucky in not receiving his marching orders. He is evidently no better in this respect than when at Leyton.'

'There was far too much of that unpleasant type of football usually conspicuous by its absence at the Crystal Palace on these occasions,' complained Laurence Woodhouse in the *Daily Mail*, castigating Turnbull for the occasional 'childish outburst of petulance'.

'Meredith,' the *Mirror* went on, 'obviously did not like the attentions of Cottle, who bowled him over heavily with perfectly fair shoulder charges on several occasions. He made too much stage show of his bruises, and did not add to his reputation thereby. Football is a game for the robust.'

United, the *Lincolnshire Echo* was in no doubt, had deserved their win. Bristol City's 'short, clever passing was nice to watch', it concluded, but 'very ineffective at close quarters'. City, the *Mirror* suggested, 'did not, and could not, play brilliant football, but they were stubborn, and fought hard to turn the tide'.

The celebrations were rather too much for some. '"There were about thirty of the men, I should say, who got left behind here on Saturday,"' an official at King's Cross told the *Daily Mail*. '"We take their names and addresses and make them promise they will send on the extra fare entailed by their travelling on an ordinary train. Last year, not one single wrong name or address was given, which speaks well for the type of men who come up."'

For all the glee in Manchester, there were some reservations. 'The football,' the *Guardian* acknowledged, '. . . was not of a very high order . . . Manchester seemed to have owed their victory to the direct and vigorous tactics which always pay in

Cup-tie football. But one could wish that League teams would devote more effort to developing an individual style, as one or two of them have done in the past.' Woodhouse called it 'peculiarly uninteresting'. Meredith, at least, stood out. 'He played beautiful football,' *The Times* reported. 'His clever footwork, rare control of the ball, sure passes and long shots at goal gave the deadliness to his side's attack.'

Above a letter from a George J. Planinsky thanking the paper for its support for Bulgarian independence, the *London Daily News* called the game 'extremely disappointing' and doubted whether the fixture should even continue. 'To those who do not follow the game closely,' it wrote, 'the fact that experienced professional players who are perfectly trained, cannot do themselves justice in the great game of the year is no doubt extraordinary, but the explanation is simple. There is too much at stake in the Cup final, and the prevailing excitement unnerves the principals. The only remedy for this defect is the elimination from the game of all forms of competition.'

It's not a remedy anybody in Manchester would have taken. An estimated 300,000 turned out to welcome United back, an indication of the scale of the club's support base (to put that in context, United's average attendance that season was 18,150). In celebration, wealthy United fans made a replica of the Cup, the design of which had never been copyrighted. That forced the FA, recognising potential problems ahead, to replace the old trophy and register the new version. In July 1910, they held a competition for the redesign, which was won by Fattorini and Sons of Bradford. Appropriately, the first winners of the updated version, the one with which we're familiar today, were Bradford City.

But whatever the design, by winning the Cup the year after winning the league, United had indisputably arrived.

It had been a long journey. The first step towards the foundation of the club had come in 1859 when the Lancashire and Yorkshire Railway had set up 'Improvement Classes' for their employees. Central to the Victorian love of self-betterment was a belief in the importance of team sports to inspire a sense of virility, resilience and comradeship, so it was nothing especially unusual when various departments of the railway began to establish sporting clubs. The records were destroyed in a fire in 1976, but it seems that in 1878 the Dining Room Committee of the Carriage and Wagon Works set up a football team.

They were good, rather too good, in fact, and soon left the LYR's inter-departmental competition to join the local Lancashire leagues, taking the name of the suburb of north-east Manchester in which they were based: Newton Heath (LYR). Their success continued. Newton Heath went unbeaten through 1882–83 and the following season entered the Lancashire Association Cup for the first time, beating Haydock Temperance 4–0 in their first game. They reached the Manchester Senior Cup final in 1885, in which they were beaten by Hurst. Other than in east Lancashire, rugby had been the preferred winter sport in the area – the *Manchester Guardian* continued to give it priority until the turn of the century – but by the 1880s that was changing.

After professionalism was legalised in 1885, Newton Heath brought in a number of gifted players, many of them from Wales, with the offer of a job in the railways. They reached the final of the Senior Cup every year until 1891, winning the competition four times, but by then their sights were set rather higher. In 1886, Newton Heath entered the FA Cup for the first time, drawing 2–2 against Fleetwood. Believing the match would go to a replay, they walked off as the referee insisted on extra-time; the FA awarded the game against them.

In autumn 1889, Newton Heath joined the Football Alliance, a rival to the Football League. They came eighth and then ninth of the twelve sides in the competition before, in 1891–92, inspired by the right-winger Alf Farman, finishing as runners-up behind Nottingham Forest. For the following season, it was decided to extend the League, incorporating the

Alliance as a Second Division and increasing the size of the First Division from fourteen to sixteen teams. Newton Heath found themselves promoted and responded by dropping the 'LYR' from their name, symbolically casting off their railway origins.

Newton Heath's rise was rapid, but success on the pitch disguised how difficult matters were off it. This was Manchester when it was known as Cottonopolis, 'the first industrial city in the world' as Dave Haslam put it in his cultural history, *Manchester, England*. Lightly disguised as 'Coketown', it was the filthy and impoverished setting for Dickens' *Hard Times*. It was where, observing the vast gulf between owners and workers, Friedrich Engels had in 1845 written *The Condition of the English Working Class in England*. There was wealth, but there was also intense poverty and limited resources for football. Clubs were low on the list of priorities. Newton Heath played home games on a piece of land leased from the railway, which leased it from the church, on North Road. The surface was far from ideal. 'In places,' said the description in the *History of the Lancashire Football Association*, 'it was hard as flint, with ashes underneath that had become like iron, and in others, thick with mud.' The soil had a high clay content, which meant that drainage was poor. Initially players would change at the Three Crowns pub on Oldham Road and then at the club headquarters in the Shears Hotel, about half a mile away.

Crowds of around 2000 were not uncommon and, in 1891, local dignitaries raised funds to build a stand that could hold 1000 fans. In a letter Percy Young published in his 1960 history of the club, the Reverend J. Wilcockson recalled the atmosphere of those early days. 'The matches were advertised largely by locally distributed "team sheets" which shopkeepers willingly placed in their windows,' he wrote. 'Often a name appeared as AN Other when the team selectors had not made up their minds. The spectators were kept off the pitch by a wire cable fixed on stumps about three feet high and the

Masseys [Charlie and his brother Ned, the groundsmen] used to patrol inside and drive back boys who had clambered underneath to get a better view.'

Upon promotion A. H. Albert, who had previously worked at Aston Villa, was appointed as secretary, becoming the club's first paid official. He leased a cottage to serve as an office and then moved into larger offices in a disused schoolroom in Miles Platting, an inner-city district east-north-east of the centre, turning it into a social centre where players and fans could mingle and play billiards.

The first season in the top flight was tough. Newton Heath finished bottom, winning only six of their thirty games, which meant a Test match against the side that had finished top of the Second Division, Small Heath (the team that became Birmingham City), to determine promotion and relegation. A 1–1 draw in Birmingham led to a replay at North Road, which Newton Heath won 5–2.

Their form didn't improve the following season, as the club was thrust into its first major crisis. The ground at North Road was also used for cricket and the LYR was concerned that the football club, to which it no longer had any affiliation, was damaging the surface for the summer game. In September 1893, Newton Heath moved to Bank Lane in Clayton, three miles way. The pitch drained better than the one at North Road, but it was unfortunately situated on the windward side of thirty chimneys at a nearby chemical plant that belched out acrid fumes. So notorious was the area that it prompted a local song:

As Satan was flying over Clayton for Hell
He was chained in the breeze, likewise the smell.
Quoth he: 'I'm not sure what country I roam
But I'm sure by the smell I'm not far from home.'

A crowd of 10,000 turned out for Newton Heath's first game at their new home, a 3–2 win over Burnley, but it was a season of struggle. Even when they won, it earned them few admirers. The following month, they beat West Bromwich Albion 4–1, prompting the journalist William Jephcott to complain in the *Birmingham Daily Gazette* that 'it wasn't football, it was simply brutality'. Newton Heath sued and, although they won, they were awarded only a farthing (¼d) in damages. Costs were split, placing a further strain on their already creaking finances. Newton Heath finished bottom of the table again and this time they were beaten 2–0 by Liverpool in the play-off.

The rest of the decade was a constant struggle as the club kept failing to win promotion. Signings came and signings went and while there were some highs – the half-back line of Hugh Morgan, William Morgan and Walter Cartwright, the 'Old Triumvirate', for instance – Newton Heath remained stuck in the second flight, their finances deteriorating by the season. Legend has it that one board meeting was held by the light of three candles wedged in ginger-beer bottles after the Corporation had cut off the power. When the *Manchester Evening News*, the region's largest local newspaper, set up a hut at the Bank Lane ground to house a phone for their reporter, they allowed the club to use it as an office. So impoverished were Newton Heath that they took to paying players a proportion of gate receipts rather than a set salary.

By February 1901, the club's debt was £2670 and there was little joy to be gleaned from performances on the pitch. 'Newton Heath,' said the *Athletic News* after a grim goalless draw with Gainsborough Trinity, 'have had such an unsuccessful season, they have got so deep in the mire that it seems hard to indulge in adverse criticism, but after recent exhibitions – notably that at Burnley – it would be impossible to endeavour to cover up their many shortcomings. It would be a pleasure to the writer to record the fact that better things were promised, but what can anyone say after the latest performance on Saturday?'

Harry Stafford, the club's captain, had got used to taking

donations from fans with his pet dog, a St Bernard called Major who would wear a collecting tin round his neck where rescue dogs might have carried a barrel of brandy, but he decided more drastic action was needed and so organised a bazaar called 'representing Sunny Lands' at St James's Hall on Oxford Road, believing it might raise as much as £1000. Manchester City were listed among the patrons. There was a military band and the Besses-o'-th'-Barn brass band, and exhibitions showcasing, as the programme put it, 'the craftsmanship of Italy, the Nile, India and the East, the Mediterranean and the Riviera'.

'We are pleased,' the *Athletic News* reported, 'to hear that the Newton Heath people are much encouraged by the results accruing from their bazaar, which was held last week. The opening ceremony each day was attended by distinguished gentlemen, from members of Parliament downwards, who had some very nice things to say about the winter game as a popular recreation, and attached suitable donations to the same. As Mr James West, the hard-working secretary, observed, "Why should men waste their Saturday afternoons in the public house when they had the opportunity of spending them amid the noise-zone of Bank Lane?" We trust that the Heathens will open a new leaf in their history. The essential leading chapters will be a new team and a ground, but these should not be impossible obstacles to surmount.'

But that was an overly rosy interpretation of the reality. Three MPs may have turned up, but the crowds didn't, even though a season-ticket for all four days cost only 3s6d and entry on the final day was just 6d. The bazaar was a huge financial disappointment. Even worse, Major went missing.

Exactly what happened next is not entirely clear, with the story undergoing various embellishments over the years. What is certain is that, with the club's financial situation increasingly bleak, creditors sought to foreclose and the contractors who had worked on the Bank Lane ground looked to have the club declared bankrupt. The Official Receiver issued a statement on 22 February outlining the debt. Newton Heath limped on until, on 18 March, a shareholders' meeting was called for at New Islington Hall. The Football Association, it was announced, had agreed to the reformation of the club if there was any way that it could achieve solvency. Stafford stood up and asked how much it would cost. A figure of £2000 was suggested, at which Stafford announced he knew of four investors each prepared to put in £500, a figure he was prepared to match.

When Major went missing, the stories seem to agree, he was found by a Mr Thomas, the licensee of a pub that belonged to John Henry Davies, a self-made man who had begun as an agent's clerk before becoming an innkeeper and then making his fortune in brewing. He later married the niece of the sugar magnate Sir Henry Tate, substantially increasing his fortune. Thomas placed an advert in the local paper describing the dog. Reading it, Davies thought the dog would be just the thing to give his daughter as a birthday present. Stafford by then had claimed the dog as his, but he agreed to sell him to Davies. As the two men spoke, Stafford outlined Newton Heath's plight, at which Davies, seeing their potential, decided to invest. He also made Stafford the licensee of another of his pubs. It's a nice story, perhaps too nice. Percy Young is sceptical of Major's part in the business, suggesting rather that Stafford 'took a chance on his slender connection with the great man through the medium of beer'.

On 26 April, another meeting was called. Davies and his fellow investors – Mr Taylor of Sale, Mr Bown of Denton and Mr Jones of Manchester – had cleared the debt, but they wanted more, proposing a change from the green-and-yellow halved shirts with black shorts to red and white and, even more radically, calling for a change of name. Manchester Central and Manchester Celtic were suggested, before a nineteen-year-old fan called Louis Rocca called out, 'Manchester United'. Or at least that was the story Rocca always told: in his account, Young maintained, 'the cold facts have been re-warmed with rather more enthusiasm than discretion.' The *Athletic News* attributed the new name to 'Brown', which was presumably a typo for 'Bown'. Whether the name was his idea or not, Rocca, always with an eye out for a deal, always looking for loopholes in the regulations, became a club fixture in the half century that followed.

United finished tenth of the eighteen clubs in the Second Division in 1901–02 and the following year they sank to fifteenth. They did finish fifth (with the top two being promoted) the following season, but of greater long-term significance was an accusation that Stafford and the club secretary James West had made illegal payments to players. Stafford moved to Crewe while West resigned.

Davies seized his chance, and appointed as secretary-manager Ernest Mangnall, who had occupied a similar position at Burnley. Mangnall was a well-educated and driven man, who had once cycled from Land's End to John O'Groats. He smoked cigars, favoured a boater and had a trim moustache that offered a distinct contrast to the elaborate whiskers sported by Davies, the effect all the more striking because the top of his head was completely bald. This was an era when secretaries, inspired by Tom Watson who won three league titles at Sunderland and two at Liverpool, rather than primarily looking after the accounts, began to take an interest in team selection and tactics.

Davies put up £3000 of his own money to sign players and offered a series of loans to the club to keep it afloat, the last of which wasn't fully repaid until after the Second World War. Mangnall, it turned out, had a keen eye for a player. He bought the giant goalkeeper Harry Moger from Southampton, the full-back Bob Bonthron and the forward Sandy Robertson from Dundee, and put together a half-back line that would become fabled: Charlie Roberts, Dick Duckworth and Alex Bell. Belief swept through the club. Crowds grew: more than 40,000 were there for a 2–2 draw against Bristol City on the opening day of the 1903–04 season. That was followed by a pair of away defeats, but there would only be four more that season as United finished third.

They were third again in 1904–05, undone by defeats in two of the last three matches, but finally, the following season, United went up, finishing second behind Bristol City. Promotion was confirmed on 28 April 1906 with a 6–0 win over Burton United in an unseasonal snowstorm as a brass band played before a clubhouse bedecked in red-and-white balloons. For the first time, Manchester had two clubs in the top flight.

Even as United celebrated, Manchester's other club was going through a crisis that would have profound consequences for both. City at the time were a bigger side than United. They'd won the FA Cup in 1904 and in 1904–05 finished third in the league. It was, though, a turbulent season. In October, they were found to have made illegal payments in transfer dealings with Glossop. The following summer, the great Welsh winger Billy Meredith, noted for his habit of chewing a toothpick as he played, was suspended for having unsuccessfully offered an inducement to the Aston Villa player Alex Leake to lose a game – although that description of his offence and punishment gives only the slightest hint of what was actually going on.

Meredith was fabulously talented but also, as far as the game's establishment was concerned, a truculent radical. Throughout his career he campaigned to be paid what he was worth, calling for an end to the maximum wage and the retain-and-transfer system that meant players were unable freely to switch clubs even when out of contract. That made him dangerous and, whatever the rights and wrongs of the match-fixing incident – Meredith claimed initially he'd been joking but later hinted he was acting on orders from somebody higher up at City – the suspicion must be that the decision to ban him, which bafflingly followed an investigation into a fracas during that game between City and Villa, was at least partly motivated by a desire to put an upstart in his place.

While banned, Meredith demanded his salary, then alleged

that under-the-counter payments were common practice at City. The club transfer-listed him in May 1906. United promptly signed him for £500, even though he was still suspended. Later that same month, the FA investigated Meredith's claims and found seventeen City players guilty of accepting illegal payments. They were fined, suspended until January 1907 and banned from playing for City again. The club put all seventeen up for sale at a mass auction to be held at the Queen's Hotel.

Mangnall acted fast. As other secretaries arrived for the sale, they found him walking away, familiar boater perched on his head, a smile beneath his moustache, having secured the signatures of four players: the forward Sandy Turnbull, plus Herbert Burgess, George Livingstone and Jimmie Bannister. Meredith finally made his debut on 1 January 1907, setting up Sandy Turnbull for the only goal of the game with a typical run to the byline and cross.

United finished eighth in their first season back in the top flight. Before the start of 1907–08, the *Manchester Evening News* wrote that 'United have never in their history opened a season with so strong a playing combination.' Their optimism was soon justified.

'Surprising Manchester Victories', read the headline in the *Manchester Evening News* on the opening day of the 1907–08 season. It led with City's 5–2 victory away to Sunderland, their first ever at Roker Park, but also noted that 'Manchester United were in brilliant form at Aston ... one of the best performances since the club was founded.' They won 4–1, a result of great significance for, as Percy Young noted, 'in those times, the smooth-playing, methodical Villa were a great power in the land, and to defeat them was worthy of lasting memorial.'

For United, the season could hardly have started better. 'A clever goal scored by [George] Wall after four minutes' play completely disorganised the Villa, and the home side were never really seen to advantage,' the *MEN* reported. '[Chris] Buckley, the Villa right-half, had the misfortune to break his ankle just before half-time, and immediately afterwards a brilliant piece of work by Meredith put the United two goals up.' Buckley was from Manchester and his brother had just joined City.

Playing against ten men, United pressed home their advantage. 'In the second half Meredith scored a third with ease, and the visitors continued to have all the serious play. Ten minutes from the end, Roberts breasted the ball, and the claim of Villa for a penalty being successful, Hampton scored. This roused the United to another effort and Bannister scored. In each half, Turnbull had a goal disallowed, and on the run of play Villa escaped very lightly.

'Roberts was in great form; in fact, the defence never looked like being beaten, and that the forwards played their part is shown by the score. In no department could the Villa equal their conquerors, and the 18,000 people who saw the game gave the Manchester men a capital reception as they left the field.'

Beating Villa, at that point the league's most successful club, on the opening day of the season was just the start. The following Thursday, United hammered Liverpool 4–0 at home and they went top of the table with a 2–1 victory over Middlesbrough. Although they then lost the return at Middlesbrough, there followed ten straight victories in which they scored thirty-seven goals. Just as impressive as the forward line, though, was the goalkeeper. The *Athletic News* singled out Moger for praise after an opening ten games in which he had conceded only nine goals. A growth spurt at the age of eighteen had taken him to six foot two, adding physical presence to his 'extraordinary reach, keen anticipation of danger, quickness of moving, and unquestioned audacity and pluck'. The profile concluded, 'We have seen him give many thrilling exhibitions and not a bad display. "Safe" rather than "brilliant" describes the man.'

When United beat Bolton Wanderers 2–1 at the end of October, Tityrus in the *Athletic News* was enraptured. 'The United have not merely a conception of the fine art of football,' he wrote, 'but they have the fine execution and deft touch of masters . . . United delighted me by passing all the time upon the ground. The ball was always rolling along as in a game of bowls – and from man to man on the same side. If the United forwards could not play with three half-backs gliding the ball to their toes they would deserve to be drummed out of the game. If the ball were hollow wickerwork with a bell inside, five blind forwards could lead an attack with this intermediate line to set them on their way with a merry tink.'

By New Year's Day, United were ten points clear of Sheffield Wednesday in second – which was just as well. The second half of the season saw an extraordinary decline. A 1–0 defeat at Chelsea was described by the *Athletic News* as 'a tame and weak exhibition of football'. When they lost 2–1 at home to Blackburn Rovers they were 'completely below form having a weak spot in defence and a disorganised forward line'. Only 12,000 turned up at Clayton for a 3–0 win over Sunderland.

United won just seven of their final nineteen games. Most shocking was the home defeat to Notts County on 13 April, when United dominated but couldn't score. 'In the first half,' the *Guardian* reported, 'little heed was paid to the blunders, and it was not until United were awarded a penalty kick early in the second half that the spectators began to cry out for "the game" to be played. The referee's decision was open to doubt, and it was evident that the United players were not anxious to take the kick; indeed, it appeared that the captain had to make a second choice of a kicker in order to fulfil the official ruling. Then Wall shot yards wide, and was heartily shaken by the hand and patted on the back by several opponents.'

Fans were furious and began to cheer for County, who scored with three minutes remaining for a victory that helped them escape relegation. 'United deserved to lose,' said the report in the *Athletic News*, 'because of their lack of spirit, poor command of the ball, and total neglect of shooting.' Turnbull was barracked as he went off with an injury in the second half as, the *Athletic News* said, 'it was thought he did so out of a spirit of resentment.'

Suspicion was widespread. 'The failure of the League leaders to win their home match with one of the weakest combinations of the First Division was due to such unwanted bungling that some inquiry into the methods of the players seems inevitable,' said the *Guardian*. 'Whatever happens, it is certainly to be regretted that there should be any misunderstandings between the club management and the men . . . it is anything but a happy family at Clayton now.'

There were other, less inflammatory allegations that the players weren't really trying. Geoffrey Green in *There's Only One United* suggested that they had been demotivated by disputes over wages and perhaps also by the poor conditions at Clayton. 'Wanderer' in the *Manchester Evening News* blamed the downturn in form on disappointment about going out of the Cup – in those days regarded as a far more glamorous competition than the league – in the sixth round against a Fulham side inspired by their goalkeeper Leslie Skene. It's true that United's worst form set in after that game, but they had been stuttering since the middle of January. 'Wanderer' insisted the decline was 'quite natural' – a slightly odd turn of phrase that seemed immediately to raise the possibility that it might have been 'unnatural'. 'Wanderer' also acknowledged that the players had been dismayed by the behaviour of some fans.

The start, though, had given United enough of a cushion and with Sheffield Wednesday losing at Bolton that day, United were confirmed as champions despite the defeat and with five games of the season remaining. United won just one of their last six games of the season and just three of their last eleven, an anticlimactic way to end a campaign that had begun with such excellence.

'When Charles Roberts,' Wanderer wrote, 'puts away tonight the big bell so far as league strife in 1907–08 is concerned, he will have much cause for pride and pleasure, and much on which to reflect in the quiet moments of the future. He will realise that he is the captain of the league champions and, if he knows as much of himself as others know of him, he will feel that he more than any man had played a big hand in the winning of league honours by a club only in its second season as a First Division member . . .

'To Charles Roberts more than any man, Manchester United owed their promotion, and to him again they chiefly owe their success in winning the league. Yes, I know well the splendid spirit shown by the team as a whole, the fine work done by every man on the side week after week, the wonderful skill and devotion to duty of Meredith, and the brilliant goalscoring and nursing of George Wall shown by Alec Turnbull . . . [Roberts] has led the side with enthusiasm that has put life and confidence into the team. In match after match, his energy has been remarkable, and he has been great alike in attack and defence – a sixth forward and a third back.'

A first league title was in the bag, but Davies was thinking even bigger. Clayton, he recognised, was no home for a club with aspirations to greatness, something made clear by William Pickford's description in *Association Football and the Men who Made It*, of an FA Cup first-round replay against Portsmouth in 1907: 'All the time the struggle was waging the thirty Clayton chimneys smoked and gave forth their pungent odours, and the boilers behind the goal poured mists of steam over the ground.' Alf Clarke, in his 1948 history of the club, said that 'it is well-known among old-time Manchester people that, if the home club was losing at half-time, the chimneys belched their noxious fumes over the playing area to the discomfort of the visitors.'

In summer 1908 Davies unveiled plans for a new 80,000-seater stadium, costing £60,000, to be built on land he had bought from the Earl of Trafford just over the city boundary in Salford. By the standards of the day, the new ground was spectacular, featuring refreshment bars and a tea-room for fans, an electric lift for the use of officials and journalists and, for the players, hot and cold plunge baths, a gymnasium and massage room, and an area for recreation and billiards.

On the pitch United were going from strength to strength as well. They beat Queens Park Rangers after a replay to lift the Charity Shield and won their first five league games of the season to raise hopes they could defend their title. Three defeats in four games from the end of October, though, dropped them to fifth and, in the league, they never recovered. The Cup was a different matter.

Success in the Cup, though, only highlighted other problems that went far beyond league form. The players had experienced the acclaim, they had seen how large the crowds were and they wanted to share the rewards – a theme that would recur frequently over the following decades. Manchester had been a home of radicalism since the Chartists; perhaps it was only natural that it was their players who should first organise to try to secure fairer reward for their efforts. That summer, they met in a hotel near what is now Piccadilly Station and formed the first players' union. The FA was predictably furious and instructed clubs to sack anybody involved. United stopped the players' summer pay. In response, Sandy Turnbull led a break-in to seize property in lieu of payment, even stealing the FA Cup, although Roberts soon arranged for it to be returned. The FA, perhaps recognising the dangers if it ostracised the players entirely, became more conciliatory and offered limited recognition of the union so long as it didn't affiliate to the General Federation of Trades Unions. Professional players were balloted and voted 470–172 to accept the FA's offer, gradually returning to work. There was peace, but no long-term solution.

Player unrest wasn't the only attack on Davies, who also faced problems with the FA. After the Manchester City scandal an amnesty had been declared on illegal payments, but United seem to have been just about the only club to take seriously the need to admit to past offences. Between 1903–04 and 1908–09, they paid out £5,743 in wages and bonuses that contravened the regulations. That drew scrutiny from the FA, which raised doubts about the nature of Davies's ownership, querying whether United was 'a genuine club', that is, to use the useful gloss in the *Athletic News*, 'one founded voluntarily by locals and with a range of shareholders rather than one dominant presence'. Davies, fairly clearly, was a dominant presence and so United were forced to float as a limited liability company with 'a subscription open to the public at a price determined by an independent valuer'. As a result, Davies's control was diminished.

Nonetheless, the new stadium was ready and the club that he had saved seemed on the brink of a gilded new era. United's final game at Clayton was played on 22 January 1910, as they beat Tottenham Hotspur 5–0, with Meredith breaking a goal drought that had lasted a year. On 19 February came the first home game at Old Trafford, with over 50,000 turning out for the visit of Liverpool. 'Along Clayton Road they came and over Trafford Bridge in trams, buses, cabs, taxis, coster's carts, coal lorries and all manner of strange things on wheels,' wrote the *Guardian*. 'Those who had not had the good fortune to find a cab or to meet a friend with a coster's cart walked it – a great stream spreading wide over the footpaths into the road, the despair of already over-harassed tram drivers, the delight of sundry small boys who trotted alongside cheerfully offering to do "20 cartwheels and a roll-over" for a penny.' Two Turnbull goals had United 2–0 up inside quarter of an hour, but they ended up losing 4–3. Still, however disappointing the result, the stadium impressed. 'It was,' the *Sporting Chronicle*'s reporter said, 'the most handsomest, the most spacious and the most remarkable arena I have ever seen. As a football ground it is unrivalled anywhere in the world.'

United went into the final Saturday a point behind Aston Villa. As Villa went down 3–1 at Liverpool, United hammered Sunderland 5–1 to ensure that the first full season at Old Trafford brought United's second league title. With a successful side and a vast stadium, the club was firmly established at the top of the English game. Everything seemed to be in place for sustained success, but it would be a long time in coming.

By 1912, the team was beginning to show signs of age. The fabled half-back line of Duckworth, Roberts and Bell was badly exposed in Meredith's benefit match against City in the September, who by then were managed by Mangnall. He had quit United a month earlier, accepting better terms across Manchester rather than face the rebuilding work United required. The following season, Roberts moved to Oldham Athletic, although he continued to run the tobacconist's in Manchester that he'd set up in 1907, selling a brand of cigars named 'Dukrobel' after the famous half-back line. Bell went to Blackburn and Duckworth had to be persuaded to keep playing. United slipped to fourteenth in 1913–14 and eighteenth the following season, avoiding relegation by a single point. By then, of course, football had ceased to be a priority for just about everybody.

They might not have avoided relegation in what turned out to be the final season before the war brought a cessation to league football had it not been for perhaps the most shameful incident in United's history. On Good Friday 1915, United met Liverpool at Old Trafford. United were seventeenth in the table, Liverpool fourteenth. It soon became apparent that something was amiss. In the first half United besieged the Liverpool goal. It wasn't so much that they played well, as that some Liverpool players didn't play at all; that it was a fix was obvious. Only a brilliant display from the Liverpool goalkeeper Elisha Scott kept the score down to 1–0 at half-time. During the break, furious shouting could be heard from the Liverpool dressing room as those who weren't in on the fix rowed with those who were. The United captain Patrick O'Connell, who would go on to manage Barcelona, put a first-half penalty 'ridiculously wide', as the *Liverpool Daily Post* described it, but walked back to his own half laughing, as though confident it would have no bearing on the result. The match officials conferred but decided to play on. The United centre-forward Enoch 'Knocker' West, blaming an ankle injury, dropped back into defence where, as 'Veteran', the *Manchester Daily Dispatch*'s match reporter, described it, he 'was chiefly employed in the second half in kicking the ball as far out of play as he could'. George Anderson added his second of the game midway through the second half and then, in the final minutes, the Liverpool striker Fred Pagnam smacked a shot against the bar and was berated by some of his team-mates. Without those two points, United would have been relegated.

Two weeks later, the *Sporting Chronicle* reported that 'a certain First League match played in Manchester during Easter weekend was squared' with a number of players having put money on it finishing 2–0. A £50 reward was offered by a betting firm for further information. Because of the First World War, football was suspended at the end of the month, the end of the season, but the Football League nonetheless set up an inquiry. On 23 December, it published its findings, concluding that there was 'a conspiracy to defraud bookmakers'. Both clubs were exonerated but eight players received life bans, while a ninth footballer, Manchester City's Fred Howard, who was found to have pocketed money from bets on the match, was given a twelve-month suspension. The Lancashire cricketer Lol Cook was also sanctioned for having helped place bets.

Liverpool's Jackie Sheldon, who had won the title with United in 1911, was named as the ringleader. It was the friendships he had formed with Arthur Whalley, Sandy Turnbull and Knocker West that led to the plot – although West was the only one of the three to have actually played in the game. West continued to protest his innocence, standing outside a wartime fixture between United and Liverpool handing out flyers printed at his own expense, urging anybody with evidence to come forward. He sued the FA and various newspapers for libel in 1917 but Sheldon testified against him and the case was lost. A year later Anderson, who had scored both goals in the game, was jailed for eight months with hard labour for his part in the conspiracy, although he maintained his only involvement had been to keep quiet having been informed of it. All the bans other than West's were subsequently overturned in recognition of the players' war service. Whalley later became a bookmaker while Turnbull was presumed killed on the Somme, although his body was never found.

Turnbull was the only United player killed in the Great War, but picking up after the conflict was no easy matter. United were in decline anyway, the core of the pre-war side ageing. Jack Robson, who'd been appointed manager in 1914, instituted a policy of 'players before points', accepting that the club's lack of resources – exacerbated by lower crowds and the wartime entertainment tax – meant there was a need to seek talent in local youth football. That had always been his way. Born in Durham in 1860, he'd become secretary of Middlesbrough in 1899 and had declined to travel to away games to save money. Subsequent spells at Crystal Palace, whom he led to one of the great early FA Cup shocks as they beat Newcastle United at St James' Park in 1907, and Brighton and Hove Albion, confirmed his aptitude for improving clubs on a tight budget.

His plan yielded the defenders Jack Silcock and Charlie Moore, the half-back Lal Hilditch and the forward Joe Spence. The side that began the first post-war season, 1919–20, with a 1–1 draw away at Derby County, cost in total just £100. Billy Meredith was still in dispute with the club and didn't re-sign his contract until late December, just as everybody was expecting him to retire.

With the financial situation bleak, Davies was criticised by many who argued that Old Trafford was a white elephant but by October, when 49,360 turned out for the derby against City, the doubts about its size had been silenced. The young side began the season well and after six games they lay fourth. United's journey back from Middlesbrough, their seventh fixture, though, suggested just how chaotic things were behind the scenes. The railways were on strike, so United hired a charabanc for the trip to Teesside. Once there, though, it was commandeered for food supplies, so United decided to return to their hotel in Saltburn in taxis. Three of the four cabs broke down with one of them catching fire, which was extinguished by players tossing loose earth onto the flames. They eventually managed to find another charabanc for their return journey but in thick fog it went off the road on Marston Moor and almost crashed into a wall. The players ended up walking the final miles back into Manchester where they were set upon by strikers who mistook them for blacklegging railway workers.

Worse followed as the chairman William Deakin caught a chill in a game at Burnley; it developed into pneumonia and he died within a fortnight, being replaced by the well-known Manchester accountant George H. Lawton.

United finished twelfth in 1919–20, a relatively promising season given the youth of the squad, but for a long time that was as good as it got. Crowds continued to grow – 70,506 packed in on Boxing Day 1920 for a 3–1 defeat to Aston Villa, an attendance record that stood until 2006. A transfer splurge at the beginning of September brought in three players for £5000 – the centre-forward Harry Leonard from Derby, the diminutive winger William Harrison from Wolverhampton Wanderers and Liverpool's Scotland international Tom Miller – but it didn't take long for any optimism that engendered to dissipate. Leonard scored five in his first six games, but it was a misleading start: he was soon dismissed as cumbersome and slow, too often offside. Harrison didn't settle either and to compound the problems with the club's transfer policy, the twenty-four-year-old centre-half Tommy Meehan was sold to Chelsea for £2000.

It had been a season of frustration: although they'd finished thirteenth, United had beaten only one side who'd finished in the top ten and the sense was that, despite a net outlay, the squad was weaker than it had been a year earlier. After a shambolic summer, it was even weaker. The forwards Miller,

Leonard, Fred Hopkin and Frank Hodges were all sold, as was Billy Meredith, by then forty-six, who rejoined City for another three years. In their place came the forward Arthur Lochhead from Hearts and the wing-half John Scott from Bradford Park Avenue, trading that yielded a profit of only £1500. When the full-back Charlie Moore damaged his ankle in a pre-season charity game, United's squad looked even more slender.

The season began badly, with one win in the first nine games. Although nobody doubted Robson's essential decency or his capacity to make money stretch as far as possible, there were questions as to whether he was the right man for a club with United's ambition. 'Robson,' Deakin had said at the beginning of the previous season, 'knows a player in the rough ... [but] he is not a showman.' The sense of United wanting to reach higher, combined with Robson's chest problems, led to him stepping aside in October 1921 to become assistant manager.

Robson's replacement was John Chapman, a stern Scot who over the previous fifteen years had turned Airdrieonians into a significant force on a limited budget. He arrived full of confidence, announcing that, 'There's only one person who thinks more about the game than I do and that's the wife,' but within thirty-eight minutes of his first game in charge, at home to Middlesbrough, United were 3–0 down. His second game brought a 2–0 defeat at Middlesbrough (games were paired in those seasons immediately after the war to make compiling the fixture list easier, a practice abandoned in 1924 partly because it heightened the advantage of coming up against a side when their key players were injured, but mainly because playing two games against the same opposition in the space of a week led to violence as immediate retribution was sought for perceived slights whereas a three- or four-month gap allowed tempers to calm). After his third, a 3–1 defeat at Aston Villa, it was decided new blood was needed, and soon.

In the space of a week, United brought in the forward Bill Henderson from Airdrie and the centre-half Neil McBain from

Ayr United for a total of £6250. It was widely believed there was still need of a right-winger, but Lawton couldn't countenance further spending and the forward George Bissett was sold to Wolves for £1200 to help balance the books. The investment looked to have paid off immediately as Henderson won the game with a 25-yard drive, but it was another two months before United won again. McBain struggled physically and ended up being shuffled out to left-half, while Henderson, having been prolific in Scotland, scored only one more goal that season.

By Christmas, United were bottom of the table. 'What have we done wrong?' asked McBain. 'We could not have had more ill luck had we killed a policeman.' Chapman organised whist drives and smoking concerts and insisted his players had tea together to build morale but none of it worked. January was the darkest month. Five days after a 4–1 defeat to Cardiff in the FA Cup, Robson died.

By the end of January, Chapman had lost patience with Henderson and selected Spence at centre-forward. He responded with a goal in a home win over Sunderland and for a brief time there was a rally as United went six games unbeaten. But the goals dried up and a run of six straight defeats effectively confirmed their relegation. Spence, going a little further than McBain, wondered if Old Trafford might be cursed and suggested digging up the pitch to see if the remains of 'a policeman or Jew or somesuch' had been buried there.

The war, perhaps, could be blamed for United's failure to make the most of the advantage Old Trafford gave them – although the decline had already begun by 1914 – but United had also spent £10,000 on signings who did little to improve the squad. Their transfer dealing, generally, was bewildering. As the battle against relegation entered its final weeks, George Sapsford, who had probably been their most effective forward that season, was sold to Preston North End. The *Athletic News* was scathing: 'At such an hour the United part with an inside-forward of the proved capacity of

George Sapsford who scored two for Preston at Birmingham on the final day of the season. Still, a club that could dispense with Hopkin could do anything.'

But that summer, at last, came an iconic signing as United finally moved to land a centre-half who could come close to the level of Charlie Roberts – even if his interpretation of the role was rather different. Frank Barson was six feet tall and weighed thirteen stone, most of it muscle. He had been a colliery blacksmith and played like it. In an era when players were hard, he stood out for his hardness, being sent off twelve times over the course of his career, a staggering figure in those days. Barson had joined Aston Villa from Barnsley and had helped them to the FA Cup in 1920, but his relationship with the club fractured when he rejected their demand for all players to live in Birmingham, preferring to take care of his business interests in Sheffield. United paid £4000 for him and promised Barson a pub if they were promoted.

Barson's arrival prompted much excitement, but after an encouraging start the season puttered out. By the end of November, after a string of draws, United were ninth. Crowds stayed at around 25,000, comfortably in the top ten in the country, but whatever optimism there may have been off the pitch, it was not replicated in the dressing room.

The first sign that something may be seriously wrong came when McBain was left out of the game at Rotherham on 9 December. When he also missed the first two games of 1923, the official programme explained that he'd been rested, but it later emerged that a delegation of United players had demanded that he be dropped and the directors had agreed. McBain released a statement saying he didn't think he was being treated fairly, at which point he was sold to Everton for £4200. His departure brought a brief upturn in form, then a slump that was broken only by a 6–1 demolition of the league leaders Notts County. The inconsistency continued, though, and any hope of promotion disappeared with a defeat to Leicester in the penultimate game of the season.

Injuries blighted the following campaign – the spine of Mew, Silcock, Barson and Goldthorpe played just forty-three games between them – and by the end of a season in which United finished fourteenth, crowds were down to 15,000, the main reason for a £1500 loss. It was a season marked by tragedy. Chapman lost his father and his brother in quick succession and in the summer of 1924, the twenty-four-year-old right-back Charlie Radford was killed in a motorcycle accident.

There was little reason to suppose 1924–25 would bring much improvement. United signed nobody in the summer and sold Bain to Everton, but the decision to move Frank Mann back from the forward line into midfield proved inspired. With Barson unencumbered by injury, there was a bedrock on which to build. Between 13 September and 8 November, they didn't concede. Even better, Henderson finally began scoring and United went top at the beginning of November.

But for United, it seemed, nothing could be easy. Henderson, having scored seven of United's previous twelve goals, was sold to Preston. Silcock fractured a cheekbone and was ruled out for twelve weeks. A groin injury sidelined Barson for eight. But Tom Jones, who had been signed from Oswestry with little fanfare the previous season, deputised and excelled.

Still there was need of a forward. Albert Pape was signed from Clapton Orient shortly before the east Londoners played at Old Trafford. The FA rushed through his registration and, inevitably, he scored for United in a 4–2 victory. But still the fans didn't trust the board. When Fred Kennedy, a promising twenty-two-year-old inside-forward, was sold for £2000 just before the transfer deadline, the reaction was furious, even when Charlie Rennox was brought in, also from Clapton, as a replacement. After a sequence of five defeats in eleven games, United found some consistency for the run-in. Leicester were relentless, but Derby faltered. As they lost at Stoke in their third-last game of the season, United beat Bradford 1–0 through a Smith goal to move above them on goal-average with a game in hand. United drew with Southampton and, with Spence scoring twice, beat Port Vale 4–0 as Derby drew with Coventry to all but secure promotion. It was confirmed with a draw at Barnsley.

Barson was given his pub. The day he took it over, he arranged a party to celebrate the club's return to the top flight; it had been going only half an hour when he decided being a landlord wasn't for him, handed the keys to his wife and walked out.

United stayed up relatively comfortably, despite more baffling transfer activity. After years of the board promising that Lochhead would thrive in the top flight because his game was better suited to the higher level, the forward was sold five games into the season. Pape soon followed him as Frank McPherson was moved into the centre from left-wing. There had been plenty of times when United had juggled the forward line and hoped for the best, but there was logic to this move. The change in the offside law in the summer of 1925 had transformed the game and far more goals began to be scored with through-balls behind the defensive line, placing a premium on pace, which McPherson had in abundance.

By November United were as high as third in the table, but their form collapsed as the Cup provided a major distraction. After an epic draw at Sunderland in the sixth round was followed by a controversial win at Old Trafford in the replay, United faced City in the semi-final at Bramall Lane, the 'biggest game of the inter-war period' as Justin Blundell put it in his history of United between 1919 and 1932. After days of feverish anticipation and squabbling over tickets, the game itself never came close to matching up to the previous round. United were furious about a push in the build-up to the goal that gave City the lead and went on to lose 3–0. Worse, Barson was called before an FA commission for an incident that left the City captain Sam Cowan flat on his back. Although the referee had restricted himself to lecturing Barson at the time, United's centre-half ended up being banned for two months, the first player ever to suffer retrospective punishment.

Without him, United lost five in a row, including a 7–0 reverse against Blackburn Rovers that remains their joint-record defeat. There were three occasions when they let in five that season – partly explained by unfamiliarity with the new off-side law, which led to a number of high-scoring games across the division – yet United still finished the season ninth. City, meanwhile, both lost the Cup final to Bolton and were relegated. With the young forward Chris Taylor scoring hat-tricks against Sunderland and West Brom in the final weeks of the season, there were plenty of reasons for optimism.

They wouldn't last. What happened in October 1926 remains a mystery, but the story really begins the previous month. United had lost two and drawn two of their opening four games of the season, when, on 13 September, the *Athletic News* carried an advertisement seeking a new manager for United to take over on 1 November, the day after Chapman's contract expired. Fans were baffled and outraged but even though a motion of confidence in the manager was carried at the club AGM, directors refused to explain what was going on. United drew with Arsenal and then won three in a row, meaning that by the beginning of October they were thirteenth in a squeezed table, just three points behind the leaders Sunderland with a game in hand, having scored twice in each of their first eight games of the season. And then, on 8 October, came shocking news: Chapman had been suspended until the end of the season by the FA for 'improper conduct'.

The reaction was one of disbelief: there were those who had criticised Chapman's dourness, but nobody had ever doubted his integrity. But what had he done? Nobody would say, not the FA, not the club and not Chapman, who merely observed he was 'surprised' by the decision, insisting, 'I have nothing whatever on my conscience.' Yet at the same time he hinted there had been some sort of wrongdoing, describing the term 'improper conduct' as 'a very vague and strong way of wording it'. Alf Clarke in his 1948 history of the club was no more forthcoming: 'I know full well all the circumstances, and I know that had John come out into the open he would have cleared himself very easily. But a player was involved and John Chapman preferred the matter to rest at that.'

But why had his job been advertised a month earlier? Was he thinking of leaving anyway? Or had the board known something? In the summer of 1927, Chapman applied for the vacant Leeds United job but was overlooked in favour of the Doncaster Rovers manager Dick Ray, who went on to lead Leeds to promotion at the first attempt. Chapman, mean-while, became manager of Liverpool Greyhound Racing Club in August 1927 and never returned to football.

If they had had warning, it hadn't been enough for United's board to formulate a plan. They appointed Walter Crickmer as secretary, which turned out to be an excellent decision, but made the left-half Lal Hilditch temporary player-manager, which was perhaps less well-advised. His first game brought a 4–0 defeat at Bolton and, but for the excellence of Steward in goal, it would have been more. There was perhaps some miti-gation in the fact that Barson missed out with a groin injury – although there were many who wondered whether that was code for him being irritated Hilditch had got the job ahead of him – while Spence was away playing for an England League XI who beat their Irish equivalent 6–1, playing well enough to earn his second England cap a week later.

Hilditch's second game brought two goals for Spence in a 3–0 win at Bury but there followed a season of inconsistency, not helped by key injuries. It wasn't until December that Silcock and Moore were back in harness in defence. When United drew at Spurs on Christmas Day, they had won only four of twelve games under Hilditch, sliding to sixteenth in the table, two points above the relegation zone. The major problem was a forward line that had been constantly rejigged without finding an effective combination. The fans had lost patience. Spence was popular, but Partridge, McPherson and Rennox were not. A defeat to Second Division Reading in a second replay in the third round of the Cup only added to the frustration.

A permanent manager finally arrived in April as Hilditch returned to the ranks and was replaced by Herbert Bamlett, the referee who'd supposedly been too weak to blow his whistle to abandon the Cup quarter-final in the snow at Burnley in 1908. After refereeing the 1914 FA Cup final between Liverpool and Burnley, Bamlett had moved into management, leading Oldham Athletic to second in the league in 1914–15, then moving via Wigan Borough to Middlesbrough in 1923. Thanks to the goals of George Camsell, they were on the verge of promotion to the First Division when Bamlett left for Manchester. United drew six and won one of the seven games that remained that season to finish fifteenth.

After the excitement of the previous season, that felt like a comedown, but there was a rationale to the board's lack of spending on players. There was a clear feeling that United hadn't built on the two league titles and the Cup win of 1907 to 1909, something that couldn't really be blamed on the war. United found themselves in a period of retrenchment and the board were looking to the longer term, saving up to buy Old Trafford outright, something that was completed in June 1927. John Henry Davies, who had been struggling with ill health for three years, died four months later, his legacy and his club secure.

CHAPTER 2

FA Cup final, Wembley Stadium, London, 24 April 1948

Manchester United   **4–2**   **Blackpool**
Rowley 28, 70   *Shimwell 12 (pen)*
Pearson 80   *Mortensen 35*
Anderson 82

Jack Crompton   Joe Robinson
Johnny Carey   Eddie Shimwell
John Aston   John Crosland
John Anderson   Harry Johnston
Allenby Chilton   Eric Hayward
Henry Cockburn   Hugh Kelly
Jimmy Delaney   Stanley Matthews
Johnny Morris   Alex Munro
Jack Rowley   Stan Mortensen
Stan Pearson   George Dick
Charlie Mitten   Walter Rickett

Matt Busby   Joe Smith

Ref: C. J. Barrick
Bkd:
Att: 99,842

OR AT LEAST THE CLUB *seemed* secure. But football between the wars was a volatile business and without John Henry Davies, United were soon struggling. Despite the early Cup exit and the impact of the General Strike on attendances, United had made a profit of £4000 in 1926–27, but Davies's interest-free loans had been a big part of United's stability in the early twenties and the difficulties of coping without that safety net were soon to be exposed.

There were more puzzling transfer dealings, with the sales of John Grimwood and George Haslam, both of whom had regularly deputised for Frank Barson during his absences with injury. Barson himself was thirty-six at the start of the season and the injuries only got worse. He managed just eleven games and left for Watford at the end of the season. That placed intolerable pressure on Frank Mann in midfield and he, eventually, was overwhelmed.

The 1927–28 season began with two wins and two draws but then came a 7–1 home defeat at the hands of the defending champions, Newcastle, which remains United's worst result at Old Trafford. When United lost 5–2 to Everton on 8 October, they were just two points off the bottom. It was then that Louis Rocca, who had begun working at United two decades earlier as a tea boy, was named assistant manager.

The exact nature of Rocca's role was never clear, not least because of his own habit of exaggeration, but his appointment coincided with a brief but vital upturn in form. Within days, Joe Spence became the third United player to reach one hundred goals for the club as he scored in a 2–2 draw against

Cardiff; the following week he scored a hat-trick in the 5–0 win over Derby to become the club's all-time leading goalscorer. By mid-November, remarkably, United were back in the top four, at which point Barson ruptured his groin in a 4–0 defeat to Burnley, effectively ending his United career. He did come back the following March for a game against Portsmouth but broke his nose and ended up playing as a passenger on the left wing in a 1–0 defeat.

When United then lost to struggling Bury, *Athletic News* asked, 'Shall we say there is no team without a Barson?' There wasn't. United did make it through to the sixth round of the Cup, where they lost to Blackburn, but their league form was woeful. It threatened to get even worse as Jack Wilson tore a muscle in a 5–0 defeat at Derby in March, leaving United with only Mann and Ray Bennion as half-backs of any experience. Fortunately the eighteen-year-old Hughie McLenehan, a former schoolboy international who had been signed from Stockport County the previous year for a freezerful of ice-cream (one of Rocca's initiatives, obviously), emerged to plug the gaps. Still, after defeats to Villa and Bolton, United were deep in trouble.

They beat Burnley and Bolton but lost to Bury and Sheffield United to be bottom with three games remaining, two points adrift having played at least one game more than their rivals. But then United won 2–1 at Sunderland and followed that up with a 1–0 win at Arsenal in which Alf Steward made a stunning late save. With six teams in danger, United knew that victory over Liverpool on the final day would see them safe.

Bamlett's eight-year-old daughter had given her doll to her father to take to four games that season, including the matches against Sunderland and Arsenal, and United had won them all. He took the doll to that final game against Liverpool, although in truth superstitious totems probably weren't necessary. In those days there was a sense of Lancastrian fraternity between the two clubs and Liverpool had, in Fred Hopkin and Neil McBain, two former United players.

Eleven minutes in, '[Jim] Hanson lifted the ball into the air for Spence to score with a beautiful header,' the *Manchester Evening News* reported. Bill Rawlings followed in the rebound after Arthur Riley had parried a Spence cross to make it 2–0 on the half-hour, and a third quickly followed, 'Johnston successfully drawing [Donald] McKinlay out of the goal area before giving a beautiful pass to Rawlings for that player to find the net.' Spence went on to complete his hat-trick in a 6–1 victory as United survived by a point. Sunderland beat Middlesbrough 3–0 to send them down with Tottenham Hotspur.

Any hope the great escape might signal a change of fortune was short-lived. United made one signing that summer, the centre-half Billy Spencer from Newcastle, who had no sooner joined than he went down with malaria. Tommy Jones, meanwhile, suffered a hernia playing tennis, while McLenehan broke his leg and Johnston suffered ligament damage standing on a ball. Wilson suffered quinsies, pus-filled abscesses on the tonsils, and played on through the autumn in a scarf at some cost to his long-term health. At the same time, the squad had been reduced in size, which was either sensible trimming of the dead wood or a reckless reliance on a handful of core players depending which way you looked at it.

But one absence outweighed all the others. 'When Barson was at United,' the *Athletic News* reported, 'they had a personality in the pivotal position. His successor, Spencer, though useful in defence, lacks Barson's dominating influence over the opposing inside men while his attempts to construct attacks are crude and ineffective.'

A run of sixteen games without a win saw United slip to the bottom, but there came an improbable recovery after the signing of the bustling centre-forward Tommy Reid from Liverpool. He scored twice in a 3–2 win over Liverpool in February that halted the slide and United took twenty-four points from the final fifteen games of the season to survive.

The pattern of desperate starts followed by improbable recovery was followed in 1929–30 as well, as United lost eight of their opening eleven games but rallied to finish seventeenth, thanks in no small part to the left-winger George McLachlan, a gift from the Davies family.

But the inevitable could not be put off for ever. Adding to all their other problems, United had lost Jimmy Hanson to a broken leg while Taylor succumbed to his knee injuries. United lacked quantity as well as quality, but the board still refused to countenance signings. 'I believe that the depression in industry will be reflected in the attendances at football games,' said the director J. Yates at the beginning of the season. 'Clubs that have paid exorbitant prices for players will regret it before the end of the season.'

Even by their standards, though, United's start to 1930–31 was terrible as they conceded twenty-six goals in their first five games, all of them lost. Liverpool's 1899–1900 record of eight successive defeats at the start of the season was soon surpassed, as was their own record (as Newton Heath) of eleven straight defeats at any stage. Charlie Roberts, not somebody given to overstatement or controversialism, suggested in the *Guardian* that United needed nine new players if they were to survive.

The ninth of those defeats was a 4–1 loss against City that United finished with eight men and City nine because of injury. 'United are the unluckiest team in the country as regards injuries to players,' the *Football Chronicle* acknowledged, before sticking the boot in, 'and they are, perhaps, the worst team in senior football.'

United had made a loss of £1341 for the previous season but the usual dividend of 7.5 per cent was paid nonetheless. That actually amounted to only £82, but when the squad was so desperate for signings, it felt like a contemptuous gesture. Certainly it riled George Greenhough, a local taxi driver whose wife ran a boarding house for music-hall acts. He had been elected secretary of the newly formed Manchester United Supporters Club and called on the board to resign en masse, demanding that the FA should investigate the club's finances.

When the board refused to meet Greenhough, he tried to arrange a boycott of a home game against Arsenal, although after Charlie Roberts had spoken against it, 23,000, the largest crowd of the season, turned out.

The boycott may have been a failure but to an extent it achieved its purpose, drawing attention to the board and giving some voice to the dissatisfaction of fans. The *Athletic News* tended to be reserved in its criticism of United but after a joint-record 7–0 defeat to Aston Villa at the end of December 1930, it turned its guns on the board. 'With the present team,' it said, 'they cannot hope to have a chance of avoiding the fate that has been threatening for some years. They have been hit hard by injuries, it is true, but where is their enterprise?

'Why is it that other clubs can secure new men and not the United? The chairman of the club, Mr G. H. Lawton, has stated that they will not pay big transfer fees for players: that, in his opinion, it is contrary to the sport, and that youngsters should be given a chance. That view is not shared by the supporters of the club in a crisis like the present one. Why is it that Manchester City have spent so freely even with a better side than United?'

The answer was simple: United didn't spend because they had no money. Perhaps if they'd admitted as much there might have been sympathy, but the board maintained its policy of silence. Their financial situation was desperate and they were locked in a downward spiral of poor results and poor attendances that meant there was no money to buy the players who might have improved results. 'Can it be wondered that the gates at Old Trafford are dwindling to under 10,000?' the *Athletic News* went on. 'If there is no immediate change, they will probably be smaller than that ... The United have been on a decline for many years, but it is since Barson left at the end of 1927–28 that the real trouble has set in. They have not had a dominating captain since his departure.'

United were ten points adrift by the midway point. There was some improvement in the latter half of the season but nothing like enough. Bamlett's contract was not renewed, his final game coming at Sunderland on Easter Saturday 1931. United won that 2–1 but finished on twenty-two points, ten from safety. By the time United met Middlesbrough on the final day of the season, their relegation already confirmed, there was no need of an organised boycott: only 3,900 showed up.

After Bamlett had been released, Walter Crickmer was put in charge on a temporary basis. His genius, though, was less for running a team than for administration and it's doubtful anyway how much even the best of managers could have done with the demoralised shell of a squad that remained. Even in the Second Division United struggled. They won just three of the first fourteen games of the season and by November they were in another relegation battle. Attempts to find a manager to relieve the burden on Crickmer faltered. United approached J. J. Commins but he preferred to stay with Barrow in the Third Division North than move to a club that increasingly looked doomed.

As attendances dipped, the board reduced prices in the Pop Side, the cheapest part of the ground, to a shilling and to 1s6d in the covered terracing of the Main Stand. An attempt to introduce a 6d ticket for the unemployed was blocked by the FA. The financial situation was so bad that Mrs Davies had had to advance the club £5000 in the summer just to cover wages, while fans would wash the players' kit to cut laundry bills. By September the deficit was £2509 and the overdraft had crept beyond £2000. Crowds of 15,000 were needed just to break even on match days but they were rarely a third of that. A request was made to the brewery, which still owned the ground, to allow the club to defer a mortgage payment; United's income tax was in arrears and the club asked Stretford Urban District Council if they could pay certain road charges in instalments.

At the Annual Shareholders' Meeting that November, the board admitted the extent of United's plight. Greenhough attempted a vote of no confidence, but his bid to present a 6000-signature petition was blocked. On 18 December, Crickmer was told by the bank that no further credit would be advanced. There was no money to pay the wages of players or staff.

United needed another Major to tug at the heartstrings of a wealthy benefactor; the nearest thing they had was Louis Rocca. He approached James Gibson of Briggs, Jones and Gibson, a tailoring company that had made its money manufacturing uniforms, initially for the armed forces and then for Manchester's tram drivers and conductors. Gibson wasn't a football fan (although given how United had been playing that might have been an advantage) but Rocca tried to persuade him that he couldn't let such a symbol of Manchester go under. Or that's Rocca's story – and he was never somebody to underplay his own role as a Mancunian Zelig. Far more plausible, as both Justin Blundell and Iain McCartney argue, is that first contact was made by the journalist Stacey Linnett, a regular lunch partner of Gibson.

Whoever initiated the move, Gibson was intrigued. He had a reputation for taking over failing companies and turning them round, so perhaps he saw commercial possibilities, but he was also motivated by civic pride. 'Manchester is suffering enough today through depression without it being known that she cannot afford to keep a famous club,' he said. 'I do not think it would help Manchester business and Lancashire trade in general if such a famous club as United was allowed to drop out without some definite stand being made to resurrect it.'

But Gibson, as he put it, had no intention of being a 'milch cow'. He agreed to take on the club from 16 December to 9 January, handed over £2000 to cover costs, paid the staff and gave them their Christmas turkeys, but he was clear that he would only maintain his involvement if Manchester proved it wanted a second club to support. 'If the public will back me up,' he said, 'and give me any justification for carrying on, I will assure them that the United will not fail.'

He seems very quickly to have grasped what United needed if he were to put them 'on a level with the great teams in the country, such as Arsenal'. There would be a new roof, he said, on the Pop Side, but there would also be signings. 'United want a good centre-half, a centre-forward and two wingers. Money ranging anywhere from £12,000 to £20,000 must be expected to be spent in securing players.' He also attacked the board for their 'unaccountable inertia' and their reliance on the goodwill of Mrs Davies.

It was precisely what fans wanted to hear, but not everybody was convinced, the *Guardian* expressing scepticism about the promises of 'jam tomorrow'. The board, though, agreed to resign when Gibson wanted them to and the FA gave their clearance for his takeover. Gibson met with Greenhough, recognising the benefits of having him onside, and on his advice put Crickmer, the trainer Jack Pullar and the local journalist Navigator in charge of team affairs until a manager could be found. Recognising what Herbert Chapman had achieved at Arsenal, Gibson said he was looking for a former player who could coach his charges. Greenhough was impressed enough to disband his own supporters' association and endorse a new, official one.

On the day Gibson issued his call for more support, 4000 turned up to see United lose 1–0 at home to Bristol City. By the next home game, though, the Christmas Day fixture against Wolves, the message had got through. The gate that day was 20,000 up on the season's previous best as 33,312 saw United win 3–2. Gibson was so encouraged that at half-time he went down to the Pop Side and promised fans that the club would go on. However, a reminder of the reality of the situation came the following day in the return fixture as United went to Molineux and, for the third time in their history, lost 7–0.

On 5 January 1932 Gibson agreed to take on United's liabilities, which were more than £40,000, then launched an appeal for £20,000 to be ring-fenced for transfers that included a patron's scheme that was effectively a three-year season ticket.

As four other investors came forward, the board resigned on 19 January and the following day the new board was elected with Gibson as its chairman. A week later he was named president.

The attempts to get fans and local businesses to commit funds largely failed but over the final three months of the season, Gibson financed the purchase of nine players for a combined total of £13,000. Just because players are being signed, though, doesn't mean they're the right ones. None of them made a huge impact other than Ernest 'Ginger' Vincent, a defender picked up from Southport, who managed sixty-five games for the club over four years. Nonetheless, with Reid, whose form underwent wild fluctuations, back on song, United's relegation fears gradually faded, a run of seven wins in eight games from the end of January carrying them into mid-table where they remained.

The search for a new manager came to an end that summer as Gibson appointed the flamboyant former Scotland inside-right Scott Duncan, a sharp dresser noted for his habit of wearing spats. He had been working as a law clerk in Dumbarton when he was offered professional terms by the local club, moving to Newcastle in 1908. He returned to Scotland five years later, signing for Rangers – although he also guested twice for Celtic during the war. After serving as a signalling instructor in the Royal Field Artillery, Duncan rejoined Dumbarton in 1918 and played briefly for Cowdenbeath before retiring after a third spell at his home-town club. His first managerial experience came with Hamilton Academical but it was at Cowdenbeath where he made his name, keeping them in the top flight despite a limited budget throughout his seven-year tenure.

For all the optimism Gibson's takeover had inspired, the 1932–33 season started with the sort of disillusionment to which United fans had become accustomed. 'There was nothing amiss at Old Trafford on Saturday except the Manchester United team,' the *Guardian* noted in its report of a 1–1 draw against Stoke City in mid-September. 'New red and white paint gleamed everywhere, there was a new pitch that even a Hobbs would not have had to pat too vigorously had a Bowes been bowling, a new idea in the shape of ball-boys wearing long white coats with red collars and cuffs, a new optimism declared by a gate of 25,000 – and the United of the bad, old days.' Stoke won 2–0.

An eleven-game unbeaten run through the autumn dragged United towards the top of the table, but they never achieved any level of consistency and lost fourteen games to finish the season sixth. The following season was far worse. United lost seven of their first fifteen games, and then their form really deteriorated. They picked up a single point in a run of nine games through December and January and although there was a slight recovery, they went into the final day needing to win away to Millwall to stay up.

The day before the game, Duncan took a walk from the club's base at Bexhill to Hastings and there popped into a palmist's. She told him all would be well. She was right, even though the inside-left Ernie Hine was injured early on and left to limp up and down the wing. A crowd of 35,000 at the Den saw United win 2–0 with goals from Tom Morley and Jack Cape. A further 3000 welcomed the team back at Manchester Central. Still, the relief couldn't disguise the fact that United were very much the second team in Manchester, City having won the FA Cup a week earlier.

Results improved the following season as the club established a new training ground at the Cliff, but United remained inconsistent, coming fifth. They did, though, make a profit of £4490, an indication of Gibson's acuity. After the final game of the season, away at Plymouth, for instance, he arranged a friendly at St Austell, splitting the gate receipts with the home club to turn a profit from a trip that would otherwise have represented a significant outlay. That same year, he persuaded Midland Railway to put in a halt stop at Old Trafford on the Liverpool and Warrington line and to run match-day specials.

Soon it was possible to get to the ground direct from Stockport, Crewe, Birmingham and London; United for the first time had begun to look beyond Manchester for support.

A run of nineteen games without defeat at the end of the season saw United go up in 1936, with promotion sealed in a fraught game at Bury. Victory, Old International (the pseudonym of Don Davies, who would later work for the *Guardian*) wrote in the *Manchester Evening News*, 'came as manna to their thousands of hungry followers, whose hurried rush to be present had left them no time for tea'. It was a close-run thing. Two goals from Tom Manley and a third from the inside-right George Mutch put United 3–0 up, but Bury pulled it back to 3–2. 'Six minutes to go,' Old International went on, 'Mutch, lamed by a kick from [Billy] Whitfield, was given a great-hearted, one-legged impersonation of [Billy] Bryant on the line, this releasing Bryant for a spell of useful tireless vagabondage all over the place. One last shot from [Thomas] Bamford, a daisycutter past the post, and the referee's whistle formally announced Manchester United's happy return to their proper sphere. Thousands of oily, begrimed, and jubilant Manchester workmen poured onto the field, eager for Red Shirts to chair.'

They were relegated immediately, though, using thirty-one players in that 1936–37 season as they finished second-bottom, two points from safety. In November 1937, Duncan resigned to take over at Ipswich Town and Walter Crickmer was re-appointed.

Duncan had entered a youth team into the Manchester League in 1932–33 as part of Gibson's desire that the club should produce its own players, something that took a great leap forward in 1937 when Crickmer set up the Manchester United Junior Athletic Club (Mujacs). Once he was manager, the emphasis on youth became increasingly pronounced. Johnny Carey, Charlie Mitten, John Aston and Stan Pearson, players who would have a major impact after the Second World War, all came up through that system.

Also in 1937, United signed the seventeen-year-old Jack Rowley, who would go on to become one of the most prolific goalscorers in the history of the club. He had first been seen as a fifteen year old but he preferred to play for Wolverhampton Wanderers in his home city. When they released him two years later and he joined Bournemouth and Boscombe Athletic, though, United pounced after Gibson had seen him playing in Dorset. United's scouts it seemed, were everywhere. Pearson was recommended by the club secretary at the Adelphi Lads Club, Mitten was spotted at the Queen Victoria Military College in Dunblane and Morris was picked up after a member of United's coaching staff heard passengers discussing him on a train.

John Carey was signed at the age of seventeen from St James's Gate in Dublin. Rocca had gone to Ireland to watch Benny Gaughran but on learning that the centre-forward had signed for Celtic, he changed plans, stayed an extra night and went to see Carey instead, making his approach at the final whistle, completing the signing and taking Carey back with him on the ferry.

With a young side, United were promoted at the first attempt and, in 1938–39, with two wins and a draw in their final three games, they maintained their place in the First Division relatively comfortably. Financially, they were on a stronger footing than at any time since the Great War, having made a profit in five successive years. 'We have no intention of buying any more mediocrities,' Gibson told the club AGM in 1939. 'From now on we will have a Manchester United composed of Manchester players.' The outbreak of global hostilities that September and the suspension of the league after one game meant it would be six years before that policy could be tested.

During the Second World War, German bombers targeted the docks at Trafford Park and factories such as Metropolitan Vickers, which built Lancaster bombers, and Ford, which made engines for Spitfires. Inevitably, there was collateral damage.

The Free Trade Hall, the Royal Exchange, the assize courts, Victoria Station, various schools, Old Trafford baths and Old Trafford cricket ground had all been hit when, on the night of 11 March 1941, a bomb fell on the Main Stand at Old Trafford football ground.

It caused significant damage and meant the stadium was essentially unusable. The War Damages Commission eventually agreed to help rebuild all ten league grounds that had suffered air-raid damage and offered United £17,478 towards the costs, although that money was only to be released in March 1948. For a while it was of largely academic importance with league football in abeyance but after the D-Day landings, as an Allied victory became increasingly probable, it became a significant problem for a club beginning to prepare for the future.

Old Trafford aside, the club had been relatively untouched by the war. Only one player died, the full-back Hubert Redwood, who succumbed to tuberculosis contracted while serving for the South Lancashire Regiment. Crickmer, meanwhile, had had a fortunate escape. He served as a special constable in Manchester, and had been buried under a bomb-hit building on the same night that Old Trafford was hit. The centre-half Allenby Chilton, who had volunteered for the Durham Light Infantry, was injured at Normandy and Caen, and the inside-forward Johnny Morris saw a close friend killed in the tank corps, but most players found less dangerous roles.

In December 1944, Louis Rocca wrote to Matt Busby, a former Liverpool wing-half who was serving as a company sergeant major in the 9th Battalion King's Liverpool Regiment and was looking for a coaching or managerial role in Scotland. The plan to turn to Busby had been drawn up remarkably early, hatched in 1941 at a cottage near Cranbourne in Dorset during a conversation between Gibson and his friend Captain Bill Williams, a sports officer for the army's Southern Command. Williams suggested Busby would make a fine manager and arranged for him to guest in a couple of games for Bournemouth so Gibson could take a look and assess his character. Gibson saw a born leader and decided that when football was ready to start again after the war, he would make Busby his manager.

Busby had been born in Orbiston, part of the mining community of Bellshill in North Lanarkshire. His father was killed during the First World War and his mother for a time planned to emigrate to the US but, in 1928, at the age of eighteen, Busby joined Manchester City. He very nearly didn't make it as a player. He found the atmosphere at the club cold, writing in *Soccer at the Top* of 'a seemingly unbridgeable gulf between first-team players and the rest, and an even wider gulf between players and management'.

It didn't help that his lack of pace meant that initially he failed to impress in his occasional run-outs in the forward line. When he fell ill with pneumonia he nearly gave up but was taken in by City's captain Jimmy McMullen. 'I vowed,' he wrote, 'that if I ever became a manager I would respect players as individuals who needed individual treatment.'

Still, after two years at the club, he was playing for the third team and had seen United baulk at a fee of £150 to sign him, when there came a stroke of good fortune. A triallist failed to show up for a reserve team game so Busby was asked to fill in at right-half. He excelled and soon afterwards the first-team right-half, Matt Barrass, was injured. Busby seized his opportunity.

In total, he played 204 games for City, helping them to the 1934 FA Cup. In 1936 he joined Liverpool and had played 115 games for them when the war ended his career. Busby was quiet and dignified, mature beyond his years, wearing a crombie coat and a trilby and smoking a pipe even in his early twenties, which, for Eamon Dunphy in his book about Busby, *A Strange Kind of Glory*, was a sign of unobtrusive rebellion, the working-class boy adopting the signifiers of the establishment. Certainly he projected an intelligence and quiet authority and, perhaps for that reason, when Rocca wrote to him, he'd already been offered a position as assistant manager to George Kay at Anfield.

Rocca, though, had become friends with Busby through their involvement in the Manchester Catholic Sportsman's Club. Sending letters via the Royal Military Academy at Sandhurst to maintain secrecy, he persuaded Busby to consider taking charge at United. Busby was still in uniform when, in early February 1945, he met Gibson for the first time at Cornbrook Cold Storage, one of the many businesses the chairman owned.

Busby had clear plans. He wanted control over team selection and to have the final say on transfers. He also warned it would take five years before the sort of team he wanted would begin to emerge. This was all relatively new. Herbert Chapman at Huddersfield then Arsenal had pioneered the notion of the manager almost as an auteur and, although the thirties saw the emergence of other dominant figures in the dug-out – the likes of Major Frank Buckley at Wolves or Peter McWilliam at Tottenham – the vast majority of managers were little more than functionaries providing a bridge between the board room and the dressing room. Gibson was impressed by Busby's ambition and the straightforward way in which he laid out his vision and, on 19 February, the thirty-six-year-old signed a five-year contract worth £350 a year plus bonuses and perks and a house in Chorlton-cum-Hardy.

Busby, though, couldn't take over straight away; first he had to be demobbed. That spring he was in Bari preparing for an army game when he saw the former West Brom wing-half Jimmy Murphy taking a training session for NCOs. 'His audience was entranced,' Busby said. 'It was as if he was delivering a sermon.' He offered him the job of assistant manager on the spot. Although the two shared a religion – Murphy was a Welsh Catholic of Irish descent – they were opposites who complemented each other perfectly: Murphy passionate and approachable, the first line of contact for players; Busby more reserved, the great authority in the background. In those days, though, he was involved on the training field: an early photograph shows him greeting players dressed pretty much as they are in a roll-neck sweater and baggy shorts.

Mujacs had been able to continue throughout the conflict, meaning that – in theory at least – there was still a supply of youth players for Busby to draw on, as well as the remnants of the 1939 squad. Jack Smith and Bill Bryant were sold straight away and only one signing was made in 1946–47, Gibson spending £4000 of his own money to bring in the thirty-one-year-old Celtic winger Jimmy Delaney, who had been born around a mile from Busby in Lanarkshire. Delaney started out at Stoneyburn Juniors, attracting the attention of Celtic, with whom he won two league titles and scored the winner in the 1937 Scottish Cup final. His career was almost ended in 1939 when his arm was badly broken in a game at Arbroath. A surgeon wanted to amputate but the arm was saved by a bone graft. Recovery, though, was a long and difficult process and it was two and a half years before Delaney returned to action. Scotland's selectors remained sceptical as to whether he would ever come back but after fans gathered outside the SFA offices and chanted his name, Delaney was picked for a friendly against England in April 1944. He played superbly but when he arrived home he found his infant son critically ill. He died a few hours later.

Celtic turned down Delaney's request for a wage increase the following year and he was transfer-listed at his own request. Busby reacted immediately. There were other changes. Henry Cockburn was moved from inside-forward to wing-half because of his lack of pace. Johnny Carey, similarly, was shuffled back in the side, from inside-forward to wing-half to full-back. Mitten had described him as 'a bloody terrible inside-forward ... a bad player, slow and cumbersome' but Busby saw something of himself in the serious, mature Carey, even if he was a teetotal vegetarian.

United finished second in that first season back after the war, despite being forced to play home games at Maine Road because of the bomb damage at Old Trafford. Their form in

1945–46, when the league was still split into northern and southern sections, had encouraged optimism and crowds remained at over 30,000 all season. They ended up missing out on the title by a point, a defeat by the eventual champions Liverpool in their fourth-last game of the season proving costly. 'There can be no doubt he has scored a personal triumph in guiding the team through its best season in years,' said Alf Clarke. 'Blackboard and easel methods are not Matt Busby's way; he believes in practical demonstrations.'

That was a tough, experienced team, full of players who weren't afraid to speak their minds, which was just what Busby wanted. Footballers, he said, had to exhibit 'flair, skill and character . . . and the most important of these is character'. Candour, he believed, kindled talent. 'Matt encouraged us to analyse each other's faults at straight-talking sessions with no punches pulled,' said Mitten. 'We found this honesty made us a much more formidable team.'

Busby had been told that he could have complete control of team affairs and he made sure that promise was kept. When Harold Hardman, a director, criticised Carey after a game within earshot of Busby, the manager brought up 'interference by directors' at the next board meeting, forcing Gibson to back him. He was also determined that the club should look after players, remembering how his own form at City had suffered and how isolated he had felt when his wife Jean had a miscarriage. That meant all unmarried players living in club houses and every player being given a club blazer and flannels. There were outings and golf days at Davyhulme Golf Club, where players would meet every Monday either for a round or a frame of billiards. 'He never browbeats a player for some blatant mistake on the field,' the journalist Tom Jackson wrote in the *Manchester Evening News* in 1947. 'He takes him to a quiet corner for a fatherly chat and a pat of encouragement. The player is refreshed and unembarrassed at being shown the right way.'

Everything was designed to inspire a collegiate spirit.

Mitten was scathing of Busby and Murphy's tactical acumen, which he claimed amounted to little more than telling his players to 'go out and play', but he admired how they inspired a sense of collective purpose. Other players, though, were adamant that Busby would give them more detailed instruction. 'I always wanted ... creative football,' Busby said. 'I wanted method. I wanted to manage the team as I felt players ought to be managed. To begin with I wanted a more humane approach than there was when I was playing. Sometimes lads were just left on their own. The first team hardly recognised the lads underneath. There never seemed to be enough interest taken in players. The manager was at his desk and you saw him once a week. From the start I tried to make the smallest member think he was part of the club.'

A run of five defeats in eight games from the beginning of September scuppered any chance of a real challenge for the league in 1947–48, but by the turn of the year United were playing bright, attacking football that was drawing huge crowds. In January 1948, a club record 81,962 turned up at Maine Road for a 1–1 draw against Arsenal. A week earlier, United had won a dramatic FA Cup third-round tie in heavy rain before a 65,000 crowd at Aston Villa. 'For dramatic content and depth of plot,' Geoffrey Green wrote, 'that Villa–United tie lives with the best ... as a match of high drama, swaying one way then another and heightened by the storm of rain, it takes some beating.'

Villa were ahead inside fourteen seconds, before a United player had even touched the ball but, as Green described it, 'Delaney, Morris, Rowley, Pearson and Mitten thought as one man and moved as one at top speed. Their approach passing was brilliant and imaginative ... Villa were cut to ribbons.' Rowley and Morris both struck twice and Delaney added a fifth before half-time. A George Edwards corner slipped through Crompton's grip just after the break, though, and in thick mud, Villa's superior strength began to tell. When Dicky Dorsett converted an eighty-first-minute penalty to make it

5–4, an improbable comeback seemed on, only for Pearson to score from a corner with two minutes remaining to seal a 6–4 victory. It was, Green said, 'a grey, damp winter's day touched by magic. It was a match of superlatives, in which football science was later challenged by undying courage.'

What followed was an odyssey of northern grounds with United unable to play at home and unable to use Maine Road if City had also been drawn at home. They beat Liverpool at Goodison Park, Charlton at Leeds Road and Preston at Maine Road to reach a semi-final against Derby County, played at the neutral ground of Hillsborough. Stan Pearson scored a hat-trick as United won 3–1.

Manchester was gripped by the excitement of the final and a possible second FA Cup. United received more than 30,000 applications for their allocation of 12,000 places and an hour before kick-off tickets priced at 3s were trading for £1. Those who made their way to London were buoyed by the news that Rowley had passed a late fitness test and would play, which only added to the optimism of the *Manchester Evening News* reporter Eric Thornton who, as he was quick to point out in pretty much every piece, had been to every Cup final since 1923. As a Wembley expert, he 'tested the turf' the day before the game and had encouraging news to report. 'It was springy – it had been newly cut and marked out – and it seems to me it will play firm, with no extra bounce and in favour of United.'

Perhaps more significant was the news that Blackpool's left-back, Ron Stuart, was injured and so had to be replaced by Johnny Crosland. Blackpool's preparations can't have been helped either by the scheduling of the inaugural Footballer of the Year dinner for the night before the final. Stanley Matthews and Stan Mortensen both attended and, although neither drank, Matthews admitted he had spent the evening, at which he won the main award, anxiously watching the clock rather than relaxing with the rest of the squad in the hotel.

Thornton was convinced United would prevail. 'The United best Wembley side in years', the headline on his preview proclaimed. 'On the one hand,' he wrote, 'we have a United acknowledged as an outstanding example of soccer artistry allied to splendid teamwork; on the other hand we exhibit a Blackpool possessing in the Stanleys two of the finest forwards the game has known over its long course. Two stars never make the bright night sky, and unless their colleagues discover sudden temporary brilliance, Stanley Matthews and Stanley Mortensen cannot make a team to beat one of better all-round strength.' He did, though, acknowledge that United's half-line might not be as good as Blackpool's.

Still, that didn't seem to worry many of those who travelled south to be met by media still obsessed by the thickness of Lancastrian sandwiches, nor the 3000 who turned up at London Road Station to wave the team off. One fan took six crates of beer south with him, leaving them in left-luggage at Euston, worried that a United victory would lead to London being drunk dry.

'By noon every strategic point in the city had been overrun and consolidated,' the MEN reported. 'The Eros statue in Piccadilly Circus was swamped under a flood of red and white. Oblivious of the traffic swirling round them, they stood and sat in the warm spring sunshine eating sandwiches, drinking beer out of bottles, ringing bells, cranking rattles, deliriously happy. More red and white outside the Palace, where gay umbrellas in United's colours promenaded up and down, mimicking the sentries. Red and white, too, astride the lions in Trafalgar Square. And here Blackpool joined forces. There were gay splashes of tangerine as every orange tulip in sight was snatched up at sky-high prices and tied on coat lapels.'

A photograph showed ten fans in suits and overcoats, most wearing rosettes, standing on the Embankment, sceptically watching a pavement artist. Suits were standard dress for fans. Even a fourteen-year-old who was reported missing from his home in Stockport over the weekend, presumed to have set off to hitch-hike to Wembley, was described as 'wearing a blue pin-stripe suit with black shoes and a blue gabardine raincoat. He had only 1s in his pocket.' Given there was no follow-up, it seems likely that William Hough returned home safely.

Hough's disappearance wasn't the only eye-catching news that day. A grocer was fined £15 for adulterating tea with Argentinian *maté* after his excuse that his pet Alsatian had knocked over two tins so their contents mixed on the ground was laughed out of court. A forger who had ripped off the Post Office for £585 blamed an underworld figure known only as 'Mad Jock'. The *MEN* radio reviewer described seeing 'television' for the first time and concluded that people on television look smaller than in a cinema but that the sound quality was good. And, the day of the final, France banned pigeon races to the dismay of Manchester Flying Club whose members had trained 600 birds for races from Rennes and Nantes. 'The ban is a big blow to our members,' said the club secretary J. A. Wood, although presumably it freed up basket-space for carrying sandwiches to London. Alternate races were sought in the Channel Islands.

But the focus was Wembley, which saw a greater influx than for any final since 1923. There were stories of fans climbing the drainpipes to get into the stadium, while one supporter unpicked a padlock on a gate using a hairpin.

As in 1909, a clash of kits meant United could not wear red, but this time it was they who turned out in blue shirts, with Blackpool wearing white. Busby had tried to calm his side, but Chilton was so nervous that he was about to leave the dressing room for the anthems when he realised he was still wearing his everyday shoes.

Blackpool were without the injured full-back Ronnie Suart, replacing him with the centre-half Johnny Crosland. They also switched Mortensen, often an inside-right, to centre-forward to try to take advantage of Chilton's lack of pace, a ploy the effectiveness of which was demonstrated after fifteen minutes as the forward swept by the centre-half, who chopped him down to concede a penalty. In the modern age there is no doubt Chilton would have been sent off; in 1948, the incident merely provoked an extended debate about whether the foul had been committed inside or outside the box. 'I was behind the play,' said the referee C. J. Barrick, 'but was certain that Mortensen was in the area when he was tackled. I did not consult my linesman but looked to him for confirmation. His flag pointed to the spot.' The television footage leaves little doubt; Barrick was right. Eddie Shimwell banged in the penalty. 'He was notorious for the whack he gave the ball from the spot,' the goalkeeper Jack Crompton noted.

Crompton was lucky to be playing and largely had Busby to thank that he was. A month before the final, the goalkeeper had suffered back pain. The club physio, Ted Dalton, was concerned and as the afflicted area became increasingly inflamed he told Busby. The club doctor diagnosed an abscess and said it would settle with time. As the final approached, though, it wasn't getting any better.

Crompton had recently lost his sister to whom he'd been close and that, he suggested, meant that he was more accepting of the doctor's decision that he wouldn't be able to take part than he would otherwise have been. With only two inexperienced keepers in reserve, though, Ken Pegg and Berry Brown, Busby was determined that he should play. On the Wednesday before the final, as the rest of the squad went to Weybridge for their preparations, Busby took Crompton to Ancoats hospital. There Crompton saw him in animated conversation with a surgeon, who eventually agreed to operate. Crompton said after surgery it was still 'painful' but after an injection it was 'more comfortable' and he was declared fit for the final.

Injury had already had a major impact on Crompton's life. He had planned to join the RAF but a chipped femur suffered playing for Newton Heath Loco in a local cup match ruled him out and he ended up passing the war in an office job for a firm that made iron pots. He was told to give up football, and for a long time he could only go up hills by walking backwards. But he worked hard at the YMCA gym and eventually recovered sufficiently to play for Goslings, a local amateur side run by three brothers who owned a greengrocer's. He played one wartime game for City and was asked back, but claimed he was injured so he could play in a vital league game for Goslings against the Army, at which City lost interest. Soon after, Rocca, working as a scout for United, approached him and he signed amateur terms, turning professional in 1945.

Midway through the first half, Pearson headed against the bar and then, on the half-hour, Carey spread the ball wide for Delaney. Eric Hayward and the keeper Joe Robinson left Delaney's cross for each other and Rowley, the master-finisher, stole in, lifted the ball over the goalkeeper and nudged it into the empty net. All season Delaney and Rowley had switched position during games, both happy playing either centrally or wide, but in the final they were far less flexible. Delaney was struggling for fitness and had been advised to stay wide where he was less likely to aggravate the injury than he would in the crowded centre. 'We kept quiet all week that Jimmy was a very doubtful starter for Wembley,' Busby explained. 'The ankle injury he suffered against Chelsea the previous week was slow to heal ... and although we passed him as fit, there was always a risk he would break down. We had an anxious moment 20 minutes after the start when Delaney got up limping after a tackle. He limped for the rest of the game.'

'I watched Johnny Morris hurry to take the free-kick,' Rowley said. He meant to get it across while the Blackpool defence was at sixes and sevens. 'Suddenly the thought came to me that this might be our last chance of drawing level. I felt we must get that ball into the net somehow else we'd never win. I saw it whip over fast. Blackpool still hadn't had time to take up position. Johnny rushed it too much for them. I threw myself at the ball ... And what a thrill to see it go in!'

'We weren't in it after Morris's free-kick,' Harry Johnston admitted. 'He took it so fast we were caught on one leg.' Hayward wondered vainly if there might have been a foul. 'Delaney's lob floated over my head as my goalkeeper called, "Right",' he said. 'I felt Rowley flash past me, he hooked the ball out of Joe's hands and dribbled into the empty net.'

Blackpool restored their lead five minutes later as Matthews played a free-kick square for Hugh Kelly to set up Mortensen to score with an awkward angled shot that seemed to catch Crompton wrong-footed, creeping into the far corner to maintain the forward's record of scoring in every round. 'I headed forward Matthews' quickly taken free-kick,' said Kelly. 'Mortensen, like a flash, picked up the pass, turned in his stride and hit the ball to the opposite corner.' Blackpool led, Geoffrey Green asserted, 'not because of any superior quality in their football, pure as it had been, but by snatching their chances. Manchester, in fact, had perhaps enjoyed the greatest share of the attack.'

That wasn't a universal view. 'It all started in exactly the same way as other English Cup finals – favourites spluttering and stumbling and looking altogether a most unimaginative lot, outsiders showing all the enterprise and getting their just reward,' wrote the former Heart of Midlothian goalkeeper Jack Harkness in the *Sunday Post*. 'Here we had Matthews in all his glory . . . And here was Mortensen, surely the finest centre-forward in Britain today . . . During Blackpool's long period of ascendancy Wee Alec [Munro] was a veritable hero in making openings and spoonfeeding the two Stans up front.'

Just before half-time, Crompton recalled in *Game of Their Lives*, 'their left-winger, Walter Rickett, went past Johnny Carey and cut inside. He whacked the ball towards the far post and I went flying and turned it wide.' Carey thanked his goalkeeper, recognising the embarrassment he'd spared him.

It was Blackpool's right wing that was the greater concern, though. Busby was obsessed by Matthews, then thirty-three but showing no diminution in his powers. Later that year he would show just how good he still was, playing a starring role as England beat the world champions Italy 4–0 in Turin.

John Anderson was told to stick tight to him, while Mitten was given instructions to track back to cover him, something that wasn't common for wingers at the time. At one point Matthews said to him, 'Charlie, you'll never be a good player if you keep following me. Now fuck off back up front.' Even Crompton had been told whenever he had the ball to play it to where Matthews wasn't – something that made such a difference to his play that his brother later commented he hadn't used the ball as well as usual.

At half-time, a number of players questioned Busby's approach. He responded by telling Cockburn to close down Harry Johnston, the Blackpool centre-half and the main supply-line to Matthews. 'Matt didn't seem perturbed,' said Crompton. 'He told us we were playing well, so all we had to do was keep doing that.'

But United lost their way in the early stages of the second half. 'For a period after half-time,' Green wrote, 'the fire and precision went out of the Manchester game; they lost touch and inspiration eluded them.' Rickett and Matthews exchanged passes to create an opening for Dick but he hesitated and the chance was gone. It would prove crucial.

With twenty minutes to go, and Blackpool on top, Johnny Morris slung in a quickly taken free-kick from wide on the right and Rowley got between Hayward and Shimwell to head the ball back across goal and into the top corner. 'I saw Johnny Morris's free-kick soaring between two Blackpool defenders,' said Rowley, 'thought, "This is it," and dived forward to head the ball into the net by the far post.' Matthews was furious. 'Somebody,' he said, 'should have stood over the ball as a delaying tactic until the others took covering positions.'

Blackpool rallied. 'Mortensen came bursting through,' Crompton recalled, 'and hit a scorching shot which, he later said, he was certain was going to win the Cup for Blackpool. But I managed to dive full-length and save it; better still, I caught it. Next second I was up on my feet and threw out to Johnny Anderson . . .' He initiated a rapid break that culminated with

Morris playing in Pearson. Hayward slipped as he went in to make a challenge allowing Pearson to beat the sprawl of Robinson with a low, angled drive. 'John Anderson's through-pass was a beauty,' said Pearson. 'All I had to do was run on and score but I placed the ball so far away from the keeper that for a second I thought it was going outside. But it hit the inside of the post and rolled across to the opposite corner of the goal.'

'If only,' Mortensen said, 'I had shot high into the crowd when I was clean through, we wouldn't have lost. Jack Cromp-ton made that marvellous save; the ball sped from one end of the field to the other; Stan Pearson scored and it was over.'

Matthews was just as convinced that that had been the turning point. 'He was at an acute angle when he shot, but I'd seen Morty score from tighter positions,' he said (as, indeed, he would in Turin later that summer in England's famous win over Italy). 'This time he fired straight into the arms of Jack Crompton. Morty ground to a halt, his head dropped for an in-stant and I saw him wince. Countless centre-forwards would have failed to tuck such a chance away but by his own high standards he knew he should have done better.'

Two minutes later, the game was done as a speculative effort from Anderson dipped past a startled Robinson, whose cousin George Strong had been on the losing side for Burnley in the final the previous year. 'Anderson's thirty-yard lob appeared to be covered by our goalkeeper,' said Johnston, 'but the ball struck Hugh Kelly's head and was deflected away from the keeper.'

'Here indeed was a final worthy of the name and worthy of the occasion, a match of overflowing talent, glorious and dramatic,' the report in *The Times* enthused. It was 'a clean and glorious game, in which both sides had brought the best out of each other, and in which, sadly, there had to be a loser'.

It had been, Harkness said, 'the game of the season': 'A perfect day. A perfect setting. A perfect result. Not for one moment would I say that the better football team won. Rather

I would say Blackpool threw the Cup away because of a series of silly mistakes at the most vital moments.' John Thompson in the *Mirror* was more sympathetic. 'Yet how cleverly Blackpool played,' he wrote. 'They make history as one of the Cup's great losers – as splendid in defeat as Manchester United were in victory.'

And there was also, perhaps, a sense of regret. In the *Mail*, Roy Pesketh observed, 'the bowed shoulders of Stanley Matthews as he walked from the field almost unnoticed . . .' Matthews was thirty-three and nobody thought he would have another seventeen years of professional football in him. He had never won a trophy and it seemed then that he never would; his consecration would eventually come in a Cup final, just not for another five years.

As numerous reports observed, United's success was reward not only for one game but for Busby's whole approach. 'United won in the end fairly and squarely after being desperately near defeat and so put the seal on two seasons of good football,' Archie Ledbrooke wrote in the *Mirror*.

Or, as Green put it in characteristic style: 'Defence is negation; attack, as we saw it, perfectly executed, is life.'

And there had been a touch of fortune, not only in the fact Blackpool had had the better of parts of the game but in the way Delaney's injury had compelled him to stay wide. 'Within the superior frame of the Manchester teamwork was the power, intelligence and thrust of Rowley, Pearson and Morris, and this was the deciding factor,' Green said. 'They saw to it that Delaney, against the inexperienced Crosland, was used as much as possible. Crosland was not disgraced, but Blackpool were never quite sure where to find Delaney next.'

Three hundred thousand lined the streets of Manchester to welcome United back. They took the Cup straight to Gibson's house, where the chairman was convalescing after an illness that had kept him away from matches that season. He would die three years later, but this was the first sign that his dream was being achieved: seven of the players who had played in the Cup final had been born within walking distance of Old Trafford.

But that was only the beginning. The 1948 side was the remnants of the side built before the war and needed rejuvenation. United had their second FA Cup but, unlike in 1909, they were able to build on that. Busby's dream was similar to Gibson's but it went further. 'Right from the start,' he said, 'I was keen and determined to develop our policy of grooming youth to our methods and standards. Some might have called it brainwashing. It was nothing of the sort. It was just a matter of bringing them up with the right values and instincts.'

His faith would be sorely tested in the two decades that followed but those values would, in the end, have their reward.

CHAPTER 3

European Cup quarter-final second leg, Marakana, Belgrade,
5 February 1958

Crvena Zvezda	**3–3**	**Manchester United**
Kostić 46, 58		*Viollet 2*
Tasić 50 (pen)		*Charlton 30, 31*

Vladimir Beara	Harry Gregg
Miljan Zeković	Mark Jones
Novak Tomić	Bill Foulkes
Ranko Borozan	Roger Byrne
Lazar Tasić	Duncan Edwards
Ljubiša Spajić	Eddie Colman
Dragoslav Šekularac	Bobby Charlton
Vladimir Popović	Dennis Viollet
Bora Kostić	Tommy Taylor
Jovan Cokić	Albert Scanlon
Rajko Mitić	Kenny Morgans

Milorad Pavić	Matt Busby

Ref: Karl Kainer
Bkd:
Att: 52,000

ON 6 FEBRUARY 1958, Dragoslav Šekularac, perhaps the greatest Yugoslav footballer of his generation, went to the cinema in the Zemun district of Belgrade. He had been part of the Crvena Zvezda (Red Star) side that had come from 3–0 down to draw 3–3 with Manchester United the day before, losing their European Cup quarter-final 5–4 on aggregate. He'd missed a late chance and, while he accepted United were the better side, it niggled at him. If that had gone in, there would have been a play-off. It was a thought that, by the end of the afternoon, would have taken on far darker connotations than he could ever have imagined.

Šekularac had enjoyed the games against United, had been impressed both by their ability and by their sportsmanship. After the game, on their way to the official banquet, he'd gone with Bobby Charlton and Duncan Edwards to the bar at the Metropol hotel. 'The Metropol was the best hotel in town at the time,' Šekularac said. 'I remember the bar was famous. I had my wedding there. I was a regular customer. I had a discount. They knew me there.'

There'd never been an opposing side for whom he'd had such admiration. 'It was not my custom to be so friendly and to go out with players from the opponent's team,' he said. 'Their friendship, their kindness, how they received us in the first leg in Manchester and how they behaved here, and how we greeted each other, even today I take my hat off to them.'

As he left the cinema, somebody ran up to him. Šekularac paused. This wasn't just a fan after an autograph; it was clear this was something serious. He couldn't quite believe the news when he was told. Even when others confirmed the story he went home, hoping there'd been some misunderstanding, until he turned on the radio. But it was true. United's plane had crashed as it had tried to take off after refuelling in Munich and there were fatalities. A team that might have been the greatest in Europe had been wiped out.

Hindsight has a tendency to blur the edges, to make progressions look smooth, as though everything was always destined to end up at the point at which it did. All the striving, all the near misses of the late forties and early fifties eventually came to fruition, but there were moments of significant upheaval and doubt along the way.

The jubilation of the 1948 Cup win soon faded to frustration among United's players that they weren't being sufficiently remunerated for their success. The Football Association had strict rules governing how players could be paid, restricting not only wages but also bonuses. Busby followed the rules to the letter – at least with his senior players – but other clubs took a rather more relaxed view. United's players, for instance, had been startled when beating Derby in the 1948 semi-final to learn that their players would have been given £100 had they gone on to win the Cup; the legal maximum was £20. 'Fresh air and physical fitness make for good health, which is better than any financial feature,' Busby wrote in *Football Monthly* in 1951. For him, young players were easier to work with, more malleable and less inclined to be seeking a little extra cash.

Money was a regular source of discontent. Busby was fair, but not generous. When, for instance, Johnny Aston discovered from Tom Finney on an England trip that clubs should include time spent as an amateur when calculating five-year benefits, Busby checked, concluded he was right, and paid arrears to eight first-team players. But he wouldn't countenance illegal payments at a time when most clubs paid them, and that led to discontent. Busby himself signed a new deal after the Cup final that earned him £3250 a year, five times his players' basic wage, making him the highest-paid employee in English football.

From his players, he demanded discipline and absolute commitment. Busby's relationship with Johnny Morris had never been comfortable, the inside-forward seeming uneasy with Busby's attempts to impose a more methodological approach. On one occasion, after United had conceded from a free-kick in a game against Blackpool, Busby had them practising with five rather than four men in the wall. After a few tries, with Busby apparently satisfied and ready to end the training session, Morris suggested the additional man made little difference and nonchalantly smacked a free-kick into the net. In itself perhaps that would have meant little, but it was part of what Busby saw as a pattern of Morris undermining him. In 1949, Morris lost his place in the team after being injured and, in his irritation, shirked training. Busby bawled him out, Morris walked off the training pitch and, a week later, found himself sold to Derby County for a world-record fee of £24,500. Johnny Downie was bought from Bradford Park Avenue for £18,000 to replace him.

When he wanted to be, Busby could be tough; loyalty meant everything. Charlie Mitten, for instance, left United in 1950 to play in the rebel league in Colombia, enticed by a £5000 signing-on fee and a weekly salary of £40 plus bonuses. He returned after a year and was banned for six months by the FA. During his suspension, Busby wouldn't even let him train with the United side, so he ended up practising with a local pub team before being sold to Fulham.

There were other changes of personnel. In 1950, Louis Rocca died and was replaced by Joe Armstrong, who set about extending United's scouting network so it stretched systematically across the whole country rather than just Manchester. Like Rocca, his genius lay less in having a great eye for a player than in knowing people and having a superb range of contacts, while he was adept at charming the parents of potential players. Busby was adamant he would never pay signing-on fees or break the laws on bonuses but he turned a blind eye to Armstrong's habit of offering inducements. Duncan Edwards' parents, for instance, were given a washing machine when their son joined United.

It was, Busby said, considered 'revolutionary' to get 'boys straight from school'. For him, though, youth was a huge advantage. 'Get them early enough . . . and they could be trained to some kind of pattern.' He – or rather Murphy – trained them in 'the Manchester United way, which was constructive football, attacking football, team football with scope for spontaneous moves of surprise by individuals capable of making something out of nothing.' Alongside that idealism, there was a determination to be the best. One season Murphy's reserve side won the Central League by nine points. When Busby congratulated him, he replied dismissively that there wasn't a single player there who would make the first team.

United recovered after an inconsistent start to finish runners-up in 1948–49, although they didn't actually go second until the penultimate game of the season. Their defence of the FA Cup ended at the semi-final, with a replay defeat to Wolves. 'Where,' asked Alf Clarke, 'is the nip of last season? The interchange of positions, the ball on the ground and so forth?'

As they returned to Old Trafford the following season, United mounted a more serious challenge, going top at the end of February and holding that position until a draw against Liverpool three weeks later prompted a run of nine games without a win. They finished second again.

A slow start undermined 1951–52: although United took thirty points from the final thirty-four available, that was only good enough for another runners-up spot.

Gradually, though, the youth policy was beginning to bear fruit. United made a profit of more than £50,000 in 1949–50 but, despite the loss of Morris and Mitten, Busby didn't spend; Murphy and the first-team coach Bert Whalley had told him of the quality that was beginning to emerge at youth level and he believed them.

Gibson, who had always championed youth, didn't live to see it. He fell ill, standing down as chairman in 1951 to be replaced by Harold Hardman who had been an outstanding amateur footballer, winning five England caps and the FA Cup with Everton in 1906 as an outside-left and taking Olympic gold with Great Britain in 1908. Hardman was noted for his modesty and frugal habits. He enjoyed lunching with friends but would rarely have more than a coffee and a bun, liked to relax with a game of dominoes and refused to take taxis even in bad weather.

After several years of deteriorating health, Gibson died the following September, shortly after United had declared themselves debt free. His wife, Violet, remained the largest shareholder until her death twenty years later. Gibson had done everything he had intended when he'd taken the chairmanship, restoring financial stability and laying the foundations for on-field success. He at least saw United win the Cup, but there were far greater glories to come.

By the beginning of 1951–52, the outside-right Johnny Berry had been signed from Bristol City and the full-back Roger Byrne, having completed his national service, had been brought into the first team. Jack Rowley scored seven in the first three games of that season, but United began inconsistently and when they lost 3–1 to Portsmouth on 17 November they lay seventh in the table. They wouldn't lose again until March, by which time they were the leaders.

A 3–1 win at Highbury in December was particularly impressive. 'The dominating factor . . .' reported the *Guardian*, 'was the leadership of Carey. The crash and thunder of attack left Carey serene and undisturbed: shrewd in anticipating a pass or going cleanly into a tackle, he invariably obtained possession of the ball then cool, poised and debonair he would glide past opponents and drive or flick adroit passes neatly to the feet or heads of forwards.'

That was part of a run of sixteen games without defeat but then came back-to-back losses against Huddersfield Town and Portsmouth. With six matches to go, United were level at the top with Arsenal, who had played a game fewer. Busby made three changes for the match against Burnley on Good Friday, moving Aston to left-back, Rowley from the wing into the centre and Byrne from left-back to left-wing. Byrne scored in a draw at Turf Moor then got two the following day in a 4–0 victory over Liverpool and another two on Easter Monday in a 6–1 home success against Burnley. Arsenal had lost at Bolton on Easter Saturday and, after playing their game in hand, were a point behind. They moved level again by beating Stoke as United, with Byrne again on target, drew with Blackpool.

But the title took a decisive turn on the penultimate week-end. As United beat Chelsea 3–0, Arsenal went down 3–1 at West Brom, meaning that, as the two contenders met on the final day, Arsenal had to win 7–0 to take the title on goal-average. That was never likely and it became even less so when injury reduced them to ten men after twenty-four minutes. United ended up sealing their first championship in forty-four years with a 6–1 victory.

The *Guardian* had little doubt that Busby's role had been vital. 'Busby,' it wrote, 'has shown himself as great a coach as he was a player, with an uncannily brilliant eye for young local play-ers' possibilities, whether in their usual or in other positions; a believer in the certainty of good football's eventual reward, and a kindly, yet when necessary firm father of his family of players ... Moreover, by eschewing the dangerous policy of going into the transfer market whenever a weakness develops and giving their chances to the many local citizens on the club's books they have made it likely that this club spirit will persist, since the club today is a Manchester one not in name only but in fact as far as most of its players are concerned.'

That's the positive view. Eamon Dunphy's interpretation in *A Strange Kind of Glory* is characteristically less idealistic: al-though his book is largely pro-Busby, he is under no illusions about the compromises Busby had to make and the disappointment he regularly felt. Even then, in the moment of that first league title, Dunphy suggests, Busby felt a sense of disillusionment, that this wasn't quite the level of football he wanted.

They may have fallen short of his ideal, but that United was built to Busby's design. His mark was everywhere, perhaps nowhere so obviously as on Johnny Carey, the 'bloody terrible inside-forward' converted into a commanding and classy full-back. Carey, the *Guardian* wrote, 'had been a model footballer – technically efficient, thanks to hard work; a fighter to the last, without ever forgetting that he is a sportsman; a steadier of the young and inexperienced, an inspirer of the older and tiring, and at all times the most modest of men, though he has won every football honour open to him.' By the time he retired in 1953, turning down the offer of a coaching job at United to become manager of Blackburn Rovers, Carey had played in every position for United apart from outside left; he even went in goal in one game at Sunderland after Crompton fell ill.

Carey wasn't the only member of United's champions nearing the end. When the championship finally arrived, it was a final validation for a lot of the side that had been at the club since the end of the war: Carey and Chilton were thirty-four, Pearson was thirty-three and Rowley thirty-two. Reconstruction was essential – and that perhaps contributed to Busby's reservations. 'The depressing thought which used to trouble me day and night,' he said, 'was the great Manchester United side was getting old . . . Had I not been so honest with myself, I might have been content to sit on my league laurels, play the over-thirty stars for a few more seasons, hoping that something would turn up in the meantime.'

He wasn't the only one whose reaction to the title was one of concern. 'The club's future,' it was announced at the 1952 AGM, 'left no cause for optimism unless radical changes were made.'

Results proved the pessimism justified. United lost seven of their first thirteen games of 1952–53 and by the end of October they were down in nineteenth. Once again, as results deteriorated, so other problems began to surface. Byrne, irritated at being played in the forward line, submitted a transfer request that, to widespread disbelief, was accepted. He was dropped for two matches then restored to the side in his preferred fullback role, at which the transfer request was withdrawn.

A friendly away to Kilmarnock offered a chance to experiment and Busby took it, fielding a swath of young players from the reserves: Jackie Blanchflower, Jeff Whitefoot, Eddie Colman, Wilf McGuinness, Duncan Edwards and David Pegg. They won 3–0 and Busby began to integrate them into the side, Pegg occupying the problem left-wing position. That December, the twenty-year-old Bill Foulkes made his debut at right-back. After moving into the centre he would become a keystone of United as they rebuilt through the sixties, an emblem of the indomitable spirit of the club. He was described by David Sadler as 'a quiet man, tough, taciturn and uncompromising'. The 'Babes' nickname came soon after, its first usage being in an *Evening Chronicle* headline after a 3–2 win over Chelsea.

The centre-forward Tommy Taylor – 'beautiful athlete . . . terrible knees', said Bobby Charlton – was signed from Barnsley in March 1953. The following month, Duncan Edwards, who would become the most iconic of all the Babes, made his debut. He was, Murphy said, 'the Koh-i-Noor diamond amongst our crown jewels'. He seemed to have been built on a different scale to other players, a huge and powerful athlete who could also pass a ball. 'Compared to him,' Charlton said, 'the rest of us were pygmies.' Edwards had been brought to Busby's attention by Joe Mercer, who at the time was the professional coach assigned to the English Schools XI. Wolves were irritated that a player from their catchment area had slipped away, but Edwards had always wanted to play for United, an indication of their reputation for youth development and the glamour that, despite their relative lack of success to that point, had, thanks largely to the scale of Old Trafford, already attached itself to their name.

Dennis Viollet, described by Charlton as 'slim and deadly quick', emerged from the youth set-up and made his debut a week after Edwards. The eighteen-year-old Billy Whelan was picked up from the Dublin club Home Farm. 'His forte,' Charlton said, 'was to scheme, to shape possibilities with his skill and excellent vision.' By the end of the season, United had risen to eighth but, more importantly, there was evidence that the youth policy instituted by Gibson and Busby might be beginning to generate something extraordinary.

That focus on youth was reflected in the fact that United won the FA Youth Cup five years in a row from 1953. The senior side came fourth in the league in 1954 and fifth the following year, by which time the average age of the side was just twenty-one. Their leader was Byrne. He had been born in 1929 and was married so tended not to socialise with the younger squad members, spending his free time working in a hospital, learning to be a physio. 'On the field Roger would shout his instructions firmly enough, let you know who was in charge of affairs,' said Charlton, 'but generally he was quiet off the field. He had the aura of a true captain.'

After a wobbly start to 1955–56 that saw them win only three of their first eight games, United hit form in mid-September. Two months later, they faced the champions Chelsea. Taylor and Edwards had returned from injury and Eddie Colman – of whom Gregg said, 'When he waggled his hips, he made the stanchions in the grandstand sway' – made his debut. United won 3–0 and, losing only three further games that season, they finished eleven points clear at the top of the table. They wrapped up the title at the beginning of April, a penalty from Berry and a goal from Taylor securing a 2–1 win over Blackpool in a game watched by 62,333 fans – but not Busby, who was travelling back to Manchester from a funeral, keeping up to date with phone calls from railway stations. Only Berry and Byrne remained from the side of four years earlier; United weren't just champions, they were the youngest side in the league. As well as the customary success in the Youth Cup, that season the reserves won the Central League: this felt like the start of a dynasty.

When United lost to Everton in October 1956, it was their first defeat in a league game for twenty-six matches. It hardly mattered. They had settled into the same rhythm as the previous season and went on to win the title by eight points. They also reached the Cup final, but were denied the first Double of the century by Aston Villa, who won 2–1. Their hopes were essentially dashed after six minutes when the Villa centre-forward Peter McParland clattered United's goalkeeper Ray Wood, knocking him unconscious and fracturing his cheekbone, forcing Jackie Blanchflower to take over in goal. 'Personally, I saw nothing vicious,' said the referee Frank Coultas. 'It was clumsy but with no foul intent.'

That United side were fluent and attacking, enjoying the mutual understanding that is only ever really achieved when a group of players grows up together. After the 6–2 win over Arsenal in early February, Don Davies had written glowingly in the *Guardian* of their 'freshness of approach . . . gaiety of mind and . . . physical resilience'. United's reputation for promoting youth became self-fulfilling. Bobby Charlton, who made his debut in 1956, had yearned to play for the club as a boy, remembering how he'd found himself wanting United to win the 1948 FA Cup final when most of his peers, charmed by Matthews, had backed Blackpool. Busby first became aware of Charlton when tipped off by the headmaster of his brother Jack's school. Busby sent a scout to watch Bobby in a game between Jarrow and Hebburn, after which the scout, suitably impressed, approached Charlton's mother, the redoubtable Cissie.

And United soon became even more glamorous and exciting. The 1956–57 season wasn't just about retaining the title, it was also about the introduction of English clubs to European football. Chelsea, the previous year, had allowed themselves to be browbeaten by the league into rejecting Uefa's invitation to take part in the European Cup. United, backed by the FA president Stanley Rous, ignored them and so began a romance between the club and the competition that has never wavered.

United's first European tie, played on 12 September 1956, was against Anderlecht. They won 2–0 in Brussels before a 10–0 triumph at Maine Road (Old Trafford still being in the process of installing floodlights). They beat Borussia Dortmund 3–2 at home, with 76,598 turning out at Maine Road, and drew 0–0 in the return leg in Germany to advance to the quarter-final.

Away to Athletic in Bilbao, United were beaten 5–3. Their return to Manchester was delayed by weather, players helping to clear ice from the wings of the plane, a portent of what was to follow. Busby was insistent they had to leave as soon as possible: he knew that Alan Hardaker, the secretary of the league, still furious at United for ignoring his warnings and participating in the European Cup, would need few excuses to penalise United if they somehow missed that Saturday's league game.

At Maine Road in the second leg, United won 3–0 in a thrilling game that sowed in the wider consciousness an image of the excitement European football could provide. 'My hands are still trembling as I write,' exulted Henry Rose in the *Daily Express*. 'My heart still pounds. And a few hours have passed since, with 65,000 other lucky people, I saw the greatest soccer victory in history.' Murphy wept when Johnny Berry hit the third with five minutes remaining, describing the game as 'the greatest night of my life in soccer'.

In the semi-final, United faced the might of Real Madrid, the defending champions. In the first leg at the Bernabéu, United held out at 0–0 for an hour before goals from Héctor Rial and Alfredo Di Stéfano in quick succession gave Madrid a 2–0 lead. Taylor nodded in a Whelan chip with eight minutes remaining but almost immediately Raymond Kopa created a chance for Enrique Mateos to restore the two-goal advantage. The experience of Athletic meant United were not without hope but at Old Trafford, under the new lights, Madrid went 2–0 up. Taylor and Charlton both scored to save face, but not the tie.

A third straight title seemed a possibility as United dropped just one point in their opening six games of the following season but a run of five defeats in eight games left them fifth by the end of October, six points behind the leaders Wolves. The European Cup campaign, though, was proceeding comfortably enough. Shamrock Rovers had been dismissed 9–2 on aggregate and Dukla Prague 3–1, setting up a quarter-final against the Yugoslav champions, Crvena Zvezda. They were a strong side, featuring arguably the greatest Yugoslav goalkeeper of all time, Vladimir Beara, and a fine goalscorer in Bora Kostić. For Charlton, though, it was their playmaker who stood out. 'They had a little midfielder, Dragoslav Šekularac, who was so good, so clever in Manchester, that I found myself asking, "Why haven't I heard of this fellow before?"' Šekularac was only twenty then; he would go on to become one of only five individuals to be named '*Zvezdina zvezda*' – stars of the Star, the all-time legends of the club.

Zvezda's policy in the first leg at Old Trafford was to attack. 'We were a big club,' said the midfielder Vladica Popović. 'We weren't intimidated. We went there to show what we could do. There was no chance that we would play defensively. We were raised that way.'

But it was United who began the more aggressively. Charlton went through one-on-one with Beara in the fourth minute but put the shot just wide. 'The visitors,' the report in the Yugoslav newspaper *Politika* noted, 'were lucky to escape those first fifteen minutes without conceding. They were under constant pressure.' At the same time, though, 'Zvezda's goalkeeper was not many times in direct danger'.

'Only after twenty minutes,' *Politika* went on, 'did Zvezda come into the game and in those moments what was noticeable was the tireless work of [Rajko] Mitić.' Zvezda's thirty-five-year-old captain had a long-range effort that went just wide and

then, after thirty-six minutes, '[Lazar] Tasić dribbled past two
challenges and shot from 20m,' *Politika* said. 'It was not so
powerful but from a difficult angle and Gregg, having seen
the ball too late, was left helpless. After that the visitors were
again under pressure.'

Zvezda led 1–0 at half-time, but the second half began with
what *Politika* described as 'a real storm' from United: 'In the
first five minutes Beara made five saves,' the best of them from
'Charlton, the best player of the opposition, who was sure the
ball was in the net, but Beara saved it and justified his nickname of "The Black Panther".'

It seemed Zvezda had weathered the worst of it. 'It might,'
Politika reported, 'have stayed at 1–0 but for two critical moments and if the nerves of the Zvezda players had not given
way.' After sixty-five minutes, 'Ranko Borozan fell in his own
half and gave away possession. It didn't look dangerous let
alone critical but in that moment the powerful Edwards hit
a well-executed diagonal pass to the left-winger Scanlon who
immediately crossed and the ball fell to the unmarked Charlton and from close range, he beat Beara.'

The pressure continued. Twice Beara made fine saves at the
feet of United players but with seven minutes remaining Vio-
lett found Colman six yards out and he gave United a 2–1 win.
'We were left to ask ourselves,' *Politika* went on, 'how this team
had such power to keep attacking for ninety minutes. Then
the French referee with his whistle finally marked the end to
all the pain of this dark night.'

The Zvezda players were left disappointed, aware of how
good United had been, but aware also that they might have
taken a positive result. 'We put in a better performance in the
first leg than the second,' Šekularac insisted. 'It was quite an
unfortunate defeat. We saw that we could play an even game.
Our coach told us to keep the ball as long as possible, to have
possession and it wasn't so obvious in the first leg that they
were the better team. We went 1–0 up and they beat us with
a late goal.'

He acknowledged, though, that United had come back strongly in the second half. 'Beara was a world-class goalkeeper,' he said. 'Maybe without him it would have been 3–1 or 4–1 at Old Trafford. We had two very strong full-backs who were eating people. There wasn't so much passing round in those times. They were hard. We were good in the air at the back so when United put in crosses to Taylor, our centre-backs coped with that well.'

Politika was less forgiving. 'Manchester United deservedly won the game,' it said. 'In golden letters should be written the names of Viollet, Charlton, Edwards and Colman.' Beara had saved the day repeatedly with his 'unforgettable jumps and saves', it noted, but concluded, 'Perhaps the fairest thing would be to name all eleven as brave heroes – although some of them were swimming in defence and had moments when they looked lost.'

Zvezda were frustrated 'with the manner of the defeat' but Šekularac was also struck by United's hospitality. 'I played against other big clubs,' he said in 2015, 'but nobody received us as we were received in Manchester. I am still a supporter of Manchester United, even though they don't have good results after the departure of Alex Ferguson.'

Their form improving, United beat Bolton 7–2 at home in the league, then Ipswich 2–0 in the FA Cup. Fourth in the table on 1 February, they went to Highbury to face Arsenal. Both teams wore black armbands in memory of the United director George Whittaker who had collapsed and died at the team hotel earlier in the day.

Ten minutes in, Edwards picked up a Viollet lay-off to fire United into the lead with a powerful drive. On the half-hour, Charlton smashed in a Scanlon cross to make it 2–0 on the counter. 'Charlton,' the *Guardian* noted, 'has grown from a limited left-sided player of little pace into a brilliant inside-forward.'

Before half-time, Scanlon crossed from one wing, Morgans returned the ball from the other and Taylor slotted in to give

United a 3–0 lead. 'It was an era,' Geoffrey Green later said, 'when even the players with the technique and know-how of "putting up the shutters" invariably bucked the inclination to do so when the alternative was to move on yet again with attack.' United suddenly found themselves facing an Arsenal comeback. David Herd volleyed in a Dave Bowen lob, Vic Groves headed down Gordon Nutt's centre for Jimmy Bloomfield to score then Nutt crossed low for Bloomfield to equalise with a diving header: Arsenal had scored three times in two and a half minutes.

With Bowen inspirational, Arsenal surged forward to make the most of their momentum. But United, Green wrote, 'by sheer force of character and will power . . . superimposed their skill to dominate events once more'. Charlton and Scanlon exchanged passes and Viollet headed past Jack Kelsey to make it 4–3. Colman and Ken Morgans then combined for Taylor to score from a narrow angle. It wasn't just Colman's ability that made him such an important part of the United set-up. 'There can have been few pairs of wing-halves,' Green said, 'with more contrasting styles and appearances as Edwards and Colman, but both shared a belief in the old dictum that attack is the best form of defence. Each complemented the other to perfection; the one the aggressive dreadnought, the other the pocket Napoleon, they prodded and prompted the forwards into unceasing action.' A late Derek Tapscott goal threatened another Arsenal comeback, but United held on.

It had been an extraordinary game, one that probably would have been remembered for years anyway, but it became far more, a monument to the style and verve of a team that was about to be destroyed. 'The thermometer was doing a war-dance,' Green wrote in *The Times*. 'There was no breath left in anyone. The players came off arm in arm. They knew they had fashioned something of which to be proud.' It became the Babes' epitaph. 'Nine goals might point a finger towards poor defence but the quality of play was sustained,' said Charlton, 'and was as thrilling to be involved in as it apparently was to see.'

The victory left United four points off the top of the table, with the leaders Wolves to come to Old Trafford the following week. Before that, though, there was the second leg in Belgrade.

There was a terrible innocence in the build-up, an awful foreshadowing in the most banal details. The *Manchester Evening News* sought advice from 'one of the leading Yugoslav sports writers', Vinko Sale. 'Tell your Manchester United players to bring plenty of warm clothes with them when they fly out here for next week's European Cup tie . . .' he said, 'for the bitterly cold spell continues and weather experts predict that match conditions will be a severe test on a snow- and frost-bound pitch.' The posts were to be painted with red stripes because of the snow. Berry, by then thirty-one, handed in a transfer request after being displaced on the right wing by the Welsh nineteen-year-old Ken Morgans. With hindsight, it all seems absurdly trivial.

Belgrade represented something of a culture shock. Charlton recalled 'great banners of Tito on the big grey buildings, a unit of tanks clanking over the cobbles, smoke rising from the street-stalls where they sold food and roasted nuts, and women in heavy boots working on the road'. But the alien environment did nothing to dampen the sense of excitement the Arsenal game had stimulated. 'The banter,' said Charlton, 'was ceaseless – and inevitably led by Eddie Colman.'

In the immediate aftermath, it hardly mattered that the game had been, as Don Davies, 'Old International', put it in his final match report, a 'battle of wits and courage and rugged tackling', a contest that highlighted United's qualities both of technique and character played out on a pitch flecked with the white of melting snow.

Confidence was high after the first leg. 'There are no terrors out there for you boys now,' Busby said as they left the dressing room for the vast concrete bowl of a packed Marakana. For a little over half an hour, it seemed there really weren't.

Viollet put United ahead inside ninety seconds, 'a beautifully taken goal', as Davies had it – 'a characteristic effort by that player – but rather lucky in the way a rebound had run out in United's favour'. Charlton had the ball in the net again quarter of an hour later after Viollet had headed on a Scanlon corner, but his effort was ruled out for offside.

The game, by that point, had already become a scrap. Davies was inclined to blame Šekularac who, he said, 'had set the fashion for shabbiness by stabbing Morgan on the knee'. A second goal, though, was coming, and it arrived on the half-hour, through Charlton. 'Dispossessing [Borivoje] Kostić about forty yards from goal,' Davies wrote, 'this gifted boy leaned beautifully into his stride, made ground rapidly for about ten yards, and then beat the finest goalkeeper on the continent with a shot of tremendous power and superb placing.' A minute later a free-kick broke to Edwards just inside the Zvezda box. He miskicked, and the ball came to Charlton who found a route through a thicket of defenders and into the bottom corner. 'We played,' said Charlton, 'with a freedom that could only be described as sensational.'

That should have been game over, but as they'd shown at Highbury, this United could be vulnerable in a lead. 'Our major aim was to save face,' said Popović. 'We said to ourselves, "If we have to lose this game, let's not make it by 5–1." To lose 5–0 or 6–0 would have been hard to swallow so we went out to fight, determined to make the best of it.'

Kostić pulled one back two minutes into the second half with a low shot from the edge of the box and, three minutes later, Jovan Cokić, teed up by Šekularac, fired a foot over. It proved a costly miss. Within a minute, Foulkes had tangled in the box with Tasić, who converted the penalty. At 3–3, the momentum would have been with Zvezda. At 3–2, United still had a two-goal aggregate cushion.

With quarter of an hour to go, Zvezda were, Davies wrote,

'wheeling and curvetting, passing and shooting in their best style, and the United's defenders had to fight their way out of a regular nightmare of desperate situations'.

As United's players were pelted with snowballs by the crowd, Morgans struck a post. 'Gregg was hurt in making a courageous dive at Tasić's feet and he had to be revived by the United trainer before he could resume,' Tom Jackson wrote in the *MEN*. 'Red Star pulled out everything in an effort to save the game and Jones, Foulkes and Colman almost played themselves into the ground in countering the Yugoslav forwards. Gregg brought off a brilliant save from a twenty-five-yarder by Kostić and so it went on tooth and nail until the eighty-ninth minute when Gregg, after making a flying save in the penalty area, was penalised for touching the ball just outside the box . . .'

That was a major chance. 'Kostić was capable of scoring all the time,' said Šekularac. 'Often I would dive near the edge of the box when the score was 0–0 near the end because he had a fifty per cent record with free-kicks.

'I made a lot of goals for Bora Kostić with passes and crosses and the fans were always making fun of him, saying Šeki made all his goals. Once, we had a free-kick, 35 or 40 metres from the goal and I told him to go into the box and I would find him with the cross, and he said, "Let me: I'll score with the free-kick." And I said to him, "Fuck off!" I didn't want to let him take the free-kick. But he took it and it was like a torpedo. Right in the top corner. I'd said if he scored I would kiss his foot, so he holds his leg up for me to kiss, and he said, "I suppose you fucking made that one as well!"'

This time the range was far more realistic. Gregg got a hand to Kostić's free-kick – the first, Charlton said, that United players had ever seen bent around a wall – but couldn't keep it out.

Suddenly there was real pressure on United. 'I had a big chance,' said Šekularac. 'It could have been 4–3. Then we would have played a third game and they would not have travelled on that day. I wasn't a goal-getter. I made assists and final passes. I missed that chance. I was to blame maybe that we didn't win the game. I curse myself for that. I was 3 to 4 metres from the goal and I put it over the crossbar. I wanted to put extra power on it and it didn't work out right.'

'The referee,' wrote Jackson, 'allowed three minutes' extra play for stoppages and these three minutes were really tense for United who were glad to kick out anywhere to save the tie. But Scanlon nearly made doubly sure with a shot that Beara saved just under the bar almost on the final whistle. United can thank the brilliant play of their forwards in the first half and the heroic work of their defence in the second for pulling them through to the semi-final.'

It had been a hard game, but it was not without sportsmanship. The mutual respect that would be demonstrated after the accident had been evident throughout, notably when Cokić refused to walk the ball into an empty net as Gregg lay injured.

'Busby Boys in Cup Semi-Final! Three Up – but they only draw!' screamed the headline in the *MEN*. 'The English team led 3–0 but they deserved to lose,' said *Politika*. After the tension and the exhaustion came the celebration at a post-match banquet. Charlton described the 'local beer and drop of slivovitz . . . the usual array of eastern European cabaret acts, including jugglers and dancers'.

There was clearly a bond between the two sides, one that the tragedy reinforced. Eight years later, United played in Belgrade again as they faced Partizan in the European Cup semi-final. Popović went to visit the three players who had played in 1958 who were still in the squad – Gregg, Foulkes and Charlton. It was Gregg with whom he got on best. 'I went to say I remembered playing against them and to wish them luck against our arch-rivals,' he said. 'I considered them as friends.'

The day after the quarter-final, even as the front page of the *Manchester Evening News* carried the headline 'UNITED CUP XI CRASH: 28 DIE', the back page carried the final article of one of the fatalities. Tom Jackson, his obituary recorded, had joined the *MEN* at fourteen as 'a chubby messenger boy'. He became a crime reporter, and worked with the Intelligence Corps during the war, helping to unmask Irma Grese, a torturer at Belsen, before taking a job on the sports desk.

'Now,' he wrote in his final report, 'I'm ready to wager my last Yugoslav dinar that even though it may be the strutting Spaniards of Real Madrid who Manchester United will be set to face in the semi-final of the European Cup, they will never have a tougher fight on their hands than the one they survived here against the challenge of Red Star.

'Believe me, this match that ended with the rivals gaining three goals each and United through to the last four stage by the barest possible goal margin on aggregate had everything to send the blood running fast through the veins.'

Foulkes, he judged, had been 'the coolest and surest United defender' over the game as a whole. 'Eddie Colman,' he went on, 'had a splendid first half, but he was out of touch when the battle was at its thickest later on, and Duncan Edwards was much below the rip-roaring form he showed at Old Trafford in curbing the activities of inside-forward Šekularac. The Yugoslav wonder-boy had a much brighter game before his own fans, but some of the shine was lost because his tackling was often too robust. It was only the spirit and courage of young Morgans that kept him going after taking a nasty knock above the knee in the first few minutes – an injury which puts him in doubt for Saturday's top-of-the-table League tussle with the Wolves. The only other United casualty was Duncan Edwards, who has an ankle injury, but he is expected to be fit for Saturday's game.' If only.

Alf Clarke was the last to board in Munich, held up by phoning the story of the delay through to his desk. They were the final words he would ever file. 'The triumphant Manchester United footballers,' read his story in the *Evening Chronicle*, 'on their way from Belgrade to Manchester, are held up in Munich by engine trouble, and they may not be able to get away until tomorrow. United, who drew 3–3 with Belgrade Red Star and so qualified for the European Cup semi-final, broke their journey at Munich, where they had lunch. They were due in Ringway this evening, but their plane developed engine trouble and it is doubtful if they will get away today as it is also snowing very heavily.'

The edition in which that story first ran also carried the result of the 3.15 from Wincanton in its Stop Press. The result of the 3.45 was never published, the section given over to far more serious developments. By 6 p.m., a special edition of the paper was listing Charlton, Foulkes and Gregg as known survivors, while there was also much misinformation and conjecture.

The plane had initially been given clearance for take-off at 14.19 German time, but had twice been forced to abort amid heavy snow and with concerns over 'boost surging' in the port engine. The passengers disembarked and returned to the terminal, where Duncan Edwards sent a telegram to his land-lady saying all flights were cancelled and he would return the following day. After around quarter of an hour, though, they reboarded, with the captain, James Thain, believing the length of the runway in Munich meant the surging problem could be countered by opening the throttle more slowly. At 14.59 the plane reached the runway holding point and secured clearance for take-off. At 15.03, they committed to another attempt.

Those on board were aware something was wrong. Harry Gregg heard Billy Whelan say, 'This may be death, but I'm ready,' while a number of passengers, including Edwards, Taylor, Colman and Swift, moved to the back of the plane believing it to be safer. With the co-pilot, Kenneth Rayment, at the controls, Thain called out the velocity in ten-knot in-crements. At eighty-five knots, the surging problem recurred and Rayment eased off slightly on the throttle before pushing forwards again. At 117 knots (217km/h), Thain called out 'V1' – the speed after which it was no longer safe to abort. At 119 knots, V2, the plane could have begun take off. But the velocity hovered at around 117 knots then began to drop, to 115 knots and then 105 knots. From then it was just a question of how bad the crash would be.

The plane ploughed through the airport fence and across a road before the port wing was ripped off as it hit a house which caught fire. The four inhabitants – a mother and three of her children – escaped unharmed. The tail was torn off but the plane carried on, the left side of the cockpit smashing into a tree as the right side of the fuselage hit a hut inside which was a truck loaded with tyres and fuel, which exploded.

Gregg, blood pouring from a head wound, kicked his way out of the wreckage and managed to pull some other passengers free. Charlton came to around fifty yards from the plane, one of his team-mates lying dead on the tarmac alongside him – for reasons he acknowledges he can't articulate he has vowed never to reveal whom. He saw Busby sitting in a pool of water groaning and clutching his chest, walked over to him and draped his overcoat round his shoulders. Replaying the details over and over, he has since wondered why he'd kept his overcoat on for take-off.

Twenty of the passengers were killed almost instantly and a further three subsequently died in hospital: the players Geoff Bent, Roger Byrne, Eddie Colman, Duncan Edwards, Mark Jones, David Pegg, Tommy Taylor and Liam Whelan; the United staff Walter Crickmer, Bert Whalley and the coach Tom Curry; the journalists Alf Clarke, Don Davies, George Follows, Tom Jackson, Archie Ledbrooke, Henry Rose, Frank Swift and Eric Thompson, the co-pilot Kenneth Rayment, the cabin steward Tom Cable, the travel agent Bela Miklos and the businessman and racing friend of Busby, Willie Satinoff. Satinoff was on the plane only because Louis Edwards had decided against travelling after George Whittaker, the director who had died on the day of the game at Highbury, had voted against him being admitted to the board.

A West German inquiry blamed Thain, concluding he had

not cleared ice from the wings but, after a ten-year battle, he was cleared and the official cause put down to slush on the runway that had prevented the plane reaching full speed.

There had been a possibility the eighteen-year-old forward Alex Dawson would be selected for the trip to Belgrade but because there was a slight doubt over Roger Byrne's fitness, Geoff Bent went instead. Dawson was playing snooker that February afternoon when he heard running footsteps in the corridor outside and recognised the sound of the short legs of his teammate Mark Pearson who told him what had happened.

Fans began to gather at Old Trafford, partly to find out the latest news, partly as an act of commemoration and partly because there was comfort in the togetherness of the crowd. On the Saturday after the crash, when United had been scheduled to play Wolves, many went through their familiar rituals, going to Old Trafford as though for a normal match day.

As ever with such disasters, there were the stories of those who escaped the disaster by strokes of remarkable fortune. Wilf McGuinness would have gone but for a cartilage problem that had flared the previous weekend. Jimmy Murphy was the manager of Wales at the time and so skipped the trip to Belgrade to take charge of the national side in a World Cup qualifying play-off against Israel. Bert Whalley took Murphy's usual seat on the plane next to Busby and was killed. Murphy returned to Old Trafford after overseeing Wales's 2–0 win with no idea what had happened. He was greeted by a secretary who broke down as she tried to explain. He took a bottle of whiskey to his office and wept.

Geoffrey Green was one of a number of journalists initially miffed to be sent to Cardiff to cover that game left pondering how close they had come. John Arlott, the great cricket commentator, had lobbied the *Guardian* for a greater variety of assignments and had covered United's 5–4 win at Highbury; he was frustrated on filing his copy that Saturday to be told that Don Davies had expressed a wish to go to Belgrade and would travel in his place. Arlott was wandering round a bookshop the following Thursday when the *Guardian* tracked him down, gave him the news and asked him to write Davies's obituary.

The Yugoslav journalist Miro Radojčić was saved when he got to the airport and realised he'd left his passport at home. By the time he returned, the plane had left. 'The memory that lingers,' he wrote in *Politika*, 'is of the banquet given after the match to both teams that night at the Majestic Hotel in Belgrade. When the lights were doused and the waiters entered with candles flaming on the bowls of iced sweetmeats the whole United side applauded and led by Roger Byrne, the captain, rose to sing, "We'll meet again".'

The day after the crash, the *MEN* was reporting that Busby was 'fifty-fifty' to pull through, that Berry was in a coma and that Edwards's condition was 'grave'. The mood in Belgrade was one of appalled shock. 'They left as friends,' read the headline in *Politika*. 'Manchester United will remain always in our hearts,' it said. 'They were a team of football masters and likeable young people.'

While those in Manchester were understandably still concerned with the disaster and who would survive, *Politika* began to look ahead. 'If in the remaining matches the opponents withdrew and played friendly games then the Cup would go to football masters who were prevented by this catastrophe from winning it,' it suggested. 'In that way would be given tribute to a great team and in the history of football they would leave a trace of that tragedy.'

Murphy visited Busby in hospital. 'Keep the flag flying, Jim, till I get back,' the manager said, although nobody was sure he would survive and, even if he did, whether he'd be able to resume management. Murphy's main task was to put together a squad that could at least see United through to the end of the season. His first signing was Ernie Taylor, the former Newcastle and Blackpool inside forward. Stan Crowther was then picked up, having been given dispensation to play in the Cup for United despite having played for Aston Villa in an earlier round.

There was little in the way of psychological support for the survivors. Charlton went to see his family GP in Ashington, Dr McPherson, who had served in the RAF during the war. His advice sounds desperately unsympathetic now but reflected the prevailing mood: he told Charlton he was like a soldier on active service and that he simply had to get used to friends dying. Charlton never did get used to it. 'It still reaches down and touches me every day,' he wrote in his autobiography. 'Sometimes I feel it quite lightly, a mere brush stroke across an otherwise happy mood. Sometimes it engulfs me with terrible regret and sadness – and guilt that I walked away and found so much.'

United's FA Cup fifth-round tie against Sheffield Wednesday had been postponed by ten days, but at some point they had to start playing again. There were 60,000 at Old Trafford to see it, a further 30,000 locked out and another 5,000 stuck at Central Station after trains to the stadium were cancelled at the news of the lock-out. One of those who did make it in was the Huddersfield Town forward Denis Law, who paid for a ticket to stand on the terraces.

Poignantly, on the back of the programme, the United team consisted of eleven empty spaces. 'We weren't just playing eleven men,' noted the Sheffield Wednesday captain Albert Quixall. 'We were playing 60,000 fans as well.' Gregg and Foulkes, two survivors, were able to take their place in the team but it was Shay Brennan, a reserve full-back, who won the game, playing at outside-left and scoring twice in a 3–0 victory, the first of them an in-swinging corner that caught the wind. At the final whistle, Foulkes wept.

Hardman's programme notes captured the mood: 'Although we mourn our dead and grieve for our wounded, we believe that the great days are not done for us. The sympathy and encouragement of the football world and particularly of our supporters will justify and inspire us. The road back may be long and awkward but with the memory of those who died at Munich, of their stirring achievements and the wonderful sportsmanship ever with us, Manchester United will rise again.'

Five days after the victory over Sheffield Wednesday, fifteen days after the crash, Duncan Edwards died. Nobody had told Busby the extent of the disaster, but he worked out that there were certain players nobody who came to visit him mentioned. About three weeks after the crash, he went through them one by one to his wife Jean, the players he knew had gone – 'Duncan? Roger? Bill? Eddie? David? Mark? Geoff?' He felt a terrible sense of guilt, reasoning that if he hadn't insisted on playing in the European Cup, the crash would never have happened. Jean remained resolute, though: he had to go on, for those who had died, for those who had survived, and for the people of Manchester.

United's form in those days seemed almost an irrelevance. Inevitably their patched-up squad, straining under the burden of grief, couldn't keep going in the league, but the FA Cup offered the possibility of an emotional pay-off, a token of the club's enduring spirit. For the sixth-round tie at West Brom, 15,000 fans travelled down to see a 2–2 draw, and there was another lock-out for the replay at Old Trafford. Before kick-off Georg Maurer, the surgeon who had treated Busby, and his medical team were presented on the pitch. A Colin Webster goal saw United through to a semi-final against Fulham.

By the time that game was played, United had lost twice in the league. There was a sense that the initial surge had worn off and they were poor in a 2–2 draw. This was not, Malcolm Brodie wrote in the *Belfast Telegraph*, the United 'who gave Sheffield Wednesday a soccer lesson. It was not the glorious United which defeated West Bromwich Albion in the sixth round. It was a mere skeleton of a once great side.'

They did pick up for the replay at Highbury. Shortly before kick-off, Murphy instructed Alex Dawson, who had been playing at centre-forward, to switch with Colin Webster and play instead on the right wing. With space to cut inside, he scored a hat-trick as United, rediscovering some fluency, won 5–3. In the *Mirror*, Frank McGhee suggested they had been inspired by returning to the scene of the Babes' last game on English soil before the trip to Belgrade.

The day Busby left hospital, 19 April 1956, Bobby Charlton made his international debut, scoring in a 4–0 win over Scotland, and Billy Meredith died, almost destitute, at the age of eighty-three. For those seeking omens, the coincidence felt significant: the end of one age, the beginning of another and, perhaps, the basis for the reconstruction for United. A few days later, Busby, walking with a stick and looking noticeably older, returned to the Cliff.

For the FA Cup final, against Bolton Wanderers, United had new shirts made, incorporating on the badge the image of a phoenix. It would take more time, though, to rise again. Two Nat Lofthouse goals, one of them following a highly controversial challenge on Harry Gregg, gave Bolton a 2–0 win – although for all the outrage his second goal inspires now, newspapers of the time saw little wrong with it.

Four days later, there came the European Cup semi-final. When the draw had been made, it was decided that United should face an opponent they could travel to play by train, which ruled out Real Madrid and Vasas of Hungary on grounds of distance. They were thus paired with the winner of AC Milan's tie against Borussia Dortmund. United were without Bobby Charlton, who had joined up with the England squad before the World Cup, but still beat Milan 2–1 at home before losing 4–0 at the San Siro. Uefa invited United to take part in the following season's competition but this time Hardaker had his revenge, pointing out that they weren't champions and vetoing the plan.

United would rebuild. They would return to European competition. And they would, in the end, achieve the continental glory of which Busby had dreamed. But the fulfilment of the quest would take a long, long time.

CHAPTER 4

European Cup final, Wembley, London, 29 May 1968

Benfica	**1–4**	**Manchester United**
Graça 79		*Charlton 53, 99*
		Best 92
		Kidd 94

José Henrique	Alex Stepney
Adolfo Calisto	Shay Brennan
Humberto Fernandes	Bill Foulkes
Jacinto Santos	David Sadler
Fernando Cruz	Tony Dunne
Jaime Graça	Pat Crerand
Mário Coluna	Bobby Charlton
José Augusto	Nobby Stiles
José Torres	George Best
Eusébio	Brian Kidd
António Simões	John Aston
Otto Glória	Matt Busby

Ref: Concetto Lo Bello
Bkd: Fernandes
Att: 92,225

IN THE EARLY HOURS OF the morning, Matt Busby cleared his throat and, in his gravelly Lanarkshire tones, sang 'It's a Wonderful World'. By the time he'd finished, most of those still left at the banquet after Manchester United's victory over Benfica in the 1968 European Cup final were in tears. Some, perhaps, remembered a similar banquet in Belgrade ten years earlier.

It had been the least celebratory of celebratory dinners. There were plenty who were in awe of United's achievement – their success, Geoffrey Green wrote, 'made giants of men who seemed to have given their last ounce of strength as they searched for the final yard to the summit' – but there was also a mood of sadness and contemplation. The memory of Munich, inevitably, suffused the evening. 'When time has come to dim the emotion of this match,' Ken Jones wrote in the *Mirror*, 'strong men will still remember it with tears in their eyes.'

Bobby Charlton, who had scored two goals in the final, didn't even make it to the dinner. Five times he tried to leave his hotel room to join the banquet only to find his limbs refusing to carry him. He said that, as had happened after the semi-final, dehydration had overwhelmed him. Others, though, Nobby Stiles among them, suspected an emotional cause.

George Best, meanwhile, was frustrated, aware he'd 'played only in snatches' during the final. He wasn't the only one. Emphatic as a 4–1 victory may appear, the final had been a nervous, scrappy affair, the dimensions of the occasion and a humid evening sapping at the players.

And there was also, as so often after a great achievement, a feeling of emptiness. 'There was an understanding,' Charlton said, 'that something was over, something that had dominated our lives for so long.' He wasn't the only one. 'There was the sense that this was the end of something momentous . . .' said David Sadler. 'I wondered if there was anywhere to go from here.'

The years that followed the crash were difficult. Even those who weren't actively grieving for friends lost at Munich felt the pressure to live up to their standards – standards that, of course, were set impossibly high because when players exist only as potential nobody ever factors in possible injury or loss of form. Plus there was greater exposure; the tale of a club trying to rebuild after tragedy attracted interest from those who would not normally have cared about football and drew support from across the country and beyond. 'Before Munich,' Bobby Charlton noted, 'United were seen as Manchester's club. Afterwards, everyone felt as if they owned a little bit of it.'

The elegant inside-forward Albert Quixall joined United in September 1958 from Sheffield Wednesday for a British record fee of £45,000. It was widely assumed that Busby's new side would be built around him, but the scrutiny to which he was subjected caused him to suffer dreadfully from nerves and he would come out in blotches before games despite his efforts to mask his anxiety with crude practical jokes.

United's new following didn't only increase the pressure on players, it also led in some quarters to resentment. Letters were sent to Old Trafford telling players that opponents were going easy on them and letting them win. The fifth game after the crash was a 3–0 away defeat at Burnley in which the young United forward Mark Pearson was sent off. Bob Lord, Burnley's controversial chairman, accused United of 'running around like Teddy Boys . . . If Manchester United continue to play like this, they'll lose the sympathy the public have for them. They must remember there are other clubs in football than Manchester United.'

The timing and tone of Lord's comments were crass and insensitive, but the sentiment would be repeated more diplomatically in the years that followed; there would be plenty who detected a sense of entitlement about United and the story of Munich lay at the heart of that self-mythologising. The ugly side of the devotion United had come to inspire was seen, for instance, in the aftermath of the 1958 FA Cup final, the Bolton bus being stoned as it passed through Salford on its way back from Wembley.

Busby returned to work a far more distant figure than he had been before Munich, rarely spending any time on the training pitch. He suffered near-constant pain in his back and leg and struggled to carry the burden. 'Deep down,' he said, 'the sorrow is there all the time. You never really rid yourself of it. It becomes part of you. You might be alone and it all comes back to you, like a kind of roundabout, and you weep.'

The first time he had returned to Old Trafford after the accident, Busby said, 'I just looked at the empty field and in all my life I have never felt such a terrible vacuum. And so I cried, and afterwards, I felt better for the tears, and because I had forced myself to go back there. It was something I had done, something I'd conquered.'

To return, though, was not the same as to recover. 'He would never,' Charlton said, 'be quite the same as he was boarding that plane in Munich.'

While other parts of the rebuilding went well, United struggled to find replacements for Pegg and Berry on the wings. Albert Scanlon appeared to have made a remarkable recovery after suffering a fractured skull and a broken leg at Munich, having a fine season in 1958–59, but memories of the crash gradually ground him down. As Scanlon's form faltered, Charlton was, despite his misgivings, moved out to the left to replace him. Scanlon wasn't the only one to find it difficult to maintain his level. Alex Dawson suggested a number of the young players thrust into action after the crash were exposed to too much too soon and never quite developed as they might have done. He himself ended up leaving for Preston North End in 1961 after scoring forty-five goals in eighty appearances for United.

It wasn't just the shadow of Munich that led players and others to question Busby. With the emergence of the likes of Don Revie, Joe Mercer and Alf Ramsey, all far more technical coaches who were happy to discuss strategy, Busby began to seem a little old-fashioned. In the *International Football Book* of 1960, he lamented the growing influence of 'the power game'. 'Results,' he said, 'are achieved by placing undue emphasis on speed, power and physical fitness.' Even his own players could be scathing of his romantic vision of the game. '"Give it to a red shirt"?' asked Noel Cantwell, an Irish full-back who joined United in 1960 and later became captain. 'You don't need a fucking manager for that.'

What Busby did do was impose discipline – up to a point – and keep the finances tight. The wing-half Stan Crowther, for instance, had been signed by Murphy from Aston Villa in the immediate aftermath of Munich but found himself sold to Chelsea that December after snapping a cue over his knee in frustration during a game of billiards at Davyhulme Golf Club. Pearson, an inside-forward who had made his debut as a seventeen-year-old against Sheffield Wednesday in the first post-Munich game, fell out of favour after following up the sending off against Burnley with a dismissal for the reserves against Leeds; he was sold to Wednesday. John Giles clashed with Busby because he wanted to play at inside-forward rather than on the wing, then suffered an undiagnosed virus and ended up being sold to Leeds.

But it was money that remained the biggest issue. In 1961 the maximum wage of £20 a week was abolished. Fulham immediately put Johnny Haynes on £100 a week but Busby offered his senior players just £25. Viollet, who had scored thirty-two goals in 1959–60, complained and was transferred to Stoke City. Results were ordinary, a runners-up spot in 1959 being followed by two seventh-place finishes. After frustration came apathy. Four years after Munich, United's popularity had dipped. In January 1962, only 20,807 turned out for a 2–0 win over Aston Villa that lifted United to seventeenth.

The Benfica of 1968 perhaps weren't quite of the same quality as the side that won back-to-back European Cups under Béla Guttmann in 1961 and 1962 but they were still two championships into a hat-trick of Portuguese league titles and featured six of the Portugal side who had reached the semi-final of the 1966 World Cup. Their progress had initially been uncertain – they'd got by Glentoran by the first ever application of the away goals rule in the European Cup – but by the semi-final Benfica had been strong enough to beat Juventus 3–0 on aggregate. This was the first time they'd been in the final since 1962 and a chance quickly to break the curse Guttmann had supposedly placed on them. The story goes that the Hungarian, enraged when the directors refused to give him a bonus he believed he was owed, stormed out of the club, telling them that 'not in 100 years from now will Benfica be a European champion'. Wembley was the first of eight European finals they have reached since without winning any.

Benfica too had suffered recent tragedy. In December 1966, seven players had gone for a dip in the heated pool at the stadium. Faulty wiring in a new whirlpool feature caused all seven to suffer severe electric shocks. One of them, the twenty-six-year-old Luciano Fernandes, was killed. 'I was in the water and suddenly I couldn't speak,' said the midfielder Jaime Graça. 'I tried to move but I was paralysed. Finally I climbed out of the tub . . . I dashed onto the wet floor and ran to the plug where the electric machine was fastened. I pulled out the plug and then I fainted.' One of those he saved was the great striker Eusébio. 'It was like a freezing dagger plunged into me,' he said.

There was no doubt Eusébio was Benfica's main threat, a

powerful, skilful forward who liked to drop deep and who was possessed of a ferocious shot. United's own centre-forward could hardly have represented a greater contrast to the revered twenty-six year old. With Denis Law ruled out by a piece of loose cartilage in his knee, Brian Kidd started on his nineteenth birthday.

United watched Lester Piggott and Sir Ivor win the Derby on television at their hotel before setting off for the game, in which, thanks to a clash of reds, they wore blue and Benfica white. From the outset it became apparent that Stiles would track Eusébio. He'd played against him three times in competitive games before and each time he'd finished up on the winning side – although Benfica had beaten United 3–1 on a pre-season tour of the USA a year earlier. The BBC coverage of the game suggested before kick-off that United would match Benfica's 4-3-3 shape, with Stiles effectively a left-half and David Sadler, although wearing the number 10 shirt, used as a second centre-back. As it turned out, though, with Stiles marking Eusébio, Sadler's role was to plug the hole in midfield, as Bobby Charlton made the play and Pat Crerand shuttled up and down in a right-half role. 'We would aim to dominate the middle of the pitch ...' Busby explained in *Soccer at the Top*. 'I impressed upon them all the disastrous consequences of losing concentration and giving the ball away aimlessly. The chasing this causes can be destroying, it saps energy and plays havoc with morale.'

Otto Glória, Benfica's coach, insisted that his side were over their 5–1 defeat to United two years earlier, when George Best had torn them apart in Lisbon. 'We have put that memory behind us,' he said. 'But we do not forget that Best is a good player. But like Nobby Stiles will mark Eusébio, so [Fernando] Cruz will do the same with Best. He is very experienced.' In the *Mirror*, Nigel Clarke predicted there would be 'shuddering tackles'.

As it turned out, Sadler's first touch of the game was in an inside-left position, functioning as the wall in a one-two with

John Aston, who was then tripped, winning United a free-kick to the left of the box. Charlton took it but it was headed clear. United's defensive structure essentially meant Foulkes dealing with the physically imposing José Torres, who drifted in from the left to the centre when Eusébio dropped deep from his nominal central striking position. Their first contact came as the two jumped for a long clearance and Foulkes was penalised for a far from obvious push. In the first minute the tone of niggliness was set, not helped by the fussiness of the Italian referee Concetto Lo Bello.

The elegant Mário Coluna, playing in his fiftieth European Cup match, floated the free-kick into the box. Foulkes beat Torres to the delivery, the ball glancing backwards off his head. It would have run through to Stepney but Crerand, taking no chances, scuttled round to run it out of the box towards the touchline. He played it down the line to Aston, who helped it inside to Charlton and he turned and spread the play out to Best on the right. At his first touch there was a great roar from the Wembley crowd. He jinked by António Simões on the outside but the left-back Cruz was in position to nip the ball away from him.

Charlton, though, regained possession and returned the ball to Best to set off immediately on a run towards the box. He went by Cruz, who took a swipe at Best's ankle, slowing him down sufficiently that he was dispossessed on the edge of the box. A free-kick was given, but a furious Best remonstrated with Cruz, jabbing a finger as the defender knelt on the ground. As Cruz stood, he barged into Best who, startled, grabbed at his shoulder in apparent pain and might have reacted further had Bobby Charlton not laid a calming hand on his chest.

Crerand dropped the free-kick between the penalty spot and the edge of the six-yard box where Sadler, stretching, reached the ball but was unable to get sufficient purchase to divert it past Henrique in the Benfica goal. Henrique cleared long, his kick carrying deep into the United half towards Stiles, about ten yards outside his own penalty area. Under very little pressure, he dealt with it poorly, miscuing a header out towards the touchline then chasing it and belting the ball out of play as Eusébio closed in. Eusébio took the throw quickly, trying to find Torres, but the ball bounced just too far in front of him and was comfortably gathered by Stepney.

It was all a little frantic and unstructured in those opening minutes. Aston played the ball in from the left to Sadler but as he turned he was dispossessed by Coluna. Languidly he advanced, turned as Dunne closed him down and was then clattered by a two-footed lunge from the full-back. Jaime Graça lifted the free-kick into the box but Stepney came and claimed confidently, before rather ruining the impression by belting his clearance far into the Benfica half, nowhere near any United players. Nerves, perhaps, were playing their part.

After a fifteenth-place finish in 1961–62, Busby recognised that a major statement was necessary. Significant investment in Cantwell, Setters and Quixall had produced little reward but, that summer, Busby persuaded Hardman to sanction the £115,000 signing of Denis Law from Torino. Law was twenty-two and had developed a formidable reputation at Huddersfield and then Manchester City before making a largely unhappy move to Italy. He had a quick temper which led to him, at least initially, often being compared unfavourably with what had gone before, but he was a very fine centre-forward, working along the front line, capable of holding the ball up and creating openings with bursts of pace and, most vitally, of scoring goals.

Law's arrival led to no immediate upturn in fortunes and United lost nine of their first fourteen games of the 1962–63 season. Dunphy, who had joined United as a seventeen-year-old in 1962, spoke of a 'poison' in the atmosphere around that time, while there was a spate of thefts in the dressing room which may or may not have been connected to the gambling culture at the club. In January 1961, for instance,

Ernest Mangnall, the first manager to lead Manchester United to the league title.

Sandy Turnbull (right) and Knocker West pretend to play cricket at Old Trafford in 1911.

(left) Billy Meredith, gifted winger and social revolutionary.

More than 71,000 packed in to Crystal Palace for the 1909 FA Cup final.

Sandy Turnbull (out of shot) beats Harry Clay to give United the lead against Bristol City in the Cup final as his teammates (in white) Billy Meredith (left) and Harold Halse look on.

Jack Rowley scores his second of the 1948 FA Cup final against Blackpool to level the scores at 2–2.

United's captain Johnny Carey is borne aloft with the Cup.

Matt Busby reinvented Manchester United after the Second World War.

Roger Byrne, United's captain, leads his team from the tunnel a week before the Munich air crash.

Duncan Edwards signs an autograph after United's 5–4 win at Arsenal in 1958, the Babes' last performance in England.

Bobby Charlton beats Vladimir Beara to put United 2–0 up in Belgrade.

The horror of the crash.

Brian Kidd heads United 3–1 in front against Benfica in the 1968 European Cup final.

An exhausted Bobby Charlton raises the European Cup.

A 17-year-old George Best warms up before a game against Burnley.

Frank O'Farrell with Ted MacDougall, another signing that didn't work out.

United arrived at Filbert Street for a game against Leicester and the card school continued long after everybody else had gone into the changing room. United lost 6–0 and on the way back a furious Busby seized the deck and hurled it out of the window.

Cantwell, as captain, was just the most vocal of the players who doubted whether the former goalkeeper Jack Crompton, who took training, was really up to the job. Yet Crompton was an expression of Busby's beliefs: he thought a few weights, some running and a match on the hard surface behind the stand at Old Trafford was enough. When John Giles moved to Leeds, he noted a 'huge transformation' in training. Under Don Revie, opponents were analysed and set-plays practised; there was a sense that the game was something to be dissected and understood.

There were divisions too within the dressing room, where Gregg and Foulkes didn't get on. Clashes of personality happen in all teams, of course, but Munich had given the uneasiness in their relationship an edge. Dunphy suspected Gregg felt Foulkes could have done more on the runway and that Foulkes resented the way Gregg had emerged as the guardian of the club's spirit, despite having joined the club only months before the crash.

Still, gloomy as Dunphy was, there was an improvement in form towards the end of the year, but the harsh winter meant there were no games between Boxing Day and the end of February, ruining any rhythm United had. During the break, though, United took a significant step forward by signing Pat Crerand from Celtic. He was the sort of player United had been missing, combining toughness and a ball-winning capacity with accurate passing that enabled United both to rotate possession and to spring forward with rapid counters.

There came a rush of fixtures: eight games crammed into March and although United failed to win any of their league matches they won every Cup tie. Denis Law scored a hat-trick in a 5–0 win over Huddersfield in the third round. Quixall got the winner against Aston Villa in the fourth and goals from Quixall and Law saw off Chelsea in the fifth. Third Division Coventry were beaten 3–1 in the sixth round and, almost without noticing, United were in the semi-final – the second of a run of five successive last-four appearances. A poacher's goal from Law saw them past Second Division Southampton and into the final, against Matt Gillies's Leicester City, who had squandered a dominant position in the league by taking a single point from their final five games, having gone top with a draw and a win over United on successive days in mid-April.

United had finished eighteenth in the league but, after an anxious start to the final in which Dave Gaskell, the goalkeeper, was badly afflicted by nerves, United won comfortably. First Crerand, intercepting a throw-out from Gordon Banks to Dave Gibson, played in Law who beat the keeper with a sharp finish on the turn – a goal that highlighted what both brought to the United side. Then Herd tapped in the rebound after Banks had saved from Charlton. Ken Keyworth headed in a Frank McLintock shot with ten minutes remaining to give Leicester hope but that was extinguished when Herd scored his second after Banks had fumbled a Giles cross. United, unexpectedly, had won the Cup for the third time.

It was, Bill Foulkes said, the 'single most important trophy in the history of our great club'. Certainly it was a key moment in the evolution of that side: Law and Crerand had been joined by confidence. 'We looked,' said Charlton, 'like Manchester United again.'

The Cup success restored Busby's credibility on the pitch, but he was also extending his influence off it. Louis Edwards, a brother-in-law of Louis Rocca, was a butcher who had first met Busby in 1950 at the Opera House. Busby and Edwards would go to shows with their wives, then slip out at the interval to a nearby pub. They were friends and Edwards understood Busby's financial thinking: that his players should not be paid fortunes but should feel that by being part of Manchester

United they were getting the best possible treatment and perks, such as the golf days at Davyhulme.

Hardman didn't have the resources to invest personally in the club as Davies and Gibson had, and his innate conservatism meant that Busby's resources were limited. In 1962, though, Edwards began buying shares with a view to a takeover. Within eighteen months, his stake in the club was 44 per cent. When Hardman died in 1965, he took over as chairman, having agreed with Busby that in time their sons would succeed them on the board. When United opened a souvenir shop at the ground in 1967, Busby was given a twenty-one-year lease for a one-off fee of £2000 plus £5 a week. It was an extremely good deal for Busby, but perfectly legal, although it says something about the nature of the agreement that it wasn't made public until many years later.

United had been warned about the danger of the Torres–Eusébio partnership and they soon saw it in action, Torres flicking on a long clearance from the goalkeeper Henrique for his strike partner after five minutes. Stiles was tight to him, but Eusébio was still able to turn. His pass, though, was poor and Dunne gathered. Charlton, dropping deep, took it from him and he hit a long ball towards Kidd who was just offside.

Neither side, it seemed, could string together three passes but then Kidd played a pass inside the right-back Adolfo Calisto. Aston ran on and crossed from the byline towards the back post. Augusto headed clear as Crerand closed in – and was then penalised for a supposed push. The free-kick was taken to Coluna who, with an abrupt change of pace, went past Best and between Shay Brennan and Stiles before being crowded out and dispossessed by Foulkes just inside his own half.

The ball was fed forward by Brennan to Best, whose every touch still produced rumbles of anticipation from the crowd. He zipped by José Alberto and was hacked down by Fernando Cruz. As the crowd booed, the defender stood, arms outspread in apparent bewilderment, before patting Best as he walked past him to take up his position in the box. Crerand's free-kick was deflected high into the air and for a time Benfica struggled to clear before Kidd was penalised for yet another minor push.

There was a general rattiness to the game. Eight minutes in, a long Stepney clearance found Kidd who laid it off towards Charlton but he couldn't quite get there and a free-kick was given for a tug on Kidd by Humberto Fernandes. The two then jostled each other, forcing Lo Bello to intervene.

Charlton took the free-kick, attempting a quick low one to Kidd just inside the box. It was intercepted, though, and Eusébio brought it clear. For the first time in the game, Benfica began to show their quality on the ball. With Adolfo down injured, Eusébio played it to Cruz who helped it on to Torres just inside the United half. He poked it back to Coluna who knocked it forward for Graça. His touch was heavy and he was forced back to Augusto in the centre-circle, who switched it left for Cruz. He went long down the line for Eusébio, who evaded Stiles's first kick at him but was felled by a second. 'That just won't do,' said a scandalised Kenneth Wolstenholme on the television commentary. Eusébio's free-kick was dreadful, belted high over the bar to derisive jeers from the crowd. Nobody, it seemed, could settle.

Stepney took the goal-kick short to Crerand and demanded the ball back, his shout of 'Give it 'ere! Give it 'ere!' clearly audible above the background hum. Crerand ignored him and instead played it to Stiles, who whacked a long ball towards Kidd. It was too long, though, and was gathered by Henrique. He also kicked long and Stiles returned it, an aimless hoof going out of play for a throw. It was all a little ugly and hectic, lacking sophistication; this was just the opposite of Busby's instructions about retaining possession.

Best, who seemed always to be surrounded by three white shirts, gave the ball away just inside the Benfica half, Graça advancing and playing it to Torres. He nudged it on for Eusébio who had pulled off Stiles. Given room, he jinked by his man and swept by Foulkes. The ball got caught under his feet but as Dunne stood off him, he regained control and hit a shot from twenty-two yards with the outside of his right foot. The ball arced slightly, moving a fraction from left to right, and pinged against the crossbar.

It was a rare moment of quality in a poor opening. Twice in quick succession Crerand overhit through-balls, the second leading to a collision between Best and Henrique. Best was penalised for it, although it seemed he could hardly have got out of the way, and reacted furiously, evidently already frustrated. Jacinto Santos, as though sensing he was nearing the edge, clearly said something to him, presumably in an attempt to wind him up.

United's only consistent attacking avenue was through Aston on the left. 'Perhaps the greatest eye-opener of the struggle,' wrote Green, 'was Aston at outside-left. Without any flowery touches, time after time he cut the right flank of the Portuguese defence open by sheer, uncomplicated speed.'

Busby had been to watch Benfica in their semi-final win over Juventus. 'I noticed,' he said, 'that their right full-back, who was quite happy and competent when the ball came to him, was very slow on the turn.' The targeting of Adolfo by Aston was a deliberate ploy, although there's little doubt that his struggles were in part the result of his early injury. Aston received the ball from Stiles, played it one side of the full-back and ran round the other before sending over a deep cross. Best, though, was crowded out at the back post. The ball was cleared to Crerand who hit it from the right over the penalty area to Aston. He again beat Adolfo, this time with a burst of acceleration, and crossed. Kidd won the header but his knock-down fell just too far in front of Sadler.

There were a lot of long balls, neither side, seemingly, comfortable enough to begin playing the passing football of which they were capable. Only occasionally were there flickers of quality. A Eusébio dummy created space for Torres but the move was let down by a poor cross. And there was a definite spite to the game. There seemed to be a deliberate policy on Benfica's part to kick Best off his stride; he was hacked down in quick succession by Jacinto and Humberto. There was an uneasiness to the play, a lack of rhythm. Crerand played the free-kick short to Charlton who, seemingly startled, struck a weak shot that Henrique saved low down. Wolstenholme, as though desperate to inject some excitement, described the shot as 'a nasty one' but in reality there had been little danger.

Another United attack came to an end as Best was held outside the box by Humberto. Lo Bello, finally, decided to take action and booked the Benfica defender. Crerand took the free-kick, dinking it into the box where Best couldn't quite get on the end of it.

Benfica, perhaps realising what a mess the opening twenty minutes had been, slowed the game and began to play some simple passes that didn't necessarily get them very far but at least settled them down. Wolstenholme felt the need to defend the 'slow-motion stuff', although by modern standards it would have taken an unusual insistence on the frenetic to find anything amiss in their play. This was an age in which 'method football', as it was known, the patient build-up favoured by the likes of Leeds and Liverpool, although increasingly widespread, was still treated with scepticism.

What was also clear was that Best wasn't quite at his peak. Leading a break, he ran into three players and was tackled by Jacinto. A little later, he was able to make space and hit a long pass out to Aston. The left-winger remained the most threatening United player, but his cross towards Kidd was claimed by Henrique.

Aside from the shot that had hit the bar, Eusébio had been quiet. It wouldn't be entirely true to say that Stiles had marked him out of the game but there were long periods when he wasn't involved. Only occasionally did the England man's stifling work cross the line into violence, but Eusébio was left limping by one crude challenge on the half-hour. Stiles 'was a great lad, very clean living off the field, always happy and smiling,' Crerand said. 'Yet on the field, he'd rant and roar and curse like blue murder to keep us going. He was a tremendous motivator.' Charlton's claim that Stiles's bad tackles were a result of his poor eyesight is likely over-generous, but it probably is true that Stiles was a better player than he's often given credit for.

As long as Lo Bello was penalising every aerial challenge, Benfica always had a chance. Twice in the space of a minute, Foulkes was pulled up for supposed pushes on Torres. The first Eusébio took himself, the second he played short to Torres; both ended up being smashed straight into the wall.

Even if he was struggling to impose himself, Best remained the principal link between back and front for United. He led a break and played the ball right for Kidd, but as he crossed, Aston was penalised for a push. Benfica could hardly get it clear. Crerand won possession on halfway and advanced. He gave it to Best who went round Cruz and chipped a cross to the back post. Aston headed it down and back intelligently for Kidd, but as he tried to strike the bouncing ball, his shot was blocked and went out for a corner.

Charlton took it from the left, Foulkes won the header amid a crowd of players and the ball seemed to brush an upraised Benfica arm on its way out of play but a goal-kick was given. It wasn't taken cleanly by Henrique and Sadler won the ball just inside the Benfica half. He laid it to Kidd, who delayed his pass cleverly before delivering it into Sadler's path as he ran on into the box. With just Henrique to beat, though, Sadler snatched at the shot and dragged it wide.

But by then, United were clearly in the ascendancy. Stiles received the ball from a Brennan throw and played it to Crerand, who knocked it into the box towards Sadler. Henrique was quickly out to smother.

Only the stream of free-kicks kept Benfica in the game. Ten minutes before the break, Foulkes was penalised again for a foul on Torres thirty-five yards out. Eusébio took a long run and caught the ball sweetly. It flashed through the wall but it was close enough to Stepney that, although he must have seen it late, he was able to get down low to save.

Both teams, by then, were playing with a certain irritation: Benfica that they couldn't get into the game, and United that they hadn't been able to score and that they kept conceding soft free-kicks as Benfica hacked away. 'It was not a great match,' wrote Ken Jones in the *Mirror*. 'Indeed at times it was an ugly one. Italian referee Lo Bello allowed it to get out of hand as players from both sides committed themselves to ruthless tackles ... Benfica's treatment of Best bordered on the disgraceful and full-back Cruz might have gone from the match long before the first half was finished.'

With ten minutes of the first half remaining, Eusébio was sandwiched between Charlton and Sadler. As the ball spun loose a free-kick was given, but Crerand carried on his challenge regardless and Eusébio followed through into him. Crerand remained grounded as widespread pushing and shoving broke out. Again Eusébio took a long run, but this time he played the ball down the side of the wall for Graça, whose touch was poor and the chance lost. Eusébio, being booed by the crowd, came again down the left. Stiles tracked him and then, as Eusébio played the ball away, clattered through him from the side. The crowd cheered and, as he walked away, Stiles chuntered away before collapsing theatrically to the ground, suggesting Eusébio had dived – although his offence could hardly have been clearer. Torres out-jumped Foulkes for the free-kick, but couldn't direct his header goalwards.

Suddenly it was United committing the fouls. Coluna was left hopping by a sliding challenge from Sadler and Brennan was then penalised in the centre-circle for a raised foot on the same player. Two minutes before half-time, Benfica broke, Eusébio carrying the ball out to the left. Only Stiles stood between him and Stepney. Eusébio went past him and was blocked but, mystifyingly, Lo Bello decided it hadn't been a foul.

Adolfo then crashed into Best on the left touchline, perhaps the worst foul of the half. Best sprang to his feet but just checked himself before exacting retribution. He pointed to his forehead, insinuating Adolfo was crazy. Humberto then went through the back of Best, raising thoughts again of a concerted policy to kick him out of the game. Charlton's free-kick was won by Sadler who headed back across goal but Kidd couldn't quite get on the end of it. And with that a bad-tempered first half came to a close. 'The first half,' wrote Green, 'was episodic and a busy dullness as a spate of ruthless tackling by the Portuguese defence and a symphony of whistling by the Italian referee broke the game into a thousand pieces.'

United had been the better side, but Benfica had come closer to scoring and, perhaps, closer to losing control. 'The evil of this night,' Brian James wrote in the *Daily Mail*, 'came in the first half when two teams, overcome perhaps by the value of that which they sought, fell upon each other in a cruel graceless frenzy ... This was the Portugal who crushed Brazil mercilessly from the World Cup, not the Portugal who so gracefully lost to England.'

With astute shaping of the squad and behind-the-scenes politicking, by 1963–64 Busby had taken control of the club again after those poisonous days of the early sixties. There was, though, still one element to add before he could reach his apotheosis: George Best. Invited over from Belfast for a trial for United at the age of fifteen, nobody from the club was there at Manchester railway station to meet him and another promising teenager, Eddie McMordie, and, intimidated, Best went home after a day. Busby's human values and desire to look after young players evidently weren't always acted upon. Best was persuaded to return but, for all his skill, many were sceptical about his apparent frailty and his unwillingness to temper what some dismissed as his 'playground approach'. In the games played on the asphalt behind the stand, others had the tricks and flamboyance beaten out of them, but not Best.

He was seventeen when he made his debut against West Bromwich Albion in September 1963, a game in which he did so little of note that Busby left him out for another three months before bringing him back for the Boxing Day meeting with Burnley. In that game, the world suddenly woke up to what the United scout Bob Bishop had seen when he'd spotted Best on a housing estate in Cregagh and sent a telegram to Busby telling him he'd uncovered 'a genius'. Best destroyed the full-back John Angus and was soon a fixture on the wing, forming a devastating trio with Charlton inside him and Law at centre-forward. Yet while they are forever linked in folk memory – and by the statue of them that stands outside Old Trafford – the three were very different personalities and far from close friends.

Best wasn't the only new feature to emerge in that Boxing Day game against Burnley; it was at that match that the hooligan element among United's fans was seen for the first time. It would become a far bigger issue over the years that followed.

In February 1964, United played the Portuguese side Sporting in the quarter-final of the Cup-Winners' Cup and beat them 4–1 at Old Trafford, apparently opening a passage to the semi-final. But in Lisbon, United were hammered 5–0. According to Crerand, Busby 'ranted and raged at us. What Matt was going to do to us was nobody's business. Murder was the least of it.' Green describes the players in the hotel afterwards being unable to eat or even look one another in the eye.

That game, though, was indirectly responsible for a major step forward in the evolution of the side. The wing-half Maurice Setters stumbled on the marble floor of the hotel and damaged his knee, opening a route for Nobby Stiles and his aggressive energy into the team. It would be almost a decade before he left it.

The second half of the 1968 European Cup final began by reprising two themes from the first as Cruz fouled Best. He stayed on his feet, but angrily approached the left-back, tapping his head. The free-kick was cleared but, as Zé Augusto came away with it, he was outmuscled by Crerand. He worked it out to Aston, who zipped by Adolfo and crossed. Sadler rose the highest but his header across goal fell into space and was cleared.

There was far more urgency about United than there had been before the break. Charlton flicked a long Dunne clearance round the corner for Aston who either mishit his cross or tried an audacious shot from a narrow angle. Henrique dropped uneasily on the ball at his near post.

Charlton, in particular, was more involved than he had been. When a Brennan pass to him was intercepted, he dropped deep into his own half to take possession after the full-back had regained it and played a one-two with Crerand on the right, then swept the ball left to Dunne, opening up the pitch in three cleverly conceived passes. Dunne fed Aston on the wing. With Adolfo and Graça in front of him, he jabbed the ball between them and ran round the outside of Adolfo, burst into the box and drilled a shot at goal. It was firmly struck, but too close to Henrique to cause him real problems.

For five minutes, Benfica struggled to get out of their own half and when they did so it rendered them vulnerable to counter-attacks. Only a cynical foul by Cruz, catching the ball as Sadler chipped a quick free-kick forward, prevented Kidd being set one on one with Henrique, but the breakthrough was coming.

A long forward ball from Brennan found Best, who lifted the ball over Cruz's head and ran on. As three defenders and the goalkeeper converged, Cruz got back to hook the ball out for a throw-in on the United left. Sadler took it back to Dunne who returned it to him, taking the one defender on that side of the pitch out of the game. Sadler had time to measure a cross from the corner of the box. Nobody picked up Charlton's run and from just outside the six-yard box, he glanced a header across goal and into the bottom corner. With fifty-three minutes played, United had the lead.

Benfica kicked off and immediately conceded possession to Crerand, who knocked a pass over the top for Best. He ran on, flicked the ball over Henrique and, from a yard out, gleefully crashed the ball into the empty net. His capering, though, was cut short by a linesman's flag; he'd been just offside.

For a brief period United were rampant and Benfica were clearly rattled. Cruz seemed to catch Kidd, but Lo Bello allowed play to continue. Cruz got the ball back, twisted and turned to try to find space and then, seeing Kidd charging in for a retributively robust challenge, raised a foot dangerously and was penalised.

Aston remained the main danger and, the confidence flowing, he beat another two men on the left and played the ball inside to Best, who suddenly was finding room. He checked inside and played a pass to Sadler who shot left-footed over the bar. Dunne was penalised for a foul on Cruz, but Benfica were careless with the free-kick and Best led another break, relishing the space in front of him. Again, though, his judgement was awry as he ran into a thicket of players in the centre when he had Crerand steaming up in support and unmarked on the right. There was perhaps a sense at that stage that Best was overly determined to do something himself, to stamp the game with his own genius. A minute or so later, Crerand played a ball to Stiles who pushed it to Best and ran on into the box for a return. Best, though, preferred to shoot. He never got hold of the shot and it scuttled through to Henrique.

Walter Winterbottom, in his weirdly strangled co-commentary, suggested Benfica looked morally broken, but gradually they began to come back into the game. The problem was that the more they attacked, the more open they became. Zé Augusto led a charge and played a pass to Eusébio, but he was denied by a fine challenge from Foulkes. Brennan kept the ball in play and hit it long. Humberto gathered but was caught in possession by Best who unexpectedly found himself through on goal. Henrique, though, was swiftly out of his box to make a sliding clearance.

Aston won a corner on the hour. Charlton swung it in, mishitting slightly so it zipped low across the six-yard box where, remarkably, nobody got a touch. Best gathered at the far post but with players in the box, he opted to shoot low at the near post and Henrique saved. At that stage it seemed only a matter of time before United added a second.

In the summer of 1964, United won the FA Youth Cup for the first time since 1957, enhancing the sense of a new era beginning. It was also in 1964 that the decision was taken to rebuild the Pop Side of the ground at a cost of £300,000. A vast cantilever roof was added, as were a number of executive boxes after Busby and Edwards had been impressed by facilities they'd enjoyed at Manchester Racecourse. They were the first such boxes in the English game and a tentative step into the modern world of marketing and commercialism. That August, the BBC screened *Match of the Day* for the first time and league football took a great leap into the television age. As they would be in 1992, when another revolution hit the English game with the advent of the Premier League, United turned out to be ideally placed to take advantage of the new opportunities.

United won only one of their first six games of 1964–65, but then won thirteen of the next fourteen to surge to the top of the table. For a long time, United and Leeds slugged it out, United eventually stealing an advantage with a 1–0 win at Elland Road in the middle of April. That was the fourth in a run of seven straight wins, culminating in a victory over Arsenal that, as Leeds drew against Birmingham City, effectively sealed the title. There was further progress in Europe too, even if United's run in the Fairs Cup, which had included a 10–1 aggregate victory over Borussia Dortmund, ended with defeat to Ferencváros after a play-off. Crerand named 1964–65 as his favourite season; as Jim White pointed out in *Manchester United: The Biography*, it was United's final year as an old-fashioned, provincial club.

It was also, perhaps, the last season before the resentment Bob Lord had forecast had really set in on the part of those fans who did not support United. The FA Cup semi-final against Leeds in 1965, an ugly, spiteful game that was followed by running battles in the streets around Hillsborough, was an indication of what was to come. There was a violent element in United's support that took advantage of the numbers in which their fans travelled to wreak havoc on towns that couldn't cope with the invasion. At the same time, there were those who felt United's players had come to act with a sense of entitlement. 'Retaliation and a veil of arrogance began to clothe United,' said Green, who seems to have effectively been a fan. 'Those who had followed them faithfully became disturbed by this new trend.'

Perhaps the biggest single factor in United becoming something more than that, becoming a club that attracted support initially from all round the country and ultimately the world, was Best. 'Everything I do is off the cuff,' he said. 'That's where the buzz is for me. I just like those spontaneous moments.' He was the perfect player for a Busby side, quick, skilful, instinctive and imaginative. Although he had started playing for the first team by then, he had played in the Youth Cup-winning team of 1964 and went with the victorious side on a summer tour to Zurich. It was on that trip, aged eighteen, that he went out drinking for the first time. Three lagers left him vomiting.

The naivety soon disappeared. As Best's talent shone and his reputation grew, so he began to be recognised beyond football. His misfortune was to become a celebrity in a football culture that had no idea how to support him. It wasn't, Duncan Hamilton agued in *Immortal*, his biography of Best, the drink that destroyed him; rather it was the pressure of his lifestyle and football that drove him to drink. The ascent to celebrity, of course, is the result of a steady accumulation of performances, but with Best it's possible to mark precisely the moment at which he ceased to be merely George Best the footballer and became something far bigger.

United, as was their wont, started the 1965–66 season slowly, winning just four of their opening twelve matches. A run of ten games unbeaten dragged them back into the title race, before a stutter round Easter ended their challenge. The season, anyway, had by then become about Europe. United had swept by HJK Helsinki and ASK Vorwärts Berlin to set up a European Cup quarter-final against Benfica.

United won 3–2 at home, a precarious lead to take to Lisbon, particularly given memories of what had happened there against Sporting two years earlier and the fact that Benfica had never been beaten at home in a European tie. Benfica fans were keen to offer reminders, hammering on the side of the United team bus as it made its way to the Estádio da Luz and holding up five fingers. It was a gesture that proved prescient, although not in the way they intended, as United produced what Green described as 'the most inspired, inspiring and controlled performance I had seen from any British side abroad . . . a masterly exposition of mobility and skill'.

At the heart of it was Best, still only nineteen. 'He set a new, unexplored best,' Green wrote. 'The rest caught his mood, and their refined actions flowed, unbelievably courtly and delicate – yet deadly.' What elevated his performance was its unexpectedness. It wasn't that nobody knew he was brilliant, rather that nobody realised it was possible to be so brilliant against that Benfica side.

'Eusébio and company,' Green said, 'began with a deceitful air of infallibility.' But after six minutes, Charlton was fouled, Dunne took the free-kick and, with Costa Pereira needlessly leaving his line, Best headed in. Six minutes later, Herd headed a Gregg clearance back for Best, who zipped past two challenges and clipped an angled shot into the bottom corner, a goal of great simplicity, born of his pace, balance and awareness. 'I dipped a shoulder and swerved inside a defender,' Best wrote in his autobiography. 'I knew from that point I was going to score. A second defender came at me but I knocked it past him. I looked up to see the keeper coming towards me. I caught the look of uncertainty in his eye and instead of waiting for him to move, I knocked it past him before he could make his mind up.' Busby had told United to keep it tight for twenty minutes.

John Connelly added a third before half-time after Law, skittering in from the right, had created space for Herd to slide a pass into the Benfica box. An own goal from Shay Brennan early in the second half gave Benfica some hope but that was extinguished when Law's perfectly weighted pass set up a fourth for Crerand, with Pereira this time rooted to his line. Charlton wrapped up a 5–1 win after Herd had touched off Connelly's pass. 'United,' *Diário de Notícias* reported, 'were fabulous in all that is most artistic, athletic, imaginative and pure in football.'

Best's socialising had begun in earnest after the Championship success of 1965, but he still wasn't a big drinker; he just liked to, needed to, go out. 'I never stay in,' Hamilton quotes him as saying. 'I can't sit in the house . . . Wednesday to Saturday it's murder. I know I've got to stay off the town and get to bed by eleven. But it drives me nuts. The only thing that keeps me sane is remembering there'll be a party on Sunday and Monday and Tuesday.' Without Busby's knowledge, Best's landlady Mrs Fullaway gave him a key so he could come home in the early hours without disturbing her.

Best admitted that even as early as 1965–66, his way of life was affecting his football. 'I was going on to the field tired and coming off it shattered,' he said. Busby, perhaps, misjudged Best and the situation. He would issue quiet admonitions, Best would apologise, promise to be more disciplined in the future, and then slide back immediately into his old ways. But life, society, had changed: there were more opportunities, more temptations, and Best was never able to knuckle down. He was even dropped for three games – a teenager needed the rest, Busby explained – but it made little difference.

However well-known he had been before, the performance in Lisbon elevated Best to a new level of celebrity. He became aware of the change as he took a walk outside the team hotel in Estoril the following morning. 'Every bikini on the beach,' he wrote in his autobiography, 'wanted my autograph.' He bought a sombrero from a local stall and made sure he was wearing it when he stepped off the plane in Manchester, giving every newspaper the photograph they used the next day; according to David Meek of the *Manchester Evening News*, Best, who had a new boutique to publicise, knew exactly what he was doing. The *Mirror* dubbed him 'El Beatle'. The geographical and linguistic signifiers may have been askew (did they wear sombreros in Portugal? Shouldn't it have been '*O Beatle*'?), but the link between Best and the Beatles was profound enough: they were young and working-class, appealing to an increasingly broad demographic from industrial cities in the north-west of England with a creative brilliance that bore an anti-establishment edge.

United under Busby had always been about youth, but this was youth not in the sense of innocence and pliability, but modernity and rebellion. Best by then was receiving 10,000 letters a week and employing three people to deal with them. He was driving a Rolls-Royce and seeing Miss England, yet he was still obeying club rules and living in digs – or at least he was when he wasn't staying at the flat he and Manchester City's Mike Summerbee had rented to facilitate their gallivanting. Busby had kept tabs on errant players before – perhaps most notably Dennis Viollet – but here he was in the dark; Best had reached a level of fame with which nobody in football was equipped to cope. He couldn't walk down the street without being hassled, while admirers were constantly knocking at Mrs Fullaway's door, asking for autographs or begging to see his bedroom. It became impossible for Best to eat in a restaurant: he would order just a main course and eat as much as he could before the pressure of the public led him to flee. He worked with the agent David Stanley and began endorsing a huge range of products. Even then there was a suspicion that football had ceased to be fun for him. 'I like to think by the time I'm twenty-five I won't have to rely on football,' he said. 'I'd like to be so well off that it wouldn't bother me.'

In the first leg of the European Cup semi-final against Partizan, Best's cartilage gave way as another European campaign ended in frustration. Law missed an open goal with United 2–0 down in the first leg in Belgrade. Back at Old Trafford, United piled on the pressure but scored only once, an own goal from the goalkeeper Milutin Šoškić, who otherwise had a fine game. The fulfilment of the quest was again deferred; the fear then was that the deferment was permanent. 'We'll never win the European Cup now,' said Law, who believed they would have won it that season had it not been for having to flog through a series of games on heavy pitches. At one stage a Treble had seemed possible, but United finished fourth in the league and were beaten by Everton in the semi-final of the Cup. Again there was criticism of Busby, most notably from Gregg, about his failure to adapt to the opposition. This time, Busby accepted that perhaps there was need of a more cautious approach. As he thought about their failures that summer, the statistic that concerned him most was that United, although they had scored five more goals than the champions Liverpool, had also conceded twenty-five more.

As the final became more stretched towards the mid-point of the second half, Charlton became increasingly involved, a classy and composed presence amid the mayhem. He played a pass to Crerand and moved to get it back. The return was weak and he had to stretch, but had the balance to retain possession, turn and spread the ball left for Aston. He played it back to Charlton, who gave it to Stiles who switched the play to Dunne advancing on the right. He helped it to Sadler but his cross towards Kidd was flipped behind by Henrique. Best's corner was high, aimed at the edge of the box where Crerand met it with a volley, slicing across the ball slightly so it arced just wide.

Kidd on a charge down the left seemed isolated but was

chopped down by Humberto, a violent – and frankly stupid – challenge that needlessly conceded a free-kick a couple of yards from the goal-line. The free-kick was taken short to Charlton who crossed from a slightly wider angle. Henrique punched it away, but Crerand gathered on the right before it went out of play. As he returned the ball to the back post, Charlton's cry of 'Leave it!' was clear. His volley took a deflection and just evaded Kidd as it bounced through to Henrique.

Slowly, though, the Benfica resurgence did come. 'We lost control in the middle slightly,' Busby said. Eusébio fired a long-ranger just wide. Dunne leapt well to beat Torres to a cross from Simões. For all the patient passes they had played in the first half, they looked at their most threatening getting balls into the box. Twice Augusto got to Cruz free-kicks but couldn't guide his header goalwards.

But the more Benfica pushed forwards, the more space there was in midfield and the more dangerous Best, in particular, looked. Aston released him on a counter and he swept between two challenges and darted past another as he burst into the box. Henrique, diving to his left, beat away his shot and the ball fell to Sadler, who had two-thirds of the goal to aim at. He didn't quite catch his shot cleanly, though, and Henrique, sprawling to his left, somehow managed to divert the ball over the bar with a flick of his trailing leg.

A Cruz cross was headed out by Foulkes, who beat Torres. Adolfo won it on halfway and played a long ball back into the box. Sadler tried to let it run but Simões kept it in and Coluna, backing him up, headed across goal where Eusébio, under pressure eight yards out, lashed a shot over. 'That should serve as a very great warning to Manchester United,' said Wolstenholme.

United fans responded by demanding their side should 'Attack! Attack! Attack, attack, attack!' It was a chant that almost half a century later would haunt Louis van Gaal but back then was an assertion that United fans preferred to see their team protect a lead by being in the opposition half rather than sitting deep.

It didn't work. Humberto was almost caught in possession by Kidd in the middle of his own half. He launched it long, but Stiles won the header against Eusébio. Sadler played it back to Dunne who, under pressure, hoofed the ball into the air. Zé Augusto won it and played it to Torres who helped it on to Graça, who moved it out to Zé Augusto as he made a run out to the right flank. He crossed deep and Torres beat Foulkes to nod the ball down. Eusébio and Stiles both went for it, but the ball was behind them and Graça, arriving late, met the bouncing ball on the angle of the six-yard box and hammered it past Stepney to level. 'Woe, woe, woe,' wrote Busby of the moment. 'I could have wept.'

The tenor of the game changed, but Cruz's robust approach did not. He committed a bad foul on Crerand – his capacity to escape a booking was astonishing even by the standards of the time. From out near the right touchline, Crerand slung in the free-kick but it was a fraction too high for Best. Suddenly both teams were committed to the attack. Cruz may have been a tough-tackling full-back, but he could also pass and he sent a perfectly weighted ball down the line for Coluna, who skipped by Sadler's slightly wild challenge and crossed to the back post. Torres won the header but his effort looped over.

United suddenly looked weary and their passing began to lose a little sharpness. Stiles and Sadler both lost possession cheaply in quick succession and then Cruz intercepted a weak pass from Best. He went past the Irishman and then Zé Augusto took over. He played it to Eusébio who jabbed a pass with the outside of his boot to Torres. He touched it off for Eusébio, who had continued his run. He left Stiles behind and, moving to his left, went past Sadler. He tried to hit a shot back across his body and across goal, but couldn't get any real power into his effort and Stepney saved comfortably.

Benfica's confidence was palpable. Graça took a pass from Coluna but dragged his shot wide. Crerand was finding room on the right as Graça became more involved from an attacking point of view and Best picked him out. He crossed and, as the ball was headed clear, Charlton lined up a volley from just outside the box. His effort was blocked by Coluna, though, and Simões broke, carrying the ball forty yards and then shaping a pass over the top for Eusébio, accelerating into the channel between Dunne and Foulkes. The ball bounced perfectly into his stride and, from the edge of the box he struck a powerful shot goalwards. There were nine minutes remaining. 'Oh no . . .' Busby was heard to mutter on the bench. 'Not again.'

Stepney had started to come, thinking he would get to the ball first, but as the ball held up on the turf, he retreated, worried about being chipped. Knowing Eusébio's preferred finish was to hit the ball with maximum power, Stepney stood up, making himself as big as he could. Positioned just outside his six-yard box, Stepney could hardly have got out of the way had he wanted to. The ball struck him – painfully, he later admitted – in the chest, he flopped backwards and, as the ball threatened to bounce loose, he had the wherewithal to grab it.

Eusébio, following in, laid a hand on Stepney's shoulder in acknowledgement. 'Oh, what a save!' cried Wolstenholme, and it's a block that has gone down in folklore. Stepney can take credit for his positioning and for the way he seized the loose ball, but the save itself was almost involuntary. Eusébio's reaction, perhaps, made the save appear better than it was; he waited until Stepney had cleared and then made a point of applauding him before trotting back to rejoin the play. 'I have always since maintained that if Eusébio had placed the ball instead of trying to bust the net with it we should probably not have survived the normal time,' Busby said.

They only just survived it as it was. A Graça cross was cleared but Dunne gave the ball away almost immediately. Eusébio spread the play back to Graça. His cross was deflected and dropped on the edge of the box. Eusébio beat Dunne to the ball but his header, with Stepney looking on with an apparent lack of concern, scooted just wide of the post.

And then, in the final seconds, a chance for United: Best nipped in as Henrique tried to bowl the ball out to Simões, but from a tight angle he sliced wearily wide. As the final whistle went, sending a European Cup final into extra-time for the second time, United looked shattered. 'With ninety minutes gone they were stretched like blue shadows on the green of Wembley's turf ...' wrote Ken Jones in the *Mirror*, 'sucking at the night air and desperately trying to slap life back into weary legs. Busby hovered over them, hen-like – encouraging, anxious and fearing, perhaps, that the worst was to come.'

Charlton and Stiles, of course, had been there before, on the same pitch, not two years earlier in the World Cup final, seeing a lead slip from their grasp and having to regain it. As the players were massaged on the pitch, Busby stalked among them, berating Crerand and Charlton for giving the ball away too cheaply, stressing the need to regain control of the middle.

Financial issues continued to fester. In the summer of 1966, Law wrote a letter to the club asking for a rise then went on holiday to Scotland. When he returned he was told that he would be transfer-listed unless he apologised in public. He did so, and then privately agreed with Busby a deal for half the rise he'd initially requested. That was typical of the way Busby operated, maintaining discipline and heading off a wider wage rebellion but without being entirely deaf to realistic requests from his players.

With Gregg suffering from the shoulder injury that would effectively end his career, Busby, aware that his rearguard needed strengthening, signed Alec Stepney in August 1966, just three months after the goalkeeper had left Millwall for Chelsea. Stepney had believed he would be replacing Peter Bonetti, who was being sold to West Ham. When the Chelsea chairman Joe Mears died, though, that deal was called off and Stepney was left as a reluctant and highly gifted reserve.

United had their familiar slow start to the 1966–67 season, losing four of their opening ten games, but they lost only twice more, taking the title by four points, a success that has come to seem important less for what it represented in itself than because it got United back into the European Cup, the tournament that had become a quest for the club. What had happened at Munich could never be forgotten or erased, but this could be a tribute to those who had died.

That at least is how it's come to feel in retrospect, as the prelude to the glory of Wembley 1968. When the title was sealed with a 6–1 win over West Ham, though, Busby described the success as his 'finest hour': only three of the regular starting eleven – Stepney, Crerand and Law – had cost a fee.

For once, United started the league season well, losing only three of their opening twenty-seven games in 1967–68 to be three points clear at the top at the beginning of February. The focus, though, was Europe. United saw off the Maltese side Hibernians in the first round and FK Sarajevo in the second, although in both ties they drew the away leg 0–0. The Polish champions Górnik Zabrze proved even tougher in the quarter-final. An own goal from Stefan Florenski and a late strike from Kidd, brought in to replace Law, who had a badly swollen knee, gave them a 2–0 win in the first leg. Conditions in Poland were difficult: the lines were marked in red so they could be seen on a snow-covered pitch, while fans lit fires on the terraces to keep warm. Włodzimierz Lubański scored after seventy minutes, but United held out for a 1–0 defeat that set up a semi-final against Real Madrid.

Madrid were extremely cautious at Old Trafford in the first leg, a game refereed by Tofiq Bahramov, the 'Russian' – actually Azeri – linesman who had decided that Geoff Hurst's shot had crossed the line to put England 3–2 up in the World Cup final two years earlier. Real sat deep and allowed United to come onto them. United had all the play, but scored just once, after thirty-six minutes, as Best flicked a loose ball on for Kidd, who advanced and spread it wide to John Aston just as a cat leapt from the stand. His initial attempt at a cross was blocked but, as the cat, having scurried down the touchline, disappeared behind the goal, he cut the ball back for Best, who lashed the ball home.

At the Bernabéu, Madrid were far more attacking. With Stiles nagging at the heels of Amancio, United held Madrid at bay for half an hour. Stiles, though, could do nothing about Amancio's free-kick delivery and, from his right-wing cross, Pirri headed in. Nine minutes later, Brennan missed a Pirri through-ball and Paco Gento ran on to stick the ball through the legs of a back-tracking Stepney. An own goal from Zoco, slicing Dunne's centre into his own net, levelled the aggregate scores but, before half-time, Madrid had the lead again, Amancio crashing in a snap shot from the edge of the box.

United had begun the game with Sadler sitting deep alongside Foulkes. Forced to attack, Sadler was advanced and they reverted to a more conventional 4-3-3. Perhaps just as important was the punch Stiles delivered to Amancio – although he always justified it by claiming Amancio had kicked him first. With Madrid seeming uncertain whether to look to kill the game or defend what they had, the second half was far more even. With seventeen minutes to go, Foulkes headed on a Crerand free-kick and, as the Madrid defence hesitated, Sadler touched the ball in: 3–3 on aggregate. Five minutes later, Crerand took a throw long down the right, Best beat Manuel Sanchis and Zoco and pulled the ball back for, of all people, Foulkes to score with a controlled finish across goal and in at the far post. United won 4–3.

The emotion was almost unbearable. Charlton, who later fainted in his hotel room, although he always claimed it was because of dehydration, recalled Busby being 'speechless' and then weeping in the dressing room. United were just one game from the European glory they had pursued for a decade.

In the league, United fell away from February, losing seven of their final fourteen games. They still went into the final day level on points with Manchester City at the top of the table but were beaten by Sunderland as City beat Newcastle to lift the title. Best was named Footballer of the Year but felt the award was hollow. After the presentation, he got drunk, fell asleep in a doorway and was awakened by a policeman who didn't believe his story until he saw his trophy. 'Get inside or it'll be posthumous,' he said.

The start of extra-time could hardly have been more different from the end of normal time as United found a renewed spurt of energy. Kidd chased a long ball and won a throw by the corner flag. He took it himself, to Charlton, who by then was wearing his socks down around his ankles. He crossed left-footed. Sadler leapt with Adolfo but the ball ran through to Aston. He was half-tackled as he turned to take the ball to the line. Humberto cleared but with a spurt Dunne got there ahead of Graça and fed Aston once more. He went on Adolfo's outside yet again but the full-back recovered sufficiently to deflect his cross behind for a corner.

Best's corner was weak and was cleared but United were back on the front foot. Dunne picked up the clearance and gave it back to Stepney. He rolled it to Foulkes and got it back again because, the keeper later claimed, the two defenders were too exhausted by that stage to do anything else. Having few other options, Stepney launched a huge kick upfield. It was flicked on by Kidd for Best, whose touch took him by Jacinto. As Henrique came out, Best floated past him before rolling the ball into the empty net. It hadn't, perhaps, been the prettiest build-up, but the execution once the chance came was devastating and United had the lead for the second time.

Benfica had barely kicked off when United added a third. Charlton spread the play to Aston who won another corner off Adolfo. Best took it. Sadler at the back post headed across goal and, with a deft nod, Kidd diverted the ball goalwards. Henrique made a reaction save but the ball came back to Kidd who looped his second header over the keeper and under the bar.

Having finished normal time so strongly, Benfica looked shattered, unable quite to understand the storm that had broken upon them. Aston surged again and was tripped by

Cruz, but the ball broke for Best and play continued. His cross was headed dangerously into the air by Humberto and, with Henrique beaten, it dropped onto the top of the crossbar. Sadler, rushing onto the loose ball, could only head the ball back into the air and Henrique cleared. There were still only five minutes of extra-time gone.

Benfica roused themselves to a slight gesture of defiance. Best made a fine tackle in his own box on Coluna and Eusébio smacked another free-kick into the wall. But then Brennan played a long low pass forward. Kidd touched it off for Charlton, and made a run down the right before getting the ball back. He skipped over a challenge from Cruz and crossed low to the edge of the six-yard box where Charlton hit the ball first-time into the far corner. It was 4–1 and the game was done.

The crowd chanted Busby's name and sang 'Happy Birthday' to Kidd. Stepney made a remarkable low save to keep out a Eusébio snap shot from eight yards – far better than his save in normal time, but far less important. For the final twenty minutes it was simply a matter of watching the clock tick down. When, at last, it had and Lo Bello blew his whistle, Charlton lowered his hands to his knees and bent forward, physically and emotionally exhausted.

'This is the most wonderful thing that's happened to me in my life,' said an emotional Busby. 'I am the happiest man in England tonight. This is not the end of the road for me. There's been a lot of talk about this but I'm staying where I am until people get fed up of me or they think I've got beyond it.'

That moment would come sooner than anybody expected.

CHAPTER 5

League Division One, Selhurst Park, London, 16 December 1972

Crystal Palace **5–0** **Manchester United**
Mulligan 10, 42
Rogers 46, 87
Whittle 89

John Jackson   Alex Stepney
Tony Taylor   Tony Young
Iain Phillip   Martin Buchan
David Payne   David Sadler
Paddy Mulligan   Tommy O'Neil
Mel Blyth   Willie Morgan
Robert Bell   Tony Dunne (Denis Law 25)
Alan Whittle   Brian Kidd
Charlie Cooke   Wyn Davies
Don Rogers   Ted MacDougall
John Hughes   Ian Storey-Moore

Bert Head   Frank O'Farrell

Ref: John Hunting
Bkd:
Att: 39,484

IT WAS A DARK, slightly misty afternoon, the pitch heavy, players' breath steaming in the dank air, a day for heart and character rather than subtle ability. In the *Manchester Evening News*, David Meek reported that 'the atmosphere was tense from the start.' But United began well, despite having won only five of their previous twenty-one league games, and despite the on-going upheaval surrounding George Best, who had been surprisingly restored to the squad following yet another club suspension.

United were, Meek wrote, 'quick to the attack with [Tony] Young finding [Willie] Morgan on the right. The winger's centre went straight to [the goalkeeper John] Jackson, though, who quickly got Palace moving. A great tackle by teenager Young stopped the burly [John] Hughes in his tracks as the Scottish international ran hard to the United goal. United immediately replied with a thrust down the left from [Ian Storey-]Moore, who beat his man cleverly but then centred tamely.' This, perhaps, was the United that had won three out of four before a defeat at Stoke City the previous week, when they had been, as Arthur Hopcraft put it in the *Observer*, 'dulled and blundering, in need of a guiding light from somewhere'. But even in those early stages the game swept from end to end; there was no sense of control, even if United were the livelier.

Nine minutes in, Martin Buchan, elegant as ever at the back, swept the ball forward to Ted MacDougall on halfway and he laid it off to Tony Dunne, advancing from left-back. He hit a swinging cross from deep towards MacDougall as he sprinted forwards. The ball eluded him but Taylor had been

MacDougall did have the ball in the net after thirty-eight minutes only for his header to be ruled out for offside before, finally, three minutes before half-time, came the second goal Palace had been threatening since they'd scored their first. Kidd played a pass in to Davies with his back to goal about twenty-five yards out. His touch was poor and the ball popped up, allowing Robert Bell to hoof the ball forward. United's shape having gone completely, the ball bounced on halfway and trundled forward into inconceivable space. Rogers won the race to get to it but was held up by Young. When he eventually crossed, Buchan headed out. But the ball went straight back to Rogers on the right flank. United, somehow, hadn't reset and so when Mulligan hurtled into the box, there was nobody to pick him up. Rogers rolled a calm pass to him and, entirely unmarked, he dug the ball out from between his feet and sliced a shot with the outside of his right foot past the left hand of Stepney. Palace's captain had never previously scored for them; that was his second of the afternoon.

Storey-Moore fizzed a shot just over early in the second half but, within two minutes, any hope of a comeback was gone. Whittle stabbed a ball behind the United backline with the outside of his right foot to release Rogers again. 'Sadler and Buchan,' said Meek, 'seemed to stand like statues as Rogers went between them.' As Stepney came out, Rogers went left and touched the ball the other side of the keeper, running on to turn in his finish from an acute angle despite Buchan's desperate slide. Given the lack of pressure on the ball in midfield, United's line was simply too high. The only question was whether that was a tactical error or whether United's players had lost their appetite for the task.

Seeking the positives, Meek saw an improvement in the second half. 'United were sticking to their task and in the last half-hour forced their way back into the game,' he wrote. 'Law had a header just over the top of the goal and MacDougall headed into the side-netting. It was a fighting finish but it looked too late.'

Far too late. Morgan, a Scottish winger with extravagant hair who had been signed from Burnley in 1968, worked the ball to Moore on the right. Hunch-shouldered, he wobbled inside and played it back to Morgan, who helped it on to Young about ten yards outside the Palace box. But the pass was a little short and Payne nipped in. The ball spurted forward into the centre-circle, where Whittle's lunge helped the ball out to Rogers. Again he had great swaths of muddied grass to run into, and did so gleefully, cutting inside the box, checking to bemuse Sadler then going again before arcing his shot just over. United's inability to deal with basic counter-attacks was startling, indicative of a complete breakdown of either will or discipline. It kept on happening. A few minutes later, Rogers ran from the edge of his own box, shook off Storey-Moore and went by Morgan before duffing his shot.

Still the agony wasn't over. With four minutes to go, Hughes won a header on halfway on the left side of the pitch, sending the ball forward to Whittle. Sadler held him up and, just as he got in the box, Whittle turned back and rolled the ball to Hughes, who had continued his run. He twisted, but couldn't find room for a shot and then, as Buchan challenged him, nudged the ball on to Whittle, who opened up his body with a touch to the right and shaped a superb shot from just inside the box into the top corner.

And it got worse. Blyth brushed Davies out of the way to win Storey-Moore's pass deep in his own half and whipped a long pass forward. United's defence was a shambles, neither sitting deep nor pushing up and Rogers capped a magnificent afternoon by taking the ball round Stepney and, with Buchan still to beat, shaping to put the ball into the right-hand side of the goal before tucking it in the bottom-left corner. 'That,' said Brian Moore on the ITV commentary, 'is total and utter confusion.'

For United, the game was a disaster, perhaps the most humiliating result in their history. 'Palace were awful and beat us 5–0,' said Law. 'What does that say about us?'

Yet perhaps the biggest issue was what Meek did not mention: George Best. Thanks to the intervention of Matt Busby and Pat Crerand, he had decided that he did, after all, want to play for United. The day before the game it was revealed he was off the transfer list and back training, albeit initially apart from the rest of the squad.

But what excitedly was reported as good news on the Friday soon became doubt. On the Saturday morning, under the headline, 'NOWT! NOWT! NOWT!' Bob Russell in the *Mirror* wrote, 'What United aren't revealing – although there are rumours galore – is who or what prompted the sudden and dramatic policy change towards a player they had washed their hands of . . . Manager Frank O'Farrell isn't saying what he thinks of the business, and the players are under orders not to talk about George. But we have a fair idea they are in a state of confusion, judging from the bewildered faces at their London hotel.'

Reg Drury in the *News of the World* wasn't the only one to see a link between United's capitulation at Selhurst Park and Best's return: 'United players surrendered as meekly as their directors had done in the confrontation with George Best . . . it's impossible to disregard the connection between the two events.'

O'Farrell clearly wasn't happy. 'You saw our display,' he said. 'It's up to you to draw your own conclusions.'

There weren't many prepared to criticise them. 'Could you blame the players, who made United great, behaving like true professionals and sportsmen, for refusing to play alongside a colleague they were convinced had let them down?' Frank Butler asked in the *News of the World*. 'Could you blame Frank O'Farrell, a proud and just man, if he resigned on the grounds that he came as a manager to manage.'

As it turned out, the defeat would have profound consequences for O'Farrell. But the loss was about more than him and about more than Best. How could it be that United had gone, in just four and a half years, from beating Benfica to win the European Cup to a humiliation like that?

*

The grail achieved, where else was there to go? It's become common practice for silverware and success to be heralded as the beginning of a brave new era of domination when at least as often great success actually marks the end of a cycle, but few had any doubt in this case that United's European Cup success had been so emotionally draining that it was a finale. 'You could almost hear the energy and ambition sighing out of the club,' said Best. 'Everybody was talking as if the good old days were over.'

In January 1969, with United sixteenth in the table, Busby announced that he would step aside at the end of the season to become general manager. He was only fifty-nine, but he'd been manager for twenty-four years and the trauma of Munich and its aftermath had taken its toll. 'He really was, I felt, an old man,' said Charlton.

'I feel it is time,' Busby said, 'for someone in a tracksuit to take over the players out on the training pitch. As it is, United have become rather more than a football club. They are now an institution. I am finding less and less time to give to the thing I consider paramount, which is the playing side.'

The final straw, Geoffrey Green suggested, had come with the two legs of the Intercontinental Cup against Estudiantes, games that proved once and for all that 'all the romantic jousts associated with ancient knights in armour had disappeared from the game he loved and he'd had enough of it.'

The worth of the competition had been called into serious question the previous season when Celtic and Racing Club of Buenos Aires had brawled over three games, the Argentinians eventually winning in a play-off in Montevideo in a game that saw six players, four of them Scots, sent off.

'You cannot stop playing these games because of certain incidents on the field,' Busby said. 'There have been no finer artists of football than the Brazilians in the last ten years and they too are South American. We can only solve these problems by playing more, not less.'

He perhaps wouldn't have been quite so diplomatic after the first leg, played in Buenos Aires. Estudiantes won 1–0 in a match that featured fifty-three fouls and culminated with Nobby Stiles being sent off for dissent. Back in Manchester, Juan Ramón Verón, father of Juan Sebastián, headed Estudiantes in front before Best and José Hugo Medina were sent off for throwing punches at each other, Medina having apparently wound Best up with a series of fouls and provocations. Willie Morgan equalised late on, but it wasn't enough. The result, though, was only part of it. 'The night they spat on sportsmanship,' roared the *Mirror* after the first game, while after the second Brian Glanville in the *Sunday Times* was left despairing for the very future of football. 'Some of their tactics ...' he wrote, 'draw us again to question how football, at the highest level, can survive as a sport.' For Busby, a world crown might have been a fitting finale; the contest, though, can only have wearied him further.

Domestically, United struggled, slipping to seventeenth in mid-March, but they then went on a run of five wins and two draws in seven games to quash any relegation fears almost before they'd begun to materialise. The defence of the European Cup reached the semi-finals, but there United lost 2–1 on aggregate to the eventual winners AC Milan, railing about a shot from Law that they felt had crossed the line but wasn't given.

The man chosen to replace Busby was Wilf McGuinness, who had been the assistant trainer to Jack Crompton, running the reserve team with a special interest in the youths. McGuinness had come through United's ranks, winning a league title medal in 1956–57, and had won two caps for England before breaking his leg in a reserve game against Stoke City in December 1959. His playing career over, McGuinness became a coach, working not only with United but with Alf Ramsey at the 1966 World Cup.

The circumstances of his appointment suggested some of the problems that lay ahead. Busby decided McGuinness would be his successor three months before telling him – although news leaked early enough that McGuinness was, according to legend at least, able to have some friends back him to be the new manager at 6–1. The first formal direct hint McGuinness had that Busby was considering him came when he was told to put on a collar and tie before coming into work the following day because he had to meet the press. He spoke of the appointment as a 'supreme honour'. Significantly, though, McGuinness was designated 'chief coach' as Busby redefined the role of the manager. Although McGuinness took training and picked the team while Busby attended board meetings, it was never entirely clear what the line of demarcation was.

Did McGuinness have a philosophy or ideas of his own? How did he think things should be done? Nobody seemed to bother to find out; he was just Busby's pawn at a time when sporting directors in the modern sense were unheard of. McGuinness wanted to sign Malcolm Macdonald, Colin Todd and Mick Mills; Busby bought him the midfielder Ian Ure from Arsenal. 'The torch,' as Eamon Dunphy put it, 'had been passed on. Wilf grabbed the lighted end.'

Best was appalled and nutmegged Ure in his first training session to make a point, first forwards and then backwards. Best was increasingly disillusioned by football as a whole. Angered by his own failure to produce a definitive performance against Benfica – even if he had scored a decisive goal – he had gone out afterwards and got drunker than he'd ever got before, so drunk he could subsequently remember only snippets of the game and virtually none of what happened after it. For Duncan Hamilton in *Immortal* this was a watershed in his relationship with booze and consequently in his career. Best never won another medal. He railed against McGuinness, who tried to impose a tactical structure Best found restrictive: too much time spent with Alf Ramsey, Best felt. But after Busby's laissez-faire approach any kind of modernisation probably would have felt oppressive.

Busby himself was subject to the whims of a board that was

capable of profound pettiness. Seemingly without being con-sulted, Jimmy Murphy was retired at the same time as Busby, reduced from assistant manager to scouting for £25 a week. In itself, that was perhaps a reasonable move for a man enter-ing semi-retirement, but what was unforgivable was that the club refused to pay any longer for his taxi to the Cliff. Murphy couldn't drive and so the pensioner who'd held everything to-gether after Munich was left to take the bus to work.

McGuinness took over on 1 June 1969 and, although United started the season slowly, the signing of Ure prompted a re-vival and they finished eighth in the league while reaching the semi-final of both Cups. Both were lost by a single goal in slightly unfortunate circumstances, but both ended up being remembered less for United's performance than for their part in the accelerating narrative of George Best's decline.

The generous perhaps saw encouragement there, but it was soon extinguished the following season. Defeat to Aston Villa of the Third Division in the League Cup semi-final com-pounded miserable league form. Back-to-back home defeats to City and Arsenal left United eighteenth at Christmas, with widespread rumours of dissent and cliques in the dressing room. 'Not everyone, sadly, would play for Wilf,' said David Sadler. 'The side as a whole did not give 100 per cent effort for him. It was as simple as that. As soon as Sir Matt returned to the scene, it changed at once.'

The fact is that whoever had taken over, the challenge would have been almost impossibly hard. After the high of winning the European Cup, and all the emotion that entailed, there was a sense of a club searching for new meaning, even if McGuinness insisted there was 'no tangible indication of imminent decline' when he took the job.

Best became particularly disaffected, increasingly a celeb-rity rather than a footballer. In his autobiography, Charlton recalls playing with Best in a Uefa representative game in Car-diff. His wife and daughters were away that night, so Charlton invited Best round for dinner. He cooked him some frozen scampi and found himself being pumped for information about married life, as though Best was considering whether he fancied it.

He didn't, or at least whatever desire there might have been to settle down was overwhelmed by other urges. In 1969, Best had a remarkable modernist house built in Bramhall. It seemed to have everything: a sunken bath, electronic curtains, a television that retracted into the chimney stack and underfloor heating. But the electronics malfunctioned and, more fundamentally, the property didn't even have a hedge, with the result that it became a glass prison, a gleaming symbol of his life in the public eye as the public came to stare, picnicking on the lawn and hoping for a glimpse of the owner.

The house demonstrated Best's naivety and a lack of understanding of the public's demands, but other episodes provoke less sympathy. Gradually his relationships became more tangled. In 1969, he had persuaded a Danish newspaper to track down an admirer for whom he'd signed an autograph, Eva Haraldsted. Within eight days they were engaged. Within ninety-one, they'd split up. She sued for breach of promise and while the case was going to trial, Best became involved in a fracas in a nightclub with her new boyfriend, the boyfriend's brother and a friend. Pat Crerand stepped in to support him and a fight broke out. Crerand, having been accused of assault, was represented by George Carman, who would later defend the Liberal leader Jeremy Thorpe on a charge of conspiracy to murder and then become famous as an expert in libel law. Best seduced Carman's then-wife as the lawyer lay drunk on the sofa downstairs. Two years later, Carman appeared on Best's behalf in another case and the affair was resumed. Carman found out and approached a local gangster, asking him to break Best's legs in retribution. The gangster, though, was a United fan and not merely refused but threatened violence to Carman if anything should befall Best.

Best's appetite was insatiable. He drank more and more, trained less and less. On the field, he became increasingly petulant. In the first leg of the League Cup semi-final against City, Francis Lee won a soft penalty late in the game, which he converted, and Best was then denied a penalty after what he thought was a foul at the other end. In his frustration, he slapped the ball out of the hands of the referee Jack Taylor, for which he was banned for twenty-eight days. He returned to score six in an 8–2 win over Northampton Town in the fifth round of the FA Cup. Best talked then about how much the Cup meant to him, how he'd always wanted to win it, but his antics before the FA Cup semi-final replay against Leeds suggested otherwise. United stayed at a hotel in Droitwich. The plan was for the players to have a nap after lunch, then gather for a tactical meeting before heading to Villa Park for the match. Best, though, ended up spending the afternoon with a woman he'd picked up in the bar. McGuinness caught him in the act and was, to use his own word, 'blazing', but rather than taking action himself he went to Busby, who said he'd sort it out. Best played, missed the only good chance of the game and United lost a second replay.

Other players were furious with Best for his lack of professionalism and with McGuinness for not having had the nerve to drop him. Perhaps another manager might have been stronger, but McGuinness was hampered by his position, unable to impose discipline while Busby, who was still close to many of the players, remained the higher authority. The contrast with Busby's ruthless treatment of Johnny Morris was obvious. When McGuinness told players to track back, the reply came that Busby hadn't asked them to do that. He was living always in the shadow of the man in English football who, at that point, beyond all others couldn't be questioned.

And yet perhaps McGuinness didn't help himself. The story about him making Bobby Charlton do press-ups in his suit in front of the rest of the squad seems to have been a joke that was understood as such by all parties at the time (the two were close: McGuinness would have been best man at Charlton's wedding had the church not raised concerns about his Catholicism and Charlton wrote the foreword to McGuinness's 2005 autobiography) but on another occasion after losing a hand of poker on the team bus the manager threw his cards at Willie Morgan. The fact he was playing cards with his team at all suggested that McGuinness was perhaps too close to them, while his reaction led Morgan to conclude he was 'too immature, too petty' for the job.

Busby in *Soccer at the Top* also spoke of McGuinness being let down by 'inexperience or slight immaturity' but his discussion of the period is oddly, perhaps significantly, defensive. The book as a whole, in fact, has a slightly uncomfortable tone, not uncommon in sporting autobiographies of the time, of slightly patronising self-assurance. No doubt is ever admitted; this is the master explaining his greatness. Insisting he had never interfered with team selection, Busby described McGuinness, after three straight defeats, asking what team he should pick for his fifth game in charge, away at Wolves. McGuinness ended up following Busby's advice and United drew 0–0, embarking on a run of ten games unbeaten (although that included four draws and two League Cup victories over lower-league opposition). Busby is then adamant that he did not interfere when it came to dropping Charlton and Law on the same day. It's not hard to imagine, though, that Busby's disapproval was readily inferred.

As fame, alcohol and gambling overtook Best's talent, others were on the wane for the more prosaic reason of age: Foulkes was thirty-six and Charlton and Brennan thirty-one. Law, at twenty-nine and struggling with knee injuries, was perhaps just past his peak. The sense of a mountain climbed and the knowledge of what followed has generated the myth that Busby left behind an ageing team, but Stiles, Crerand, Dunne and Stepney were all in their prime, while Best, Aston, Kidd and Sadler were under twenty-three. The problem was rather that the sense of purpose that had sustained the club for a decade had gone and McGuinness was unable to rekindle his players' hunger.

After a 4–4 draw at Derby County that took their run without a win to six games, McGuinness was relieved of the job on 28 December and reappointed reserve-team manager. He was, Busby said, 'too close' to the players and, as a result, 'they resisted Wilf and it did harm to the club'. McGuinness responded to his dismissal by banging his head against the wall and tucking into the boardroom sherry. 'I felt as though I had been punched in the stomach,' he said. 'This was grievous news and I just hadn't seen it coming.'

When McGuinness and Busby met the players to inform them of the change of roles, Brian Kidd turned on his teammates, shouting, 'It's you lousy bastards that have got Wilf the sack.' McGuinness always wondered whether he was talking purely of their performances or whether there'd been lobbying of Busby.

McGuinness stuck out the reserve-team job for two weeks then left for Greece, where, at the age of thirty-three, his hair fell out – apparently the delayed reaction to the stress he'd been under.

Best had been a major part of the problem. He was drinking more and more and, as he later acknowledged, caring less and less for football. McGuinness was never able to get him back – and nor, initially, it seemed, was Busby. His first game back in charge was away at Chelsea; Best didn't turn up. It later emerged that he'd had a heavy night and overslept, missing his train. Rather than taking another train, Best decided to skip the game but to fulfil the appointment he'd made for later that evening, visiting the actress Sinéad Cusack at her flat in Islington, north London. Once the press found out, the flat was besieged and it would be four days before Best was finally smuggled away to be suspended and fined by Busby.

But the old authority hadn't deserted Busby and Best returned to score fourteen goals in the second half of the season. Law recovered from injury to score fifteen and United climbed away from the relegation zone to finish eighth. Busby, though, had no wish to return to the job full-time. He sent Crerand to

Glasgow to try to persuade Jock Stein to succeed him and the Celtic manager agreed to meet Busby at a motorway services. He supposedly said he would take the job if United got rid of Law and Charlton; Busby was reluctant to do so, at which Stein decided that his wife didn't fancy the move. Busby suspected that Stein had never been especially interested but was using United to help negotiate a better deal at Celtic. Stein, anyway, was apparently unimpressed by Busby's football acumen. Asked if the two ever discussed football, he's supposed to have replied, 'Och, no, I wouldnae embarrass the man.'

Eventually, in July 1971, Busby stood aside again. United approached the Chelsea manager Dave Sexton and when he turned them down they gave the job to Frank O'Farrell, who had been a wing-half for West Ham and Preston before managing Leicester City to promotion. At West Ham he had been part of the so-called Academy, the group of thinkers which included Sexton, Malcolm Allison, John Bond, Noel Cantwell, Ernie Gregory and Ken Brown that had become hugely influential in the development of the English game, but just as important to Busby was the fact that he was a rigorous Catholic with a reputation as an honourable man.

The board had authorised Busby to offer O'Farrell a salary of £15,000 a year. He initially proposed £12,000 only for Edwards to announce the higher figure when he met O'Farrell on a B road between Manchester and Derby, forcing Busby to admit he'd 'made a mistake'. 'Our whole relationship was damaged from that moment onwards,' O'Farrell admitted in his autobiography. 'I felt something wasn't right and Matt knew that I knew he had tried to cheat me.'

O'Farrell anyway had seen what had happened with McGuinness and was determined not to exist in Busby's shadow. He insisted on taking the manager's office, moving Busby out, upped Best's wages and got Johnny Aston, by then the chief scout, a club car.

There was a sense, too, of the squad evolving as Stiles left for Middlesbrough and Crerand retired to become a youth coach, while Alan Gowling and Sammy McIlroy emerged as first-team regulars. But there was a culture to be changed as well. 'They weren't an easy side to bring up to speed with the modern game and tactics,' O'Farrell said. 'They felt they were free spirits, and none of them became successful managers.'

Circumstances could have been easier. United were banned from playing home matches within twenty-five miles of Old Trafford at the start of 1971–72 after a knife was thrown from the crowd during a game against Newcastle the previous season. O'Farrell, though, began well, largely thanks to a run of inspired form from George Best – as it turned out, the last of his career. United won fourteen and lost two of their first twenty games of the season. Even with three draws in a row over Christmas, they were top heading into the new year, prompting Busby to describe O'Farrell as the best signing he had ever made. But United lost 3–0 at West Ham on New Year's Day, the first in a run of seven straight defeats. Looking to arrest the slide, O'Farrell signed the central defender Martin Buchan from Aberdeen for £170,000 and the forward Ian Storey-Moore from Nottingham Forest for £200,000 (despite the best efforts of Brian Clough's Derby County). 'The Manchester United I joined,' said Buchan, 'was a curious mixture of legends and guys who wouldn't have got a game in Aberdeen reserves.' United ended up finishing eighth.

Best, again, was a major part of the issue. He'd failed to turn up to training in the first week of 1972 and O'Farrell seemed to have no idea how to handle him. An experiment of billeting him with the Crerands lasted three days. 'When George Best first went off the rails,' said Bill Foulkes, 'Sir Matt was sympathetic and lenient. George, who says he hates publicity but attracts it like a lightning conductor, wouldn't have got away with it the second time. But by then Mr O'Farrell was in the chair and being an important player whom he needed, that was that. All this has helped undermine morale.'

Well, perhaps. But Best's slide had begun under Busby and by that stage the player had begun to doubt the former manager, accusing him of being over-loyal to Charlton. By September 1972, when a testimonial was staged for Charlton, the frostiness between them was so marked that Best refused to play in the game. He watched for five minutes at Old Trafford, then went to his familiar haunt of the Black Bull where he threw beer and two dozen eggs at the photograph of Charlton that hung on the wall. Besides, as Foulkes noted, the squad was nothing like as strong as it had been even five years earlier; whoever the manager was would have naturally been tempted to try to accommodate Best. O'Farrell was, as Charlton noted, 'left a difficult legacy'.

O'Farrell brought in two forwards in the summer of 1972, Ted MacDougall from Bournemouth for £17,000 and Wyn Davies from City for £65,000. Neither really settled and both were offloaded the following summer. The acquisition of Buchan had been a clear success, although standards had slipped to such an extent that his professionalism was seen by some as an attempt to suck up to the management, with Morgan regarding him as O'Farrell's spy. 'I hear whispers here and there and things seem to have gone sour in the dressing room,' Busby admitted. 'As for the buying, I must say I'm concerned.'

He wasn't the only one, but it perhaps wasn't the most judicious thing for somebody in Busby's position to let on such doubts. O'Farrell, not surprisingly, felt undermined, not least because he suspected Busby, who played golf with Morgan and Stepney, was obstructing changes he wanted to make to the squad. He wanted to move Charlton and Law on, was never convinced by Stepney, wanting to replace him with Peter Shilton, and thought Morgan was guilty of shirking challenges at the back post. The difficulties in the relationship were made clear in *Soccer at the Top*. O'Farrell, he wrote, 'was brought to the club to manage players. It seemed as if he wanted to manage the board too.'

Matters came to a head after a 4–1 defeat to Tottenham in October at the club's annual dinner dance when Busby, having had a few drinks, spoke to O'Farrell's wife Anne, saying her husband was 'an independent sod' and asking her to try to calm him down. O'Farrell and Busby met most Mondays and the next time they saw each other, the manager asked his predecessor what he had meant. Busby said he thought Charlton shouldn't have been dropped and that Buchan was playing poorly. This, for O'Farrell, was blatant interference in team affairs.

Busby denied both direct interference and the conclusion many drew that his presence was intimidating. At the same time, though, he issued a direct riposte to his critics, those who felt he should have stepped fully aside. 'How could I leave the place?' he wrote. 'How could I walk out of a club I built on the ashes of war and rebuilt after the mass tragedy of Munich, a club I love dearly, a club I have nearly killed myself for?' How indeed? And nobody at United had the ruthlessness to force him to leave. The contrast with Liverpool and their almost brutal handling of Bill Shankly's retirement in 1974 is striking. They may have looked heartless, they may have left Shankly feeling unappreciated, but by banning him from the training ground they allowed Bob Paisley, his successor, to get on with the job.

The awkwardness of Busby's relationship with O'Farrell was far from the only issue. Storey-Moore had suffered a knee injury that had effectively ended his career. Best, already on the transfer list, had told the club he would never play for them again, a conclusion the board had already reached. And it was becoming increasingly apparent that, for all Buchan's quality, Foulkes had never been replaced at the heart of the defence. But the biggest problem was the squad had lost any sense of belief during the slump in the second half of 1971–72.

The following season began appallingly: three defeats, followed by four draws, followed by a further two defeats that left United bottom of the table. In the November, Best was charged with slapping a woman in a club (he was subsequently convicted by a magistrate). O'Farrell fined him £200 and suspended him. Best went on a bender to London. In the four weeks that followed, Best failed to show at a meeting with directors to discuss his conduct, had his white Rolls-Royce vandalised, saw his name taken off the boutiques he had once owned by the company that had taken control of them and lost his boot deal with Stylo to Kevin Keegan.

O'Farrell would actually probably have been sacked in the November had it not been for a trenchant piece written by David Meek for the *Manchester Evening News.* Acknowledging that players and manager had to take responsibility, he also pointed out the culpability of the board in bungling the Busby–McGuinness handover, creating the mess O'Farrell had inherited. Two days earlier, the board had taken the decision to dismiss the manager. Meek didn't know that but Busby assumed he did and banned Meek from travelling on the team bus, while giving O'Farrell an extra couple of weeks.

November brought a flurry of three wins in four games, but when United lost to Stoke on 9 December, they were back in the relegation zone. The following week, United went to bottom-of-the-table Crystal Palace, who had won just one of their previous thirteen games. This, it seemed, was a chance to get the season back on track. The Scotland manager Tommy Docherty was in the stands at Selhurst Park, he said to watch the full-back Tony Taylor. With Morgan, Buchan, Law and Mac-Dougall all playing and eligible for Scotland, only the most suspicious – or those who saw Busby approach him at the final whistle – suspected an ulterior motive.

The 5–0 defeat was perhaps the most humbling single event in United's post-war history. 'Final humiliation of Manchester United', screamed the headline in the *Sunday Telegraph.* 'United have never been so bad,' the subhead went on. 'Only the old hags with their wicked grins and clicking needles were missing . . . as Manchester United, sullen, silent and without hope, went to the guillotine.'

The mood everywhere was not exactly one of surprise, but

disbelief that things had been allowed to get so bad. 'The best of teams have lost five goals and survived and prospered,' wrote Bob Ferrier in the *Observer*. 'United have done it in the past. But there are wider issues here. Everyone cares about Manchester United. Their achievements over the past twenty-five years have made it so. But their astonishing benevolence to George Best, which reached a preposterous climax last week, is at last being reflected in the work of the rest of the staff and the very core of the club now seems to be at risk.'

O'Farrell made clear that he had not approved of Best's recall by refusing to attend the press conference the following Monday at which Louis Edwards read out a statement outlining the rationale behind Best's return. 'This morning I mentioned to Mr O'Farrell that I was going to meet the Press and make a statement and I invited him to come along,' Edwards said. 'He said that he had a lot of things to do and would rather not come.'

The splits behind the scenes were clear. 'Their main problem, I believe,' wrote Bob Russell in the *Mirror*, 'is simply that Best and O'Farrell have become incompatible as player and manager.'

The following day, both were sacked, as were O'Farrell's assistant Malcolm Musgrave and the coach John Aston. The manager knew what was coming. Tuesday, 19 December 1972 was unseasonably warm. 'Pleasant day,' said a journalist as O'Farrell arrived at Old Trafford. 'Aye,' he replied. 'Nice day for an execution.' Or perhaps he said it to Johnny Aston; accounts vary.

'We've finally had enough of George,' said Busby, who was pictured walking on a carpet of ripped-up photographs of Best that had been thrown by angry fans. 'We've finally had to decide to get him out of our hair once and for all. All of us on the board were at the end of our tether. We'd had enough of George and his nightclubs and his way of life.'

Best announced he was quitting football altogether. 'I came back hoping my appetite for the game would return,' he said, 'and even though in every game I like to think I gave 100 per cent, there was something missing.' But why had the board ever brought Best back? 'The idea,' said Busby, 'was only that if we got him training again someone might buy him.'

O'Farrell was, to a large extent, merely a victim of circumstance, although the sense of many players was that he had never had the personality for the job. 'Mr O'Farrell,' said Law, 'came to the club as a stranger and went as a stranger.' Best, not unreasonably, became the scapegoat, but there were others who more consciously attacked the manager. Crerand thought that it was a visit by Bobby Charlton to Louis Edwards that fatally undermined O'Farrell, although it's not clear whether any such meeting took place. What certainly did happen was that Busby invited Charlton to visit him at home on Kings Road in Chorlton, the first time Charlton had ever been there. By that stage Charlton had lost patience with Best's lack of professionalism.

For all the talk of United doing things the right way, O'Farrell was afforded little dignity. Pettily, the club demanded he hand over the keys to his company car there and then; Musgrave had to give him a lift home. He was initially offered a severance package of £20,000 but, eleven months later, they eventually settled on £45,000. In the interim, he was forced to sign on to make ends meet. That was part of a pattern: when Stiles had left the club in 1971, he hadn't been given a testimonial despite his thirteen years of loyal and successful service.

On 22 December, Docherty, fast-talking and controversial, was appointed to replace O'Farrell on £15,000 a year. At Busby's insistence, Crerand was installed as his assistant, a relationship that never worked out. Docherty also brought back Murphy and Crompton, explaining that they didn't have specific roles but were there essentially to bring their experience and a sense of continuity with the past.

Docherty had won the League Cup with Chelsea, but after that he'd had less than impressive stints with Queens Park Rangers and Aston Villa (as well as Rotherham United and

Porto). He spent £420,000 on signing a raft of Scots – Alex Forsyth, Stuart Houston, Jim Holton, George Graham, Lou Macari and Jim McCalliog – and placed faith in young players such as Brian Greenhoff, Gerry Daly and McIlroy. Dunne, Sadler and Kidd soon followed MacDougall and Davies out of the club, while Storey-Moore's injury-ravaged career came to an end after he turned his ankle in the gym.

But the most important thing Docherty brought was his personality. Discipline may have been lax and training basic but he was, Morgan said, 'a breath of fresh air ... very outgoing, very positive'. A run of eight games unbeaten staved off the threat of relegation, but come that summer there was no doubt that the team that had won the European Cup had gone, barely a trace of it remaining.

Charlton was still physically fit but was mentally tired and wearied by the attitude of some of the younger players. Even when things had been going well, he had seemed a man apart – a 'bit of a moaner', as O'Farrell put it, something Charlton's wife, Norma, acknowledged in a frank interview in the *Daily Mail* on the eve of the 1968 European Cup final. 'People think Bobby's standoffish,' she said, 'but he's not really. He's not a born leader but he's easy with the people he likes. I don't think he's all that popular with the rest of the team. He's too outspoken.' She perhaps occupied a similar position among the wives. 'Some of them,' she said, 'get a bit of reflected glory and it goes to their heads.'

Once the threat of relegation had been seen off, Charlton approached Docherty and told him he'd had enough. Docherty had recalled Law to the Scotland side the previous season but the striker was struggling with injury. Docherty spoke to Law of a contract extension, a testimonial and a place on the coaching staff, but recommended to the board that he be offloaded; Law discovered he'd been given a free transfer to Manchester City when it was announced on television. With that, the Holy Trinity was gone: Best had quit to spend more time with his demons, Charlton retired and Law shunted across town for a sad, valedictory season at City that would come back to haunt Docherty and United. Docherty, lamenting that the great side of the late sixties had been 'allowed to grow old together', offloaded thirteen players in the summer of 1973.

But there was one return. Best hadn't quite gone; there was heat in the embers, yet one more final chance to be squandered. In that summer of 1973, he was hospitalised with a thrombosis. Busby visited him, and Best, making familiar promises about renewed discipline, vowed to return. He did so, playing twelve games and scoring two goals, but he looked bloated and was clearly off the pace. When United lost 3–0 to QPR on New Year's Day, he was fairly evidently suffering a hangover. He missed training the following day, claiming he'd had a twenty-four-hour bug and had been too ill to ring the club. Docherty was suspicious but picked him for the FA Cup third-round tie against Plymouth. Best turned up smelling of booze. Docherty suspended him for two weeks but the day before that sanction was set to expire, Best retired from football.

United were struggling. Holton and Buchan were a fine central defensive pairing, but the team couldn't score goals. That defeat to QPR left them third bottom, having conceded thirty but scoring just twenty in twenty-three games. At Christmas, the goalkeeper Alex Stepney, who'd started taking penalties, had been their joint top goalscorer with two.

In the spring, Busby took Docherty aside and told him that if United were to go down, they should at least do it while staying true to their principles. Docherty unleashed a 4-2-4 with McIlroy partnering Macari up front, Morgan and Gerry Daly on the wings and Jim McCalliog replacing George Graham in the centre. A flurry of four wins and two draws in six games through April raised hopes, but it was too late.

United faced City in the penultimate game of the season, needing to win to have a chance of staying up. They had the better of the game but couldn't score and, with nine minutes remaining, Law backheeled the winner. He turned, an arm clutched uncertainly across his chest, and walked disconsolately back to the centre-circle. There was a mass pitch invasion trying to force an abandonment but as Birmingham and Southampton had won, United's result was irrelevant. The referee ended the game and United were relegated for the first time since 1937. 'That night as I sat at home I had no enthusiasm for anything,' Docherty wrote in his autobiography. 'I felt like an empty shell.'

O'Farrell rang to commiserate, a conversation that became one of the classic Docherty after-dinner anecdotes. O'Farrell told him he had decided to leave Cardiff City. 'I've taken a job,' he said, 'where I can get on with things in peace, where there'll be no turmoil or animosity flying around.' Docherty asked him where. 'Iran,' O'Farrell replied.

More importantly, Busby told Docherty that his job was safe and delivered a crate of champagne. Relegation, it turned out, had a galvanising effect both on the club and the fans. The first game of 1974–75 was away at Leyton Orient. Around 10,000 United fans made the journey to east London, many of whom couldn't get in, leading to a riot during which the gates were smashed down. A linesman was hit by a missile thrown from the crowd and had to be replaced. Violence was to become a familiar theme as thousands of fans realised that local police forces simply couldn't cope with their numbers. Unsavoury as it was, for those involved the sense of freedom was undeniably thrilling. As the music producer Tony Wilson pointed out, United's popularity in the second half of the twentieth century was based on three things: Munich, the Holy Trinity of Best, Law and Charlton, and the hooligan fringe of the seventies. There were serious fights at Portsmouth, Sunderland, Millwall and Cardiff. A pitch invasion at Hillsborough led to 105 arrests. A fire was lit in a stand at Norwich. At home United's gate averaged 48,388, the highest figure for any club at that level for a quarter of a century.

On the pitch, United thrived. After an attempt to sign Peter Osgood from Chelsea was rebuffed, United bought Stuart

Pearson from Hull, allowing Macari to drop back into midfield to replace McCalliog. Jimmy Nichol emerged from the youth set-up to take over at right-back. The winger Steve Coppell, still finishing his economics degree, arrived from Tranmere Rovers on Bill Shankly's recommendation after Liverpool had decided not to pursue him. There was a run to the semi-final of the League Cup that included a famous victory over Manchester City, Daly scoring the only goal from the penalty spot in front of 56,000 at Old Trafford.

The emphasis was on youth and adventure. 'This defensive football,' Docherty said, 'is a bore. Spectators want to watch goals. That is what we try to supply.' Macari's goal in a 1–0 win at Southampton sealed promotion at the first attempt as United topped the table by three points from Aston Villa.

Docherty capitalised on the success to strengthen his position, selling Willie Morgan back to Burnley and forcing Crerand out of the club. He had been warned before taking the job about the back-biting that characterised life behind the scenes at Old Trafford. Sure enough, Docherty found the board 'riddled with political subterfuge'. Part of the problem, he felt, was Busby, Crerand and their drinking partners, many of whom had vice-president season tickets, entitling them to tea and sandwiches before the game and at half-time – an early version of modern executive boxes. Busby's influence remained problematic; Docherty was aided by the passage of time and the obvious need to rejuvenate the squad but, unlike his predecessors, he had the strength of personality to assert himself – up to a point.

United won five of their first six games of the 1975–76 season and went on to finish third in the First Division. They reached the Cup final as two goals from Gordon Hill, a winger signed from Millwall in the November, gave them victory over Dave Mackay's Derby County in the semi-final. Docherty slightly foolishly declared that to be the real final as Second Division Southampton beat Third Division Crystal Palace in the other semi. He wasn't the only one to get carried away: in *Match of*

My Life, Buchan was scathing about the attitude of some of his team-mates, saying they were distracted by the players' pool before the final and that 'some of them thought we just had to turn up' to win the Cup. Docherty admitted that 'we began to believe our own publicity in the build-up to the final'.

At Wembley, McCalliog made a personal point, laying on the only goal of the game for Bobby Stokes as Southampton became the second Second Division side in four years to lift the Cup. If his remarks after the semi-final had shown the worst of Docherty, his remarks after the final showed the best of him, as he picked up despondent players and fans by telling them United would simply go back and win the Cup the following year. Beneath the surface, though, he was suffering. 'At the time,' he wrote in his autobiography, 'I remember thinking, "This must be worse than dying. At least when you die you don't have to get up in the morning and read about it in the newspapers."'

On the day of the final, Mark E. Smith, a shipping clerk and college dropout, took significant quantities of dexadrine and went to a cinema in Hulme where he watched a film about Jimi Hendrix. In the following two months, he saw the Sex Pistols and the Buzzcocks at the Lesser Free Trade Hall. The three events provoked him into setting up The Fall. 'Manchester,' Paul Morley wrote in the *NME*, 'was a very boring place to be. It had no common spirit or motive. It was probably a reflection of the country at large.' But those two gigs in the summer of 1976 were hugely influential, seeding Manchester's rise as a centre of British music just as Liverpool had been a decade earlier. Hindsight offers the tantalising thought of just how close United came to being swept along on larger cultural tides, as Bill Shankly's Liverpool had been in the early- to mid-sixties. But it was not to be: the football club fell short, its rise deferred, for reasons that had little to do with football.

The more Docherty thought about the defeat, the more he wondered whether it were not too easy to blame the mood and United's application. 'To be honest,' he said, 'I thought Alex was too slow off his line and should have cut down Stokes' angle of vision.' Was Stepney, by then thirty-four, past it? With Stoke City forced to sell off players to raise funds after storm damage to a stand, Docherty signed Jimmy Greenhoff and tried to buy Peter Shilton. A £275,000 fee was agreed, but the United board baulked at his wage demands and Stepney remained the number one for a further two seasons.

As far as the league went in 1976–77, an injury to Buchan proved costly, United losing five and drawing three of eight games with him out of the side in the autumn. A rally of eight wins in nine matches in spring ensured United finished as high as sixth, Buchan suggesting it was their inability to grind out 'a 1–0 at Coventry on a wet Wednesday' that cost them by comparison with Liverpool. That would become a familiar lament over the decade that followed.

Again, though, it was the Cup that claimed the attention. There was some measure of revenge over Southampton with a 2–1 win in a sixth-round replay. A 2–1 victory over Leeds in the semi-final set up a final against Bob Paisley's Liverpool, who had won the league and would go on to lift the European Cup. On a gorgeous sunny afternoon, the perfect weather of Cup final stereotype, it was a game decided in five second-half minutes. Fifty-one minutes had gone when Jimmy Greenhoff helped a bouncing ball on for Stuart Pearson to muscle his way past Joey Jones and fire an angled shot past Ray Clemence. Within two minutes, though, Liverpool were level, Jimmy Case taking down Jones's long pass, turning on the edge of the box and lashing in a shot that Stepney perhaps should have saved. But three minutes later United were back ahead, this time decisively. Macari beat Emlyn Hughes in the air to flick a long ball on for Greenhoff and as he battled with Tommy Smith, the ball popped loose for Lou Macari, whose shot deflected off Greenhoff and looped over Clemence.

Docherty danced around Wembley with the lid of the Cup on his head. By dawn, after a night of celebration, he was wandering across Hyde Park with Coppell and Brian Greenhoff clutching a bottle of champagne. Nobody could have blamed him for thinking this was just the beginning, that his young side was getting stronger and stronger and that a serious tilt at the league title was a realistic prospect. A month earlier he had turned down a £28,000-a-year offer to manage Derby County – £10,000 more than he was on – and in the glow of Wembley, that must have seemed an excellent decision. But Docherty never took charge of another United game.

The night before the final, Docherty had invited the BBC cameras into the team hotel. Hill was shown getting a massage from the club physio, Lawrie Brown. As he lay reading a tabloid, he expressed mock surprise at the exploits of his manager. 'Blimey, Lol,' he said, 'the gaffer gets absolutely everywhere, don't 'e?' His words would soon take on a significance far greater than was surely intended.

A month later, Docherty called a press conference at a house in Mottram to announce that he had left his wife to set up home with Mary, Brown's wife. He had spoken to Louis Edwards after the Cup final and been told that the club would support him. Ten days after the announcement, a board meeting voted to sack him. Edwards and his son Martin may not have minded what Docherty got up to in his private life, but other directors did. 'I have been sacked,' Docherty said, 'for falling in love.'

When he'd found out about the affair, Brown had punched Docherty. The physio ended up being retained, and given a pay rise.

Busby's role remains unclear, but a letter O'Farrell sent Docherty on 12 May 1977 before the Cup final is intriguing. 'Dear Tommy,' the letter reads, 'You will have found out by now, as I did to my cost, that the "Knight" is not covered in shining armour as he makes out to many who do not know him so well. He must be suffering torment at not being able to get rid of you as is rumoured he has been trying to do. Long may you continue to torment him. All the best. Remember us all to Agnes and the children. Yours, Frank.'

Why on earth would Busby have been trying to get rid of Docherty nine days before the Cup final, that is, several weeks before his relationship with Mary Brown became public knowledge? Docherty in his autobiography links the letter to the failed attempt to sign Shilton, the implication being that Busby had acted to protect Stepney, one of his golfing partners. Docherty, of course, had also offloaded Willie Morgan and pushed out Pat Crerand, two other Busby allies. If Busby really were acting to protect his clique, then of course it makes his post-managerial influence over United far more malign than merely being an intimidating presence in the stand.

The sack was never going to be the end of it. Always willing to embrace controversy, Docherty claimed Busby had a mistress in London but had got away with it because he'd kept it secret. Morgan, angered at being sold on and perhaps still loyal to Busby, said on Granada TV's *Kick-Off* programme that Docherty was 'the worst manager there has ever been'. Docherty sued, only for Crerand and Stepney to testify on Morgan's behalf. Further allegations surfaced that Docherty had helped tout Cup final tickets – something Docherty admitted, insisting he had merely sold directors' unwanted spares to players involved in the game who needed extra tickets for friends and family. Early in the trial Docherty gave evidence about the transfer of Law to City that he later admitted was inaccurate. The case collapsed and Docherty was accused of perjury, although those charges were subsequently dropped.

It was all unsavoury and unnecessary and, worst of all from the point of view of fans, it stifled in its infancy what may have been a great era of success for United. They had come back from the humiliation at Selhurst Park, had found a manager who had led them through relegation back to prosperity and then, entirely avoidably, they had thrown it all away.

CHAPTER 6

*European Cup-Winners' Cup, quarter-final second leg, Old Trafford,
Manchester, 21 March 1984*

Manchester United   **3–0**   **Barcelona**
Robson 23, 51
Stapleton 53

Gary Bailey	Urruti
Mike Duxbury	Gerardo
Kevin Moran	Josep Moratella
Graeme Hogg	Julio Alberto
Arthur Albiston	José Alexanko
Remi Moses	Víctor Muñoz
Ray Wilkins	Periko Alonso
	(Paco Clos 58)
Bryan Robson	Bernd Schuster
Arnold Mühren	Juan Carlos Rojo
Norman Whiteside	Diego Maradona
(Mark Hughes 72)	
Frank Stapleton	Marcos Alonso
Ron Atkinson	César Luis Menotti

Ref: Paolo Casarin
Bkd: Schuster, Moratalla
Att: 58,350

TEN YEARS AFTER HE HAD replaced Tommy Docherty at Chelsea and six years after he had first been offered the job, Dave Sexton replaced him at United. It was a classic swing from one extreme to the other. After the reserved O'Farrell, United had turned to the extrovert Docherty and after him they went back to a cerebral, thoughtful figure who would read Ludwig Wittgenstein, John Stuart Mill and Robert Frost on away trips. Like O'Farrell, Sexton had been part of the Academy at West Ham, had won the FA Cup and the Cup-Winners' Cup with Chelsea and had just led QPR to second in the league. His credentials were excellent but after Docherty he couldn't help but seem a little drab.

Sexton bought a video camera and a screen and analysed training, which took on a rigour it had never previously had, even if Tommy Cavanagh, who had been assistant to Docherty, remained in charge to ensure a level of continuity. Sexton began to focus far more on the tactical side of the game, pushing the wingers deeper and practising pre-planned moves. Steve Coppell thrived under the new approach, Gordon Hill never really did, even if he finished Sexton's first season as top scorer.

United finished tenth in 1977–78, failing to recover from a run of four successive defeats in the autumn. The Cup-Winners' Cup campaign never really got going either. United were expelled from the competition after crowd trouble at Saint-Étienne in the first round – United fans bore the bulk of the culpability but the lack of segregation and the characteristically heavy-handed approach of the French police were at least in part to blame – but that sanction was commuted to a fine and a ban on playing the second leg within 125 miles of Old Trafford. After a 1–1 draw in France, United won the home leg 2–0 at Home Park, Plymouth, but were then hammered 4–0 away to Porto in the second round. A 5–2 win at Old Trafford wasn't enough.

The Scotland centre-forward Joe Jordan and his compatriot, the centre-back Gordon McQueen were signed from Leeds in the summer of 1978 but after the euphoria of the Cup win the season before, everything felt flat. Stepney, by then thirty-six, moved to Dallas Tornado and was replaced in goal by Gary Bailey, the son of the former Ipswich keeper Roy Bailey. He had grown up in South Africa before being picked up by United in 1978 following a trial.

The sense of the club entering a phase of dourness was enhanced when Hill was sold for £300,000 to Derby, by then managed by Docherty. The winger Mickey Thomas, who had helped Wrexham to promotion from the Third Division, was signed for £350,000, but he never seemed quite at home at Old Trafford, crashing his car on his way to his first training session – supposedly because he was so nervous.

By November there was sufficient frustration for United to be booed off after a home draw against Southampton. United went on to finish ninth in the league, but the Cup offered encouragement. Liverpool were beaten in the semi-final after a replay, setting up a final against Arsenal that, after a largely uneventful game, would produce one of Wembley's great climaxes. Goals from Brian Talbot and Frank Stapleton had put Arsenal 2–0 up by half-time but, with four minutes remaining, McQueen turned the ball in after Jordan had returned a Coppell free-kick to the centre of the box. Three minutes later, Sammy McIlroy ran on to a Coppell ball over the top, twisted past two men and stabbed a shot past Pat Jennings to level. Extra-time seemed inevitable, and United had the momentum but, within a minute, Alan Sunderland had arrived at the back post to turn in a left-wing cross from Liam Brady and restore Arsenal's lead. Bailey acknowledged the goal was at least partly his fault; he had misjudged the cross so badly that he came for it but didn't get close to getting a touch, although as McQueen noted, Thomas and Macari didn't help matters by lunging in on Brady when they could simply have tracked his run down the United left.

That summer, Sexton continued his restructuring of the squad, selling Brian Greenhoff, Stuart Pearson and David Mc-Creery and signing Ray Wilkins from Chelsea for £825,000. By November 1979, United were top of the league playing, as Sexton put it, 'football as it should be played'.

Just as everything had begun to go right on the pitch, though, a boardroom row that had been brewing for several months erupted. In 1978, United made a loss of £134,000. Turnover was falling and, at the same time, Edwards's meat business was struggling. He launched a rights issue to raise funds, a policy that was opposed by three board members. Significantly, one of them was Busby, angered at the refusal to honour the agreement reached in 1962 to elevate his son, Sandy, to the board. The split prompted the ITV current affairs programme *World in Action* to investigate. In January 1980, it alleged that Edwards's meat empire had been based on bribing local councils. Edwards died a month later – 'of shame', said his son Martin, who became chairman.

Martin Edwards, concerned by the club's worsening financial situation, drew up a budget that demanded numerous cuts, among them the nights the team traditionally spent at Mottram Hall Hotel before home games. Twenty years later it was an incident in the ladies' toilet at the hotel that led to Edwards quitting the board.

Despite the financial restrictions, in February 1980 United signed their first continental European player, the Yugoslav defender Nikola Jovanović from Crvena Zvezda. He made just twenty-one appearances before returning to Belgrade with a chronic back problem and his club car. He pronounced himself bewildered by what he saw as a culture of unprofessionalism at the club characterised by casual drinking. It wouldn't be until the end of the decade that the accusations really went away.

A run of eight wins in their final nine games meant United pulled level with Liverpool at the top of the table at the end of April, but while they had one game left, Liverpool had two and a far superior goal difference. As United lost their final match, against Leeds, Liverpool beat Aston Villa 4–1 effectively to secure the title. Sexton was rewarded with a three-year contract on double the money.

Fans, though, were unconvinced. Sexton may have spoken of playing football the way it should be played, but he and United fans had very different ideas as to what that entailed. Moreover there were worries that the local core of the club was being eroded. It took time for Wilkins, a Londoner, to win the crowd over, and in the summer of 1980, the Manchester-born twenty-year-old Andy Ritchie, who had already scored two hat-tricks for United, was sold to Brighton for £500,000 as Garry Birtles was signed for £1.2 million from Nottingham Forest. Perhaps that wouldn't have become such a source of resentment had Birtles been successful, but he failed to score at all in his first season at Old Trafford.

The contrast with Docherty, who was constantly on television and in the newspapers giving his opinions on his former club, was obvious. Sexton was, his predecessor said, the only man ever to survive a 'total personality bypass'. Whereas Docherty had entertained journalists in his office every Friday with a couple of bottles of wine, Sexton gave nothing away. He always seemed nervous in public and his habit of swallowing before speaking was soon mockingly imitated. To make it worse, while Sexton was boring journalists, across town at Maine Road, Malcolm Allison and then John Bond sparkled, loving the attention of a press conference.

And however calm and cerebral Sexton may have appeared, his approach didn't filter to the training pitch. Gary Bailey described a brutal culture in which only the hardest could survive, suggesting Andy Ritchie was in part let go because he didn't toughen up. Then again, Bailey, university-educated and having grown up abroad, was perhaps never going to fit in comfortably. He built a house by the Mersey on Northenden golf course with Kathy Plowright, the niece of Laurence Olivier. At their housewarming, to which all his team-mates were invited, he released twelve ducks to go on their lake. Although their wings had been clipped so they couldn't fly away, they waddled out of an open gate, made their way into the river and swam off down the Mersey. It was an incident often recounted, perhaps a little unfairly, to suggest that Bailey was a slightly ridiculous figure, somebody with ideas above his station who didn't fit in. Yet Bailey was a gifted goalkeeper, a regular in the England squad and Peter Schmeichel's idol. It says a lot about what was wrong with the culture of the club that he spent much of the early eighties racked by doubt, suffering from ulcers between 1981 and 1983.

The 1980–81 season featured a remarkable fifteen draws in the first twenty-four games. While it was easy to wonder what might have been had Birtles found a cutting edge, it effectively undermined any chance of a title challenge. After a run of five successive games without a goal in February and early March, Sexton was summoned to a board meeting. He urged the club's directors to wait until Wilkins had returned from injury to judge him – and that call for patience was at least partially vindicated as United won their last seven games of the season to finish eighth – but the decision had already been taken and Sexton was sacked in May.

Just as Sexton had been the polar opposite of Docherty, so his successor could hardly have been less like him. Ron Atkinson was big and brash and flamboyant, and had taken West Bromwich Albion to third in the league in 1978–79, a season in which they beat United 5–3 at Old Trafford, and fourth in 1980–81. Atkinson was probably only the fourth-choice candidate behind Lawrie McMenemy, Bobby Robson and Ron

Saunders, which gives some indication of the declining lustre of the club at the time. He found out he'd got the job during a tour with West Brom after a chance meeting with the striker Frank Worthington in a bar in Fort Lauderdale, Florida.

The story goes that when Atkinson arrived at Old Trafford, there was a discussion as to what car he would be given. Martin Edwards told him that Sexton had had a Rover. 'My dog's called Charlie,' Atkinson is supposed to have replied, 'but what about the car?' Edwards dismisses the story as 'a Ronism' but whatever the truth of it, Atkinson ended up with a champagne-coloured Mercedes coupé. Atkinson held his first press conference at the Millionaire's Club, a flash venue frequented by the wealthy and those who wished to appear so, wearing a bright-yellow suit and pouring champagne.

But there was more than bling to Atkinson, who was only too aware of the size of the task facing him. 'When people look back on the years between Busby and Ferguson,' Atkinson wrote in his most recent autobiography, *The Manager*, 'they talk about Manchester United's quest for the Holy Grail of the league title. By 1981, the league title wasn't an issue at Old Trafford – Manchester United just wanted to compete.' He signed Frank Stapleton from Arsenal for a fee a tribunal set at £900,000, ostensibly as a replacement for Joe Jordan. Although both were good in the air, Stapleton was far less of an orthodox battling target-man, capable of dropping deep and creating. He was startled by the difference in training he found at United compared to what he'd been used to at Arsenal. Atkinson, he said, appealed 'to the heart rather than the head'. That's the common view, but the long-serving full-back Arthur Albiston was keen to praise Atkinson's 'knowledge and memory'.

The right-back John Gidman, who was blind in one eye after being hit by a rocket at a Bonfire Night party several years earlier, arrived from Everton and then, two months into the season, Atkinson splashed out £1.5 million to bring Bryan Robson from West Brom. Busby was so appalled by the size of the fee and how contrary it was to his belief in youth development that he quit the board in protest. Robson, though, would go on to become the iconic United player of the era.

He was, Atkinson said, 'the finest, the greatest, the most rounded and accomplished footballer I have ever worked with.' The respect was mutual. 'His banter and enthusiasm were infectious,' said Robson. 'His man-management was excellent and the players respected him for the way he treated and trusted them.' Yet Robson, at the time the most expensive British footballer there had ever been, felt the pressure, the constant knowledge that United hadn't won the league since 1967. 'The weight of expectation was much heavier at United because of the club's illustrious past,' he said.

Almost as significant was Atkinson's decision to revamp the backroom staff as he sought to sweep away the culture of cliques and backstabbing. Central to that was the appointment of the ferocious Eric Harrison, whom Atkinson had known from their days doing National Service in the RAF. He was put in charge of the youth set-up and soon unearthed Mark Hughes, Norman Whiteside and Clayton Blackmore (although he also allowed the future England internationals Peter Beardsley and David Platt to leave).

There was an immediate improvement under Atkinson as United finished third in his first season in charge. Birtles, almost visibly more relaxed, scored eleven – and was then sold back to Forest. United had only actually scored eight more goals than they had the previous year, but the perception was that their football was more expansive. 'I sensed that most people accepted we had made reasonable progress,' said Robson, although he was frustrated with his own lack of consistency.

The Netherlands international Arnold Mühren, although thirty-one, arrived from Ipswich to offer creativity on the left, as Atkinson changed the emphasis of training away from tactics. Mühren's willingness to tuck in alongside Wilkins freed up Robson, who responded by scoring ten league goals, twice as many as he had in the previous campaign. With the sixteen-year-old Whiteside a regular presence, United finished third again, a distant twelve points behind the champions Liverpool, but they did reach both Cup finals. Whiteside opened the scoring in the League Cup final, but a Gary Bailey error let Liverpool back into the game before Ronnie Whelan claimed the winner with a superb curler in extra-time. It might have been different had the Liverpool goalkeeper Bruce Grobbelaar been sent off for clattering McQueen, who had been moved upfield because of cramp, but he wasn't, adding to a sense in Manchester that Liverpool in those days got the decisions.

The first hint that something might be brewing in the FA Cup came in the sixth round in which United were for a long time frustrated by Everton. Just as a replay at Goodison began to look inevitable, though, Atkinson took a typical gamble, withdrawing Duxbury for Macari. The substitute promptly chested the ball off for Stapleton, who volleyed in the winner.

United were trailing to a Tony Woodcock goal in the semifinal against Arsenal when Kevin Moran suffered a head injury. As he was stretchered off with blood pouring from a gash, he raised himself on one arm and punched the air with the other, a gesture of defiance that rallied fans and teammates alike. Goals from Robson and Whiteside turned the game. Having been stitched up, Moran joined the celebrations in the dressing room, only to require further stitches after being caught by a flailing arm as the players threw the assistant manager Mick Brown into the bath.

Brighton and Hove Albion, United's opponents in the final, had been relegated from the First Division that season, but they took a fourteenth-minute lead at Wembley as Gordon Smith planted a back-post header across goal and past Bailey. Stapleton forced in an equaliser as Whiteside helped on Duxbury's cross ten minutes into the second half and when Wilkins curled in a second after seventy-two minutes the game seemed won. But with three minutes remaining a corner was cut back to Tony Grealish and his half-hit effort fell in the box to Gary Stevens, who grabbed an equaliser. And then, in the final seconds, Michael Robinson laid in Smith ten yards out with just Bailey to beat. 'And Smith must score . . .' said Peter Jones on BBC radio, but Bailey charged from his line and the forward's shot lodged between his legs. It finished 2–2 after extra-time, necessitating a replay.

Roy Bailey had come over from South Africa for the final. Pointing out that in three matches at Wembley his son had conceded seven goals, he gave him a padlock around which a red-and-white ribbon had been tied. He told him to lock it at the start of each half and place it in his goal, then unlock it at the end. In three subsequent games at Wembley, Bailey didn't concede. The first of those was the Cup final replay, staged on Busby's seventy-fourth birthday: two goals from Robson, a Whiteside header and a Mühren penalty gave United a 4–0 win and Atkinson his first trophy. It was lifted by Robson, who had assumed both the United and England captaincies after Wilkins had suffered a depressed fracture of the cheekbone in a League Cup tie against Bournemouth.

That was United's first silverware since 1977, but it didn't presage a rush of success. Atkinson's teams produced some great performances, notably raising their game for matches against Liverpool, but they were never consistent enough really to challenge for the league. They were capable of dreadful performances in the Cups as well, as they proved in 1983–84 by going out of the League Cup to Oxford United and then being sent packing from the FA Cup by Bournemouth, both clubs in the Third Division.

Atkinson's plans suffered a major blow that October as Coppell, who had struggled with a knee injury since suffering a wild challenge in a World Cup qualifier against Hungary in 1981, was forced to retire. The twenty-one-year-old Wales international Alan Davies, who had played in the FA Cup final and was regarded as a major talent, might have been able to replace him, but he never fully recovered from a broken leg and was sold to Newcastle United in 1985. He went on to make over

100 appearances for Swansea City before, in February 1992, he committed suicide. The thirty-one-year-old Arthur Graham, who had been picked up from Leeds United that summer for £50,000, ended up taking a regular place on the flank.

But despite the issues on the right and despite the failures in the domestic Cups, 1983–84 represented the closest United came to genuine success under Atkinson as a sixteen-game unbeaten league run carried them to the top of the table in mid-March. They'd also edged past Dukla Prague on away goals thanks to a superb display by Bailey in the away leg and beaten Spartak Varna 4–1 on aggregate to reach the quarter-final of the Cup-Winners' Cup. There they faced a Barcelona side featuring Diego Maradona, although he had a back injury and was far from his best.

United played well in the first leg at the Camp Nou, Robson hitting the bar with a half-hearted volley when he'd mistakenly thought he was offside and missing another decent opportunity before Graeme Hogg scored an own goal against the run of play ten minutes before half-time. Juan Carlos Rojo smacked in a late second from twenty-five yards – the best goal ever scored past him, Bailey said – but most at United felt the 2–0 defeat was not an accurate reflection of the game. Deserved or not, the defeat left United with what the MEN described as 'an almost impossible task': 'United need a miracle,' said their headline.

In the league, United beat Leicester City to stay second, but then came dispiriting news: Juventus wanted Robson. Under the headline 'The Lira Era', the MEN spoke of a possible £3 million deal and quoted Atkinson apparently giving the offer serious thought. 'What has to be considered is the use that could be made of that kind of cash to strengthen the team and squad overall,' he said.

United's good form went on and they thrashed Arsenal 4–0 to go top of the table. Barça, meanwhile, seemed enveloped in doubt. The MEN proclaimed them 'worried men' in a headline, the strap reading, 'Below-strength Barcelona fear a

Cup cave-in.' The hard man Migueli was suspended, the right-back José Sánchez, their captain, was injured, and the winger Francisco Carrasco was suspended. Most significantly of all, Maradona had a cold. The miracle had begun to seem possible.

There was a clear sense of expectation about a packed Old Trafford. Bryan Robson had seen reasons for hope in the Camp Nou. United had been frustrated by Barça's offside trap but, Robson suggested, 'there were signs that if you put them under pressure they could crack'. He blamed himself for the chances he had missed. 'I knew,' he said after the game, 'I had to make up for my mistakes in the Camp Nou and thankfully I did.'

Fans picked up on his positivity. After the Arsenal win all things seemed possible. 'A crowd of more than 58,000 simply refused to countenance the possibility of defeat,' wrote David Lacey in the *Guardian*, 'and in the end their raucous, passionate support persuaded United of the truth of it. Manchester United turned Old Trafford into a bullring . . . [and] cast Bryan Robson as chief matador.'

Over shots of the Stretford End surging and swirling, Martin Tyler, commentating for ITV, described the atmosphere as 'extraordinary'. Frank Stapleton believes many more than the official 58,000 got in. Robson described it as the best atmosphere he experienced at Old Trafford. 'It was one of those nights you dream about and treasure for the rest of your life,' he said.

It was the biggest home game in fifteen years and even several hours before kick-off, as the players made their way to the ground from the Midland Hotel, where they'd had their pre-match meal, they saw thousands of fans streaming towards Old Trafford. 'I had never before heard such fervour and I haven't experienced it since,' Norman Whiteside wrote in his autobiography. 'It almost lifted me off my feet so I could play at the very limit of what my body was capable of doing.'

Before kick-off, Wilkins went round each player individually, giving them advice. He may not have been captain any more, but he remained influential tactically, with Robson preferring to gee players up emotionally.

For half the first half, Barcelona resisted. Whiteside found himself up against José Alexanko, who had tried to intimidate him physically when Northern Ireland had beaten Spain at the 1982 World Cup. 'Within five minutes of the start,' he said, 'I found myself racing into a 50–50 challenge with him by the touchline. I knew that if I bottled it he would see it as licence to take liberties for the rest of the game so I went in wholeheartedly . . . bundled him over the line and smacked him into a perimeter advertising board.'

As United won three throw-ins in a row down the right, there was audible irritation from the crowd; United didn't seem to be making inroads. Wilkins took the third of the throw-ins to Hogg, who returned it to him. He crossed from deep towards the edge of the box. The goalkeeper Urruti had looked skittish all night. 'The crowd was so intimidating and piled so much pressure on him,' Bailey said. 'He just couldn't cope.' Urruti came and leapt with Alexanko, the libero. The ball fell to Periko Alonso, the father of the Liverpool, Real Madrid and Bayern Munich midfielder Xabi Alonso. He could perhaps have hooked it clear, but he dithered and Whiteside, who wondered whether his early reducer might have made Alexanko a little hesitant, jabbed a foot at the ball, sending it goalwards, high into the air. At the top of its parabola it was maybe thirty feet off the ground but it dropped sharply and, as Urruti hurtled back, it bounced on the top of the bar.

It would, perhaps, have been a freakish goal – although Whiteside was clearly trying to direct the ball goalwards – but what it did was expose just how shaky Urruti was under aerial balls. Barcelona, though, kept possession well, frustrating United. But, with twenty-three minutes gone, Alexanko gave the ball away to Duxbury. He played it to Wilkins who touched it off for Robson. United's captain spread the play left to Albiston, whose attempted forward pass was blocked by the West Germany midfielder Bernd Schuster. The ball came back to Hogg and he returned it to Albiston on the left. Alexanko headed out his cross to Schuster, but he was dispossessed by Mühren who worked it out to Stapleton. Perhaps a little over-anxious to get forward, he trod on the ball, overran it and checked back before playing a clever disguised pass down the line into the path of Albiston, an ever-willing runner from full-back. Josep Moratalla conceded a corner.

On the television commentary, Tyler questioned Barça's ability to cope with United in the air. Wilkins swung it to the near post, Hogg got between Schuster and Alexanko to win the header and flicked it across the face of goal where Robson was one of two United players unmarked as he dived forwards and nodded over the line. United were back in the tie.

Barça were prompted into a response. Their left side looked the flank more likely to yield a goal for both sides as Julio Alberto swept forward from full-back. On another sally he de-livered the ball to the left-winger Juan Carlos Rojo, who tried to play it back to him, only for Remi Moses, in an unusual right-sided role, to block. The ball came back to Rojo on the top corner of the box. He slipped it inside for Julio Alberto and this time got the ball through. Julio Alberto took a touch with his right foot and shot with his left. Hogg got in the way and the ball ricocheted back to Rojo, who moved right across the top of the box trying to work space. From a central position fifteen yards out, he shot. Moran charged it down and the ball bounced out to Marcos on the right side of the box. As Albiston hurled himself in the way, the striker fired his effort over the bar. Bailey was furious, although at what was unclear, unless he perhaps felt Albiston should have been closer to Marcos to begin with.

Still it was United, tails up after the goal, who looked the more threatening, particularly when they were able to get crosses into the box. Wilkins spread the ball right to Duxbury, who sent it forward for Whiteside, making a run out to the right touchline. He was bundled over by Julio Alberto. Dux-bury took the free-kick short to Wilkins, who advanced slowly and slid a pass outside for the advancing full-back. He crossed. Schuster at the near post got his head to the ball, sending it high into the air. As it dropped towards the back post, Moran, soaring above a crowd of players, put his header over the bar. Urruti was notably lacking in authority.

Maradona had barely been involved for most of the first half but, five minutes before half-time, he took down a goal-kick from Urruti and found Julio Alberto on the Barça left. The full-back pushed the ball inside for a charging Rojo, who skipped by Duxbury and got to the byline. Moses slid in and blocked with his body. With a slightly anxious glance at the referee, Moses sprang up and played the ball long towards Whiteside. It was at an awkward height and the forward couldn't control it. Alonso headed it forward and Schuster at the corner of the box turned it on for Maradona. He went left of Moran and, with very little backlift, struck a shot goalwards from twenty yards. It was close enough to Bailey that he gathered comfortably, but it was a reminder that, even out of sorts, even with a cold and a bad back, Maradona was capable of game-changing moments of brilliance.

Duxbury hit a long ball forward and Stapleton, who clearly had the beating of Barça in the air, headed down for Wilkins moving into space on the right side of the box with Julio Alberto seemingly unaware of the danger. He struck the bouncing ball while slightly off balance and it skewed well wide but the half was ending with a United flourish.

Moran, receiving the ball from Bailey, rolled it to Duxbury who fed it inside to Robson. He laid it out to Wilkins, who had moved to the right touchline and, shaping to cross, he turned inside Rojo and fed the ball in to Whiteside. He was tackled and Julio Alberto played the ball forward towards Maradona. Moran, though, was alert and intercepted, giving it to Stapleton. The ball got caught under his feet but, as Rojo and Schuster closed in, he was able to work it out to Duxbury. He went inside to Robson, who turned away from Alonso and played the ball behind the retreating Maradona for Hogg.

The defender went square to his right to Moran, who passed it inside to Wilkins in the centre-circle. There was a smooth rhythm to United's passing. Their game-plan may have been based on crosses, understandably enough given Urruti's shortcomings, but there was far more to them than just that.

Wilkins swept the ball left for the sprinting Albiston, whose first attempt at a cross was blocked by Moratalla. The ball bounced back to him, though, and a second effort was deflected behind for a corner.

For United, every set-play was a chance. Wilkins took it. Gerardo headed clear at the near post, but it was gathered by Mühren on the left. He slid the ball down the line for Wilkins, whose cross was half-blocked. It looped to the edge of the box, where Whiteside struck a volley that hit a defender and rebounded to Moses in the D. He perhaps could have shot but instead turned smartly and slid a pass in to Moran, who was just offside. The message, though, was clear: United were matching Barça on the ball and were far more dangerous in the air.

The United surge continued into the second half. Stapleton and Whiteside kicked off and played it to Wilkins, who worked it right for Moses. He played it forward to Stapleton, who headed right for Robson. He beat Julio Alberto and crossed low to the near post, where Stapleton, seemingly caught between an effort on goal and trying to control it, ended up doing neither, the ball bouncing off him for a goal-kick. United, though, were very much in the ascendant.

Urruti took a goal-kick short to Gerardo, who was pressured by Stapleton. United simply looked hungrier than Barça. At the time in England the Catalan side had a ferocious reputation, largely because of their brutal approach to the Super Cup game against Aston Villa in 1982, but here they seemed timorous, cowed perhaps by the atmosphere and United's fervour, and perhaps also by the absence of Migueli.

Gerardo turned it back inside to Moratalla, who played it to Schuster, deep in the right-back position. He seemed to consider a backpass but, with Whiteside lurking, knocked the ball square for Victor, who, without a glance, sent it back towards Urruti. Whiteside slid in with the keeper and the ball squirted out to the right where Moses gathered. His cross was pulled back behind Whiteside at the near post and came to Wilkins in the centre of the box. He didn't quite strike it cleanly, but Urruti spilled the shot and Robson turned in the loose ball. Six minutes into the second half, United were level.

Straight from the kick-off, Marcos surged forward and fired wide from twenty yards, but the momentum was with United. Wilkins advanced, swinging his arms to encourage Duxbury forward. He gave it to Stapleton, who turned by Alonso and slipped it inside to Robson, who sprayed a pass out wide to the left, completely changing the angle of attack. His ball might have been meant for Mühren but it was Albiston, hurtling down the left once again, who took over. He crossed deep, where Whiteside outjumped two defenders to win the header, sending the ball back across goal for Stapleton. Unmarked, six yards out and with half a goal to aim at, he lashed the ball in with evident relish. 'The world,' Stapleton said, 'seemed to explode.' With thirty-seven minutes still to play, United had the lead in the tie.

Barça were badly shaken, evident in Schuster's booking for protesting after Marcos and Moses had run into each other. United, knowing an away goal would see Barça through, kept pressing. A Bailey clearance was aimed long towards Whiteside. Alexanko headed out. Stapleton nodded down for Robson and, at the top of the bounce, he hit a fierce shot that was charged down by Moratalla. The ball cannoned off Julio Alberto into the path of Moses, who burst into the box. Alexanko did well to force him wide but, from a narrow angle, he still got in a shot at goal. Urruti saved with an outstretched left foot. The corner was flicked on by Whiteside and Robson headed over.

Forced onto the offensive, Barcelona withdrew Alonso for the forward Paco Clos, but at least initially United's dominance continued. Wilkins took a throw to Duxbury who helped the ball on to Moran, who spread it left to Albiston. He headed it infield to Mühren, who nodded it back, and Albiston returned it to him. The Dutchman played it forward to Whiteside who had moved into an inside-left position, and he shaped a left-footed ball into the box. As Urruti recklessly left his line once again, Robson headed just over from fifteen yards.

But a Barça response was brewing. Victor played the ball out to Gerardo, who went inside to Alexanko and then forward to Maradona on halfway. He took the pass neatly and turned by Duxbury, then pushed it outside for Rojo who helped it on for the overlapping Julio Alberto. The full-back's low shot at the near post was shovelled wide by Bailey.

United, suddenly, began to look a little anxious. Mühren picked up a loose ball and went past two Barça players before being dispossessed by Gerardo. His pass was weak and Robson almost regained possession, but Moratalla came away with it. He fed Clos on the left, who turned it inside to Schuster. He drove forward and turned inside Moran then helped the ball on to Maradona. The Argentinian's first touch was heavy, but he was able to turn and tried to cross from the corner of the box. Hogg blocked, but Maradona reclaimed possession and, stabbing the ball with the outside of his boot, played the ball to Marcos. Under pressure and with his back to goal, he worked it to Schuster. His first touch took him away from goal, but he managed to clip a curling effort on the half-turn that, with Bailey scrambling, sped just wide of the far post.

Atkinson brought on Hughes for Whiteside, presumably looking for another figure to play alongside Stapleton who could hold the ball up if United were forced back and reduced to long clearances. There were eighteen minutes remaining. The switch almost paid off immediately, as a Clos pass was played behind Maradona, allowing Robson to come away with it. He played it forward quickly and Hughes, although only a few yards inside the Barça half, would have been away had Moratalla not hauled him back. A modern interpretation would probably have been a red card, but the Italian referee Paolo Casarin showed yellow.

With nothing to lose, Barcelona pushed on with ever greater abandon. Victor spread the ball right to Schuster, who hit a remarkable left-footed pass low across the pitch for Alexanko, up from sweeper. From twenty-five yards he hit a firm low shot that Bailey got down well to save.

But the attacks kept coming. Duxbury gave the ball away to Schuster, who played it down the right touchline to Maradona. Albiston got in a tackle but conceded a corner. Schuster took it short to Clos, who slipped a pass into the box for Gerardo, who collapsed as Hughes ran behind him. Casarin waved play-on and replays offer no definitive evidence either way, but it's at the very least possible that Hughes clipped him. Atkinson certainly thought he had.

Moratalla advanced through the centre-circle and played the ball out right to Marcos. He turned inside Albiston and the ball was moved on through Moratalla to Maradona. With Duxbury one side of him and Moran the other, he hurled himself to the ground with a flick of the heels – an obvious dive that didn't fool Casarin or impress the crowd which struck up a lusty chorus of 'Ma–radona is a wanker, is a wanker!'

The free-kick went to United. It was taken short to Duxbury and, as he played it inside, Moran was fouled. Moran lofted the free-kick forward and, for once, Alexanko won the header. The ball fell to Wilkins, whose pass out to the right drifted out of play. As Schuster received the ball from the throw, Wilkins tripped him and was booked.

Time ticked away. Old Trafford, exuberant half an hour earlier, had become anxious. Robson drove towards the right corner and was fouled by Julio Alberto. There were only seconds remaining but United threw men forward. Barça broke, Julio Alberto winning a corner off Mühren. As though accepting United had the advantage in the air, it was taken to the edge of the box to Schuster. Perhaps the idea was for him to volley it, but it came at an awkward height and his attempt to control was poor. As Moses won the ball and surged forwards, the final whistle went and United had completed a remarkable comeback.

César Luis Menotti, Jeff Powell reported in the *Mail*, was 'dismayed that his team had been too apprehensive to seize the attacking initiative until it was too late'. United were ecstatic, their fans carrying Robson shoulder high from the pitch at the end. In the *Mirror*, Bob Russell described the game as United's best in Manchester since the victory over Athletic twenty-seven years earlier. 'Seldom,' he went on, 'have I seen Robson play with such power and purpose.'

In his post-match interview, Robson hinted it was his intention to resist the lure of Juventus and stay. If any game was likely to persuade him to remain at Old Trafford, it was this one – although he subsequently suggested that, while he hadn't been desperate for a move, United's valuation had effectively priced him out of a transfer. Usually Stapleton slept soundly after games; that night the adrenalin was such he barely got a wink. 'People criticise the English game,' said Atkinson. 'But we won tonight because of our fighting spirit, our grit and determination and our aerial strength.'

By the time of his second autobiography, Atkinson seemed to have had second thoughts about the game. The crowd, he said, 'drowned out everything and coloured everyone's impressions of the night. If you watch Manchester United versus Barcelona with the sound turned down, it is quite an ordinary match. However, the noise and the emotion of the night made it something special. I don't think we actually played that well except for the fact that we knew Barcelona had a weakness at corners and it was something we exploited.'

That sells the game short. United might not have been especially fluent, but their energy and the willingness of Albiston in particular to get forward made them irresistible. Barcelona simply couldn't cope.

Whatever Atkinson's reservations, for him, that was as good as it got at United: a thrillingly memorable night that hinted at great things to come, the best of a number of outstanding occasions under Atkinson, but ultimately it led nowhere. It was a great peak when United needed a sustained plateau of excellence. Injuries, it's true, played their part in dragging United down but there are those who would suggest United's casualty list was itself a result of the culture at the club.

The weekend after the victory over Barcelona, United should have played away at Nottingham Forest, but heavy rain led to the game being postponed. That seemed to cost United their momentum, with some blaming Atkinson for taking the players for a break in Mallorca rather than training. They lost away at West Brom, then Robson injured himself on England duty and missed six league games.

By the time the Cup-Winners' Cup semi-final against Juventus came around, United were without Robson and Mühren through injury and Wilkins through suspension. Gidman then pulled a hamstring early in the home leg. He was replaced by Alan Davies and the Welsh winger's close-range finish made it 1–1 after Paolo Rossi had put Juve ahead with a deflected shot. Wilkins returned for the second leg but, although Whiteside cancelled out Zbigniew Boniek's opener and Bailey produced another outstanding display, Rossi pounced on a loose ball after Gaetano Scirea's shot had been blocked for a late winner.

United were out, and the league campaign also turned sour as they won only two of their final ten games of the season to finish fourth, six points behind the champions Liverpool. It would be a little misleading to suggest United were dependent on Robson, but it was probably true that Atkinson's preference for a small, tight-knit squad meant that they were disproportionately susceptible to injuries and disproportionately affected by them when they did occur. 'When you are out,' Alan Brazil, who signed that summer from Ipswich, said of Atkinson's way of structuring the squad, 'you are out.'

Atkinson took action to alleviate the issue of the size of the squad in the summer of 1984, selling Wilkins to Milan and bringing in Gordon Strachan and Jesper Olsen as well as Brazil, but the old problems persisted and were compounded by an unbalanced squad that was heavily focused on attack. United ended up fourth again, but they were never realistically in a title race despite being second for long spells. By the December, frustration had set in. A month after throwing away a 2–0 lead to lose at Sunderland, they did the same at Nottingham Forest. After the game, a furious Bailey blamed his defence, McQueen in particular, accusing him of lacking positional sense. McQueen responded by calling him a coward and as Bailey approached, red mist descending, McQueen punched him in the face before team-mates separated them. Bailey began kung-fu lessons the following day. McQueen subsequently apologised, but nonetheless felt that Bailey, who was still only twenty-six, wasn't of the quality United required, that he had been elevated to the first team before he was ready.

The Cup, though, again offered an opportunity. Liverpool were beaten after a replay in the semi-final and a Whiteside goal in extra-time settled the final against Everton, despite United having Kevin Moran sent off for a foul on Peter Reid after seventy-eight minutes – the first man ever dismissed in a Wembley Cup final. It was a mark of how radically Atkinson had changed the team that only six of those who played in the 1983 final also played in 1985.

United began the following season superbly, winning their first ten games. After fifteen games they had forty-one points. At one stage they had a ten-point lead. 'We believed,' said Robson, 'that we were at last on our way to claiming that title.' But once the first defeat came, against Sheffield Wednesday in the sixteenth game of the season, the collapse was rapid. United won only nine of their final twenty-seven league games of the season and slipped back to finish fourth, twelve points behind the champions, Liverpool.

Part of the reason was Mark Hughes's complete loss of form, the result of his imminent transfer to Barcelona. He'd scored twenty-five goals in 1984–85 and, with his contract expiring in the summer of 1986, he'd been offered a seven-year extension. His existing deal was worth £200 a week; the new deal was worth £300 a week, increasing each season by an additional £100 a week. Barcelona offered £2000 a week and Atkinson accepted their bid of £1.8 million, pointing out Barça had matched Hughes's buy-out clause and that his hands were tied. Because Barcelona already had three foreigners, though, Spanish regulations meant they couldn't sign Hughes straight away. A plan was hatched for him to stay at United until the end of the season, but an attempt at secrecy failed and Hughes struggled to cope with the pressure.

United also suffered a series of injuries. Gidman broke his leg, Strachan dislocated his shoulder and Moses twisted his ankle. Perhaps it was bad luck, but many linked United's constant injury problems to the background issue Jovanović had highlighted four years earlier: booze. Robson, McQueen, McGrath, Whiteside and Moran were the heaviest drinkers, the so-called A-squad. Robson, who as a teenager at West Brom had been told to drink a bottle of Mackeson's stout each night to build him up, was of the opinion that the drinking was beneficial, that regular sessions were a way of getting grudges out into the open and binding the side. He continued to insist that the drinking wasn't excessive, although in his autobiography he eventually conceded that what he meant by that was that he didn't feel his own game was adversely affected. 'My metabolism was such that I could drink loads with the lads in the early days,' he said. 'I also knew that if we had a decent training session the next day, I could run through it.'

Others, such as Frank Stapleton, felt the alcohol held them back. If the United he'd played for had had Alex Ferguson 'or someone of similar stature', Stapleton insisted, they would have won the league 'at least three times'. Atkinson, he said in *Match of My Life*, 'was a gung-ho manager, fine when everything was going well, but lacking when we were in a crunch situation. It could be said, too, that he didn't exercise enough discipline where drinking was concerned.' His words echoed those of Buchan a decade earlier. 'When we were flowing, the football was great,' he said, but he believed with greater prag-matism they might have 'ground out' more wins. Atkinson saw Stapleton as a born moaner. 'In the sad art of grumbling,' he said, 'he was world class.'

Even McQueen, who was the main organiser of social events, admitted things got out of hand. 'The drinking was a serious problem,' he told Andy Mitten, 'but we never realised that at the time because it was pretty much the norm.' His own behaviour, which placed him at the centre of an array of anecdotes, many of them scatological, was at times, he acknowledged, 'disgraceful'. Atkinson himself remains doubt-ful, dismissing the 'pasta preachers' and insisting 'bonding is an essential part of team-building'. He points out that in his four years at the club, United were never out of the top four, having finished that high only twice since winning the European Cup, and had won the FA Cup twice; between 1968 and Atkinson's arrival their only trophy had been the 1977 FA Cup.

After the defeat at QPR in mid-March, Atkinson offered his resignation, but he was persuaded to stay. That summer United were blighted by a series of poor transfer decisions. In came John Sivebæk, Colin Gibson, Peter Davenport and Peter Barnes, none of whom really settled. Those were misjudge-ments, but there was also misfortune. Seven United players went to the World Cup in Mexico; on their return, five required surgery.

The sense of drift that had characterised the end of 1985–86 continued into 1986–87 as United took just four points from their first eight games. There were those who blamed the drinking and those who blamed the lax training regimen – although that hadn't been such an issue in previous sea-sons – while Whiteside believed Atkinson's personal life had become a distraction. Most notoriously, the manager missed the ground staff's annual party claiming to be ill, only for it to emerge that he'd been in a restaurant in Bowden.

Amid the doubts there came a training-ground fight as Moses left Olsen needing stitches after the Dane had gone over the top on him in a five-a-side. United claimed Olsen's wound had been caused by an accidental clash of heads but when the truth came out it looked as though Atkinson had lost control, however much players of the time insist similar incidents were commonplace.

Bobby Charlton, by then a director, had seemingly never been convinced by Atkinson and it's widely believed it was he who had vetoed an attempt to sign Terry Butcher after the World Cup. According to Atkinson, Edwards told him the money wasn't available for a move for either Butcher or Kerry Dixon because it had been set aside for the redevelopment of the club museum. Atkinson described Charlton as 'a relentless boardroom adversary', and he had taken advantage of the World Cup to sound out a possible replacement. On 4 November, after a 4–1 League Cup defeat to Southampton and with United languishing at nineteenth in the league, Atkinson was sacked. Characteristically, his response was to throw a party in the manager's office.

In the early hours of the morning, Strachan called Atkinson in a panic. He'd taken a wrong turning after driving away from the ground and was lost. All he could see that might help work out where he was, he said, was a football ground, which he thought might be Maine Road. It turned out, appropriately enough given where Strachan ended up, to be Elland Road.

Two days later, United unveiled their new manager, the greatest in their history and arguably the greatest in the history of British football: Alex Ferguson.

CHAPTER 7

FA Cup semi-final, Maine Road, Manchester, 8 April 1990

Manchester United   **3–3**   **Oldham Athletic**

Robson 29   *Barrett 5*
Webb 72   *Marshall 75*
Wallace 92   *Palmer 113*

Jim Leighton   Jon Hallworth
Colin Gibson   Denis Irwin
Gary Pallister   Earl Barrett
Steve Bruce   Andy Holden
Lee Martin (Mark Robins 106)   Andy Barlow
Mike Phelan   Neil Redfearn
Paul Ince   Mike Milligan
Bryan Robson   Nick Henry
  (Danny Wallace 71)   (Paul Warhurst 84)
Brian McClair   Rick Holden
Neil Webb   Ian Marshall
Mark Hughes   Andy Ritchie
                                        (Roger Palmer 95)

Alex Ferguson   Joe Royle

Ref: Joe Worrall
Bkd:
Att: 44,026

PALM SUNDAY 1990 DAWNED BRIGHT, sunny and anxious. For well over a decade football had existed in a constant state of self-analysis, beset by violence and tragedy, but the issues seemed particularly acute that morning as, a year on from the disaster at Hillsborough, England prepared for the FA Cup semi-finals which for the first time were played back-to-back rather than simultaneously.

There was trepidation but, after four hours of gripping, unpredictable football – broken only by the *EastEnders* omnibus – it was being hailed as the day on which English football was reborn. Three months later, Paul Gascoigne's tears at the World Cup semi-final in Turin performed the symbolic baptism. More than that, although it wasn't recognised at the time, it was the day on which the balance of power in English football began to tip from Merseyside to Manchester. This was not the moment at which United knocked Liverpool from their perch, but it was perhaps the day on which Liverpool's grip began to weaken as United, by somehow keeping themselves in the Cup, edged towards the trophy that would mark the beginning of a period of success rivalled in the English game only by what Liverpool had achieved in the seventies and eighties.

The FA had previously insisted that the spirit of the Cup demanded teams should not go into a game knowing whom they would face in the final, but Hillsborough persuaded them at last to give in to the demands of television. 'Tragedy,' as David Lacey put it in the *Guardian*, 'has led to telethon. Hillsborough has made it desirable that fans without tickets should be discouraged from turning up on the day, so live TV coverage makes good sense in the circumstances.'

Odd as it may seem today, screening back-to-back games was perceived as a risk. Would viewers be able to cope with three hours of football – extra-time didn't bear thinking about – on the same day, particularly on a weekend that also featured the Grand National and the US Masters? They needn't have worried. As the usually staid *Rothman's Football Yearbook* put it, 'There have never been two more exciting FA Cup semi-finals in the same season.'

Not that anybody was expecting too much. United had been having their difficulties and although Oldham Athletic, their second-flight opponents, had already disposed of Arsenal, Everton, Aston Villa, Southampton and West Ham in Cup competitions that season, a run of three straight league defeats suggested fatigue was taking its toll. As for the other semi, while Liverpool had not exactly hit the heights, Crystal Palace were languishing in fifteenth in the First Division, and had, humiliatingly, lost 9–0 at Anfield earlier that season. When Palace followed that up with a 2–0 home defeat to Liverpool, their manager Steve Coppell noted drily that 'at least we're moving in the right direction'.

Liverpool seemed to be stumbling towards a repeat of the Double they had achieved in 1986, although they'd struggled for consistency all season and had come nowhere near the heights they'd achieved in 1987–88. But Palace exploited their vulnerability in the air at the back and won a breathless game 4–3 after extra-time.

The nation composed itself, calmed down during *EastEnders*, and prepared for the second semi, scarcely daring to hope it could match the drama of the first. It did, and, if anything, the quality was even better. Oldham's challenge on three fronts drew an exuberant analysis of their tactical flexibility from Peter Ball in *The Times*. Joe Royle, it was noted, had gone to the same school as Coppell: on his forty-first birthday, could he repeat his schoolmate's feat? United, mired in introspection and self-doubt, seemed there for the taking.

The appointment of Alex Ferguson on 6 November 1986 was probably the best managerial decision any club has ever made, although it took some time for that to become apparent. Ferguson had achieved remarkable things with Aberdeen, breaking the Old Firm hegemony to win three league titles, four Scottish Cups and a Scottish League Cup. Most remarkably of all, in 1983, on the night a young Tony Blair begged Labour Party officials in Sedgefield to extend the deadline for applications to be the parliamentary candidate at the general election, Aberdeen beat Real Madrid to win the Cup-Winners' Cup. If John Hewitt hadn't dived to head that extra-time winner, who knows whether those Party officials, who'd gathered to watch the game together, would have been prepared to bend their rules? Less auspiciously, Ferguson had led Scotland at the 1986 World Cup, taking over after the death of Jock Stein, but they were eliminated from a brutally tough group.

Ferguson was from Govan – in which he took such pride that his office bore a sign reading 'Ahcumfigovan'. His family had worked in the shipyards but Ferguson made machine tools, serving the latter part of his apprenticeship at Remington Rand, the US manufacturer of typewriters and electric shavers. He became involved in the Amalgamated Engineering Union, serving as acting shop steward for the apprentices during a strike. At the same time, he played football as a forward for Queen's Park, gaining a reputation for his determination and willingness to use his elbows.

In 1960, he joined St Johnstone but found it so difficult to practise with the Perth club while working in Glasgow that he trained with Third Lanark and then Airdrieonians, joining up with his team-mates only on match days. It was far from an ideal arrangement and there came a time when Ferguson was so disillusioned that, like Busby, he contemplated emigrating to Canada. Just before Christmas 1963, trying to skip a reserve game, he got his brother's girlfriend to telephone the club pretending to be his mother to claim he had flu. The manager Bobby Brown wasn't fooled and, after a couple of injuries, summoned him by telegram to turn out for the first team away at Rangers. Ferguson had a quiet first half but in the second hit the bar twice and scored three times as St Johnstone won 3–2, their first ever victory at Ibrox. Ferguson, suddenly, had arrived and the following summer got a move to Dunfermline who had become a rising force under Jock Stein, although he left for Celtic just before Ferguson's arrival.

Ferguson was Dunfermline's leading scorer that season but was left out of the side for the 1965 Scottish Cup final. The manager, Willie Cunningham, only told him in the dressing room on the day of the game. Ferguson was furious and bawled him out in front of the other players. More importantly, he learned a significant lesson about how to handle leaving players out.

He moved to Rangers in 1967 for £65,000 and there came under the manager who was probably the greatest direct influence upon his own style, Scott Symon, who was noted both for being a disciplinarian and for refusing ever to criticise his players publicly. Rangers were top of the league, unbeaten, and Ferguson had scored six goals in sixteen games when, unexpectedly, Symon was sacked on 1 November, the demand for a tracksuit manager sparked by Stein's success at Celtic leading to the appointment of David White, who had been Symon's assistant. He and Ferguson never got on. Rangers took sixty-one points from thirty-four games that season, but still somehow finished behind Celtic, much of the credit being given to Stein, who had ramped up the pressure before the end of the season by suggesting Rangers were so far ahead they could not be caught. A section of the fans found a scapegoat in Ferguson.

During an end-of-season trip to Denmark, the club began to brief that Ferguson was leaving. Ferguson found out through Cathy, his wife, and was furious, getting drunk and then haranguing the club's press officer Willie Allison in a Copenhagen hotel while wearing red pyjamas.

Ferguson survived that storm but his time at Rangers was never happy. He was blamed for losing Billy McNeill as the Celtic captain headed his side's opener in a 4–0 win over Rangers in the 1969 Scottish Cup final. Ferguson was relegated to train with the reserves and the youths, the suspicion nagging away, he said in his autobiography, that he might have been treated better if he hadn't married a Catholic. While there's no direct evidence that that was the case, he could legitimately feel aggrieved at the club's ruthlessness. That, he said, taught him 'how to treat players'; there are plenty who played under him who may wonder exactly what the lesson was.

In autumn 1969, Ferguson joined Falkirk, who were managed by Willie Cunningham, whom Ferguson clearly respected despite the volatility of their relationship. Falkirk were promoted that season with what is widely considered the best team in the club's history, but Ferguson doesn't appear on any of the club's official photographs, refusing after a spat with a photographer. His temper was volcanic and led to him being sent off six times over his career, an astonishing tally in an era when dismissals were much rarer than they are today. That spikiness was demonstrated again when the club physio had to separate Ferguson and Cunningham after the manager refused to allow him to sign for Hibernian. The upshot was an improved deal for Ferguson that included a role as assistant manager.

He also served as chairman of the Scottish PFA for three years from 1970 and was involved in a threatened strike action in 1972 after Cunningham reacted to a 6–1 League Cup defeat to St Johnstone by withdrawing the players' lunch and travel allowances.

Cunningham resigned in the summer of 1973 and was replaced by the former Scotland manager John Purchase, who demoted Ferguson back to being a mere player. He left for Ayr United soon afterwards, where he played for Ally MacLeod. The end of his career was coming, though, and Ferguson, who had worked as a sales rep while at Rangers, took over Burns's

Cottage, a pub in Govan, renaming it Fergie's, and the following year bought a stake in another pub, Shaw's. His break in management came quickly and he was put in charge of East Stirlingshire in 1974. His achievements there were remarkable as he imposed discipline – once banning the chairman's son-in-law for skipping training – but after 117 days he left to take the job at St Mirren.

There was potential there, but shortly after Ferguson's appointment the chairman who had given him the job, Harold Currie, was succeeded by Willie Todd. Ferguson never got on with the new man, even though in the four years he survived there he increased crowds by a factor of six and took the club to promotion. After St Mirren had finished third bottom in their first season back in the top flight, Ferguson was sacked. Nobody thought it had anything to do with their league position. Within forty-eight hours he had been named the new manager of Aberdeen.

Ferguson took the unusual step of taking the St Mirren board to a tribunal, claiming £50,000 compensation. He lost and the picture that emerged was of a dictatorial approach that demanded extreme personal loyalty. In his final six weeks in the job, for instance, he refused to speak to his secretary, conducting all communication with her through a seventeen-year-old assistant. The club physio, Ricky MacFarlane, who had worked closely with Ferguson and eventually led the team they had built together to unimagined highs, refused to follow Ferguson to Aberdeen, preferring to keep his family in Glasgow; Ferguson's autobiographies, written at various points over the following twenty-one years, make no mention of him at all. MacFarlane was considered disloyal and so was airbrushed from history. Loyalty outranked almost everything else. Ferguson dropped Eric Black for the 1986 Scottish Cup final because the player had revealed two weeks earlier that he would be leaving for Metz; the final was not to be his grand farewell.

Aberdeen hadn't won the league since 1955, but they were

rising, thanks to MacLeod, who had led them to the League Cup in 1977, and then Billy McNeill, who took them to second in the league and the Scottish Cup final before moving to Celtic to replace Stein. The team Ferguson inherited hadn't lost in the league since the previous December. But there was no doubt that he made them better – eventually.

His first eighteen months were turbulent, not helped by a lengthy touchline ban imposed after he had defied a prohibition on speaking to referees to berate an official after a 2–2 draw at St Mirren in which two Aberdeen players had been sent off. As he approached the referee at the end of the game, he shook off a club official who had come to tell him his father had just died.

He fell out with the prolific goalscorer John Harper, whom he felt didn't offer enough to the team and essentially wasn't serious enough about his football. Aberdeen came fourth in the league in his first season, got to the semi-final of the Cup and lost to Dundee United in the final of the League Cup in a replay. While the Dundee United manager Jim Jeffries made two changes to his team, Ferguson, despite wondering whether he should freshen up his side, stuck with the same line-up. He later admitted he'd been too 'frightened' to upset players; it wasn't a mistake he'd ever make again.

Anxiety was a notable feature of his early years and manifested as a dry cough that would come on quarter of an hour or so before kick-off. He developed a reputation for volatility, although nobody was ever sure which of his outbursts of temper were real and which premeditated and feigned for effect. Even during the 5–0 win over Hibernian that confirmed Aberdeen's league title in 1980, Ferguson managed to earn a year's touchline ban for foul and abusive language. Yet while there clearly were times when Ferguson lost control, even his rants at referees were part of a wider strategy: everything, he insisted, was set up to favour the Old Firm. He created a siege mentality that gave games between Aberdeen and Rangers or Celtic a bitter, often spiteful, edge. Unsavoury as some found it – Gordon Strachan said one of the reasons he left Aberdeen was to get away from the poisonous atmosphere of games against the Old Firm – it worked.

Ferguson was a perfectionist. Ten days after winning the Cup-Winners' Cup in 1983, for instance, Aberdeen faced Rangers in the Scottish Cup final. They played poorly but after ninety minutes the scores were level. 'You're Rangers' best player,' a furious Ferguson told Leighton before extra-time. An Eric Black goal four minutes from time gave Aberdeen the win, but Ferguson wasn't happy. In his post-match television interview, he called Aberdeen 'the luckiest team in the world. They were a disgrace in their performance.'

Yet he could be sentimental when it suited him. In Gothenburg, for instance, Ferguson had named Stuart Kennedy, who had been injured in the semi-final win over Bayern and couldn't play, among the substitutes. He later described it as 'one of my best man-management decisions'.

In retrospect, the traits that emerged more fully at United are clear. There was, for instance, a belief in youth. In 1984–85, Aberdeen had won the Scottish Youth Cup, coming from 3–0 down to win the final 5–3 after a Ferguson rant had reduced several players to tears. And there was a capacity to regenerate, a relentlessness to the success: Aberdeen retained the Scottish title in 1984–85 despite the loss of Strachan, Doug Rougvie and Mark McGhee. But Aberdeen, with their crowds of twenty-odd thousand could only go so far; he needed a bigger challenge.

Ferguson's start at United was inauspicious. Strachan had warned his team-mates of the ferocity of Ferguson's temper, but when he arrived he seemed nervous; when he read out the starting line-up for his first game in charge, a 2–0 defeat away at Oxford United, he referred to Peter Davenport as 'Nigel', confusing him with the actor. Afterwards, Ferguson admitted that he hadn't been able to believe how unfit his side was.

Gradually, Ferguson began to impose his methods. Under Atkinson, training had begun at 10.30, which often meant closer to 11.00, and was done by 12.00. Ferguson ordered play-ers to cut their hair and insisted on club blazers for official trips. Healthier food, including porridge, was introduced to the canteen at The Cliff training ground.

For three weeks, Ferguson kept his temper in check, to the extent that players wondered what Strachan had been warn-ing them about. They drew at Norwich and beat QPR at home. And then they lost at Wimbledon. Ferguson erupted, singling out Peter Barnes for criticism. The winger had been taken off after an hour and had hidden in the bath to try to avoid his manager, despite Wimbledon having turned off the hot water. 'Trying to win the championship with my lightweight crew would be like going to war with a pop-gun,' Ferguson said.

Barnes was one of the first offloaded as Ferguson reshaped his squad. Graeme Hogg, Arthur Albiston, John Gidman, Frank Stapleton and Kevin Moran all left within a year. A disgrun-tled Hogg gave an interview to the *News of the World* in which he described Ferguson as being out of his depth, ranting to cover his inadequacy. He made public for the first time the process that Mark Hughes had termed 'the hairdryer' when Ferguson stood in front of his victim and bawled at them so furiously that their hair could be seen being blown back by his breath. United finished eleventh that season and went out of the Cup in the fourth round; the sense was of a club with major structural problems. 'If Alex Ferguson had any illusions about the task when he took the job,' said Bryan Robson, 'he can have had none by that summer of 1987.'

Ferguson told the board he needed eight new players, but the poor transfer business of the previous summer meant resources were limited. The only two arrivals were the right-back Viv Anderson from Arsenal and the forward Brian McClair from Celtic. Anderson's time at the club was afflicted by injury, but McClair proved a versatile and intelligent sign-ing. 'When major success came to Manchester United in the nineties,' Ferguson said, 'nobody deserved it more than the good soldier McClair.' United almost landed Peter Beardsley from Newcastle, but he ended up going to Liverpool instead, prompting Ferguson to rail against what he saw as institutional bias in their favour, a perceived mass conspiracy that incorporated everybody from referees to *Match of the Day*.

He had come to view Liverpool with suspicion before he even got to Manchester. In rejecting an approach from Arsenal in 1983, Ferguson had suggested that the only two clubs he would move to England for were Liverpool and Manchester United. In November 1980, he took charge of his first match at Anfield, a European Cup second-round second leg. Aberdeen had lost the home leg 1–0; they were then thrashed 4–0. Kenny Dalglish suggested the result 'scarred' Ferguson and it's at the very least intriguing to consider what happened to the three players who played that night who were available for Ferguson's Scotland squad for the 1986 World Cup. He left out Alan Hansen, unconvinced of his commitment to the national side. Dalglish then withdrew with a knee injury, while Graeme Souness was controversially left out of the final group game against Uruguay.

United's issues weren't just about Liverpool or personnel or their position in the wider landscape. The booze culture had to be tackled; whereas previously United's squad had been banned from drinking in the forty-eight hours before a game, Ferguson demanded full prohibition while they were in training. A number of players in those days liked to drink in The Park, a pub in Altrincham run by Pat Crerand, but the biggest issue was with McGrath and Whiteside, who shared a flat. Matters came to a head the night before an FA Cup tie against QPR in January 1989 when the pair appeared on Granada's *Kick Off* programme. Both gave the impression of being drunk – although they denied it – and Ferguson transfer-listed them. McGrath was sold to Villa and Whiteside to Everton. Fans were outraged.

There had been signs in 1987–88 of Ferguson shifting the club in the right direction, although many remained to be convinced. United lost only one of their first fifteen games but drew eight of them and when a 2–0 defeat at home to South-ampton in mid-January left them fifth, they were booed off. Home gates had fallen below 40,000. United got by Ipswich and Chelsea in the third and fourth rounds of the FA Cup, and then, in the week leading up to the fifth-round tie against Arsenal, Bryan Robson injured his calf while training with England for a friendly against Israel. Ferguson was furious; United lost 1–0.

A 1–0 defeat at Norwich in the March was the last straw. Ferguson packed the players onto the bus thirty-five minutes after the final whistle – before they could have a drink in the club bar – and so they had to crawl through the same traffic as the fans. The next day, he brought them in for a meeting.

It worked. United went unbeaten through the ten games that remained that season, including a 3–3 draw at Liverpool on Easter Monday, despite going 3–1 down and having Colin Gibson sent off. Strachan celebrated the equaliser in front of the Kop by cupping a hand to his ear and pretending to smoke a cigar, but more significant was Ferguson's interview afterwards as he laid into Liverpool and the way, he claimed, referees favoured them at home. 'The provocation and intim-idation he [the referee] is under are incredible,' he said. This was Ferguson doing precisely what he had done in Scotland, generating a siege mentality by claiming everything was fixed in favour of the dominant club(s). As Ferguson was talking, Kenny Dalglish walked past with his six-week-old baby, Laura. 'You might as well talk to my daughter,' Dalglish told the tele-vision crew. 'You'll get more sense out of her.'

United finished second, their best league finish since 1980, while McClair had become the first player since Best to score more than twenty league goals in a season. They'd lost only five times, fewer than in any season since 1906. But they were nine points behind Liverpool and had twice attracted fewer than 30,000 fans to Old Trafford (against Luton and Wimbledon).

In May, Hughes returned to the club having spent one season at Barcelona and another on loan at Bayern Munich, but Ferguson missed out on Paul Gascoigne, who was persuaded to join Tottenham while the manager was away on holiday in Malta.

After the glimmers of hope in 1987–88, 1988–89 was a disappointment. United won only three of their first fourteen games and crowds had dipped to their lowest level since the early sixties, even before the sales of McGrath and Whiteside. United's transfer activity remained bewildering to many. Strachan was sold to Leeds in March 1989, while new arrivals such as Mal Donaghy and Jim Leighton failed to impress. The winger Ralph Milne, whose diffidence had frustrated numerous previous managers, was signed from Bristol City, but he never looked at home and played just twenty-three games. United finished eleventh after a run of nine games without a win, in eight of which they'd been ahead. It was the FA Cup sixth round defeat to Nottingham Forest, though, that prompted Ferguson to decide he needed a clear-out. Gordon Strachan left five days after that game and within two years McGrath, Whiteside, Anderson and Donaghy had all left the club.

Amid all the frustration, there was a demand for change, any change. In August 1989, before the opening game of the season, a 4–1 win over Arsenal, a slightly tubby thirty-seven-year-old with a moustache, wearing United shorts and a training top, performed some keepie-ups on the pitch and then smashed the ball into the net at the Stretford End. This was Michael Knighton, and the ball-juggling was his way of announcing to fans his takeover of the club; he wanted them to know, he said, that he was not just another businessman. A former apprentice at Coventry City, he had become a teacher and then a headteacher before leaving education to manage his property portfolio full-time. The directors, according to Edwards, 'cringed' at his antics. Ferguson later spoke of a 'terrible gut feeling'. Bryan Robson called him 'a head case . . . on a massive ego-trip'.

It had been little secret that Edwards was happy to sell his shares. In the summer of 1983, the publisher and former MP Robert Maxwell had offered £10 million for them. Edwards was seemingly initially willing to sell, but after fan protest and amid boardroom suspicion as to Maxwell's motives, he asked for £15 million, leading Maxwell to turn away and devote his attentions to Oxford United, which was probably a fortunate escape given how things turned out there as he tried unsuccessfuly to merge the club with Reading and ended up quitting to take over at Derby while leaving his son Kevin as chairman. When Maxwell drowned in myserious circumstances in 1991, the club fell into insolvency.

Knighton's bid for United was worth £20 million but it soon became apparent that the deal was not quite so close to completion as it had appeared. Edwards says two of Knighton's backers pulled away; Knighton claims he had no need of other backers and the problem was a campaign against him by the Maxwell press. Either way, although he took a seat on the board for three years, Knighton's takeover never happened.

He ended up taking over Carlisle United in 1992. In a controversial and increasingly bizarre decade as owner, he saw them twice promoted and twice relegated, the second demotion coming after he had appointed himself head coach. After standing down, Knighton took to writing poetry and had a series of artworks depicting the crucifixion exhibited at King's College, Cambridge, in 2006, under the pseudonym Kongthin Pearlmich (an anagram of Michael Knighton PR). He also claimed to have seen a UFO in 1976.

Knighton's failed takeover seemed to focus Edwards's mind on the potential for growth and he decided to fund major rebuilding – or perhaps undertook it expecting investment. Gary Pallister, Paul Ince, Mike Phelan, Neil Webb and Danny Wallace all arrived in 1989. After three years, only Blackmore – 'huge ability', said Ferguson but lacking 'the yard of pace needed to make him truly outstanding in his natural midfield position' – remained of the side that had lost to Oxford in Ferguson's first game.

None of the new signings settled quickly, which ramped up the pressure. 'No manager on earth can have a grievance if he gets sacked after spending that little lot,' said Atkinson. Pallister, who had joined for the highest fee ever paid between two British clubs, was described by George Best as 'the biggest mistake United have made'. It perhaps didn't help that, as was common at the time, the new signings received little support in helping them to settle. Pallister lived in the ugly Ramada hotel overlooking Piccadilly Gardens, eating in Pizza Hut and spending his afternoons in the bookmakers with Ince.

Having beaten Arsenal on the opening day, United thrashed Millwall 5–1 in their sixth game of the season, but in between they lost three times. Even with that background of inconsistency, what happened in the seventh game, away at Manchester City, was unexpected and devastating. United lost 5–1. Ferguson was distraught, went home to bed and buried his head under a pillow. 'I was as close to putting my head in the oven as I have ever been,' he said, 'and I think there would have been plenty of volunteers to turn on the gas had I done so.'

Just before the City debacle, Ferguson had signed a new three-year deal, but the doubters were queuing up. Emlyn Hughes awarded him, in classic tabloid style, the OBE – 'Out By Easter'. Leighton, who acknowledged Ferguson had lost the dressing room, began to be attacked by fans as a proxy for his manager. In his own words, Ferguson became 'something of a hermit, driven into a self-imposed hiding by a failure I hate. I shut the world outside my door and just felt miserable. I went through my team talks, everything and couldn't find anything wrong.'

That did nothing to alleviate the sense of shame. 'Every time somebody looks at me,' he told Hugh McIlvanney in the *Sunday Times*, 'I feel I have betrayed that person.' The feeling was mutual: the majority of fans had lost faith. 'What really hurts, Alex,' said a piece in the fanzine *Red News*, 'is that under you we've had shit football, shit atmosphere, shit boardroom shenanigans and our support is drifting away.'

The next month, Ferguson took the players to Dunblane to play golf and generally try to raise spirits. They played a friendly against St Johnstone, but that only made things worse. In his autobiography, Ferguson spoke of the 1–0 win as a 'monstrous embarrassment, a really stinking performance'.

The nadir came with a 2–1 defeat against Crystal Palace at Old Trafford at the beginning of December, a result that left United twelfth. Only 37,514 turned up; one of them, Pete Molyneaux, brandished a banner that became notorious: 'Three years of excuses and it's still rubbish . . . ta-ra Fergie.' 'If I had paid attention to letters from fans,' said Martin Edwards, 'it would have been easy to sack the manager.'

On 10 January, United went to Nottingham Forest in the third round of the FA Cup. Webb, Robson, Ince, Wallace, Sharpe, Donaghy and Colin Gibson were all out injured. The widespread assumption, although Edwards says it is inaccurate, was that Ferguson would be sacked if United lost; bookmakers were offering 5–2 on him leaving. Best said he 'wouldn't walk round the corner to watch United play'. And somehow, amid the gloom, a prescient voice rang out. 'If his team can get a draw or pull off a win,' wrote Rob Shepherd in *Today*, 'it could prove the catalyst for a complete change in the club's fortunes.' On the morning of the game, Ferguson backed United to win the Cup at 16–1.

In the BBC's coverage of the game, Jimmy Hill commented that United 'looked beaten in the warm-up'. Ferguson happened to be passing a monitor at the time and never forgot or forgave the line. However despondent United may have looked before the match, and however much players may have begun to doubt their manager, they played with great energy and determination to withstand significant pressure and won thanks to a second-half goal from Mark Robins, who stole in front of Stuart Pearce to nod in a cross shaped from the left by Hughes with the outside of his right foot. 'I think we did it that day with defiance,' Ferguson said.

Had Nigel Jemson had a better day in front of goal, English

football might have looked very different over the following twenty-five years, but he didn't and Ferguson survived. The foundations were in place. As Terry Gibson, assuming Ferguson's exit was a fait accompli, put it in the *Sun* before the Forest game, 'Whoever takes over will be the luckiest boss in the land ... there is so much talent there that one day they could be a real force.'

United's league form remained indifferent. They didn't win a game between 18 November and 10 February, but the Cup offered solace. They squeaked by Hereford in the fourth round on a mudbath at Edgar Street with a late goal from Blackmore; only a fine save from Jim Leighton had prevented them going behind after a whistle blown in the crowd had caused the defence to stop. They beat Newcastle 3–2 and then Sheffield United 1–0. If they were to go on and win it, the statisticians pointed out, they would be the only side to lift the Cup without having played a match at home (although in 1948 they'd won it without playing a game at Old Trafford).

While the draw had been unkind to them in that way, at the same time they hadn't had to face top-flight opposition since Forest, even if Oldham, as Ferguson said were 'a top-flight team in all but name'. They were promoted the following season, but Royle looks back on the 1989–90 season as his fondest time at the club. They had reached the League Cup final, in which they lost to Nottingham Forest, and had challenged for promotion before faltering as fatigue caught up with them and finishing eighth in the Second Division. They even produced a single with Cannon and Ball. 'It was called "The Boys in Blue",' said the former United player Andy Ritchie. 'It didn't exactly take the charts by storm, but for the fans it was absolutely brilliant. The whole town was just blue. I believe at one stage they even dyed the meat pies blue.'

There were those who put Oldham's success down to the artificial pitch at Boundary Park, but that was to underestimate how good they were, on grass as well as plastic. 'Joe wanted to play swift, attacking football,' said Ritchie. 'There was a myth about the synthetic pitch. Actually, you couldn't lump it. You had to play fast, attractive football, but people came with preconceived ideas. But we'd won away at Everton and down at Southampton in the Littlewoods Cup, which showed we could play anywhere.'

For United, Robson returned after three months out with groin and hernia problems, taking his place alongside Ince in the centre of a cautious line-up. Mike Phelan was selected at right-back to deal with the threat of the Oldham left-winger Rick Holden, with Colin Gibson used on the left of midfield in front of Lee Martin. Brian McClair operated on the right side of midfield, with Neil Webb, himself only recently returned from injury, in a free role behind Mark Hughes. 'There was a major worry about the form of Jim Leighton,' Ferguson wrote in his autobiography. 'He had lost confidence and his decision-making had become suspect.' His assistant manager Archie Knox, though, persuaded Ferguson to stick with his regular keeper.

Although 36,000 gallons of water had been pumped onto the Maine Road pitch in the week before the game, it still looked hard and a little dry, and for several minutes both sides struggled to get to grips with it. There were a lot of poor touches and a lot of misplaced passes and a general sense of anxiety.

Others, in their first game back following a lengthy absence, might have been tempted to play their way into the game, but Robson's first challenge was ferocious, clattering into the former United forward Andy Ritchie as he completed the task of robbing him of the ball begun by an almost equally forceful challenge made by Steve Bruce. 'The ball must have squealed,' said an approving Barry Davies on the BBC commentary.

But Oldham had not achieved what they had without quality. There was far more to them than merely effort and energy. Four minutes in, Phelan dinked a ball infield from the right and Hughes headed it on towards Webb. Andy Holden, the centre-back, read the situation and covered the run, helping the ball to Mike Milligan, the captain, who turned calmly and drilled a pass from his own box to Ian Marshall on halfway. His first touch was excellent, trapping the ball into his turn; his second rather less so as he sprayed a pass out of play several yards in front of its intended target, Neil Redfearn.

Ritchie picked up a loose ball just inside the United half and made a forward surge, whipping in a low cross. Leighton came for it, and should have claimed comfortably, but presumably didn't call and Phelan intervened, the ball dribbling away for a corner with Rick Holden only three or four yards from seizing on the error to turn the ball into an empty net. It didn't matter – an open goal would present itself soon enough.

Rick Holden slung in the corner towards Marshall at the near post. It was headed out, and Holden regained possession on the right of the United box. As Phelan went to close him down, he sent over a mishit cross that bounced awkwardly at the near post. Ritchie went for it but missed and Leighton, behind him, was distracted enough to misjudge the bounce of the ball, patting it on. From five yards, Earl Barrett nudged the ball into an empty net. Had Ritchie touched it he would have been offside, but he didn't and so, after six minutes, the Second Division side led.

United were unsettled, rattled by the ferocity of Oldham's start and repeatedly caught out by their offside trap. Martin lifted a free-kick into the Oldham box but Barrett got high above Webb to head clear, then Redfearn punted it long for Ritchie, whose energy and willingness to chase offered Oldham a regular out-ball. On this occasion Phelan covered and played it back to Leighton. He cleared long and Hughes won the flick but as Gibson closed in, Andy Holden lunged in on the edge of the box to help the ball back to Jon Hallworth.

A couple of United corners caused problems, Ince having a shot charged down on the edge of the box and Hallworth claiming an awkward swirling ball tumbling backwards under pressure from McClair, but there was little rhythm to their play. Webb kept being caught in possession, not yet up to speed as he returned from injury.

Dawdling, Webb was dispossessed by Redfearn after quarter of an hour, before Milligan swept it forward for Marshall. He was beaten by Bruce and, at last, United got some proper possession. Robson played it to Martin and it was worked on to Hughes to Robson to Pallister to Bruce, advancing to halfway and working it back again before Bruce went long down the left for Hughes to chase under pressure from Barrett. The striker played it back inside for Ince who drifted infield looking for an opening. He found none and was tackled by Milligan, who immediately played it forward for Ritchie. He dummied to turn Pallister and set off on a charge down the left, only for Marshall to be caught offside as he swept a cross-field ball towards him.

Oldham's threat on the break was obvious, but the rat-a-tat of passes seemed to calm United. Phelan took a throw to McClair, who turned under pressure. Andy Holden poked the ball away from him but only to Ince, who returned it wide to Phelan. He shaped a ball in for Hughes, who headed on for Webb. From the byline, he chipped a cross to the back post, where Denis Irwin headed away as Gibson closed in. Redfearn completed the clearance, putting it out for a throw, which soon became a corner as Irwin headed out of play. Andy Holden beat Bruce in the air to clear Webb's delivery but Gibson was bundled over by Redfearn about thirty-five yards out on the United left – a needless free-kick to give away that allowed United to maintain the pressure. Webb took it quickly towards the near post, where Bruce was moving into the ball with menace only to be ruled offside.

United at last had some sort of control, but they were restricted largely to long balls. A Leighton clearance was taken down by Webb who slid a pass towards Hughes, but Barrett outmuscled him before being hit by a late challenge from Robson – a sign, it seemed, of United's frustration.

Another Leighton clearance was flicked on by Hughes, and Andy Holden put it out for a throw when he might simply have nudged it back to Hallworth. Phelan took it to Hughes, who flicked the ball up and drove it across the face of goal, where Irwin, unfussy as ever, cleared.

It would be an exaggeration to say Oldham were on top, but they seemed comfortable and posed a persistent threat. Ritchie, receiving the ball from an Andy Holden challenge on Hughes, saw Leighton off his line and sent a chip goalwards that drifted just wide. Barrett kept intercepting Webb through-balls. Ince clattered into Marshall and then, clearly irritated by United's scratchy start, harangued the referee Joe Worrall. A foul by Phelan on Rick Holden gave Oldham a free-kick on the left. Holden crossed deep for his brother, who, at full stretch, headed it up into the air. Marshall kept the ball alive and Pallister, clearing under pressure, could only head out as far as Milligan. He switched the ball left for Rick Holden and his cross arced dangerously across the six-yard box before being claimed by Leighton.

There was little to suggest United might be about to level but, just before the half-hour, they did. It began with a long clearance from Leighton that Webb flicked on. Andy Holden beat Hughes in the air but Robson turned the ball back towards the Oldham area. Barrett volleyed clear but slightly mistimed his kick and Bruce, sliding in front of Marshall, forced the ball forward to Webb. He took one touch to control and then, on the turn, at last got a pass beyond Barrett. Robson ran on and, although Hallworth got his hands to the shot, Robson's arm was up in celebration before the ball had crossed the line. It was the fourth semi-final in a row in which he'd scored.

Oldham swung back into the attack almost immediately and Pallister got in front of Marshall to head a Redfearn ball back to Leighton. The goalkeeper rolled the ball out to Phelan, who advanced down the right then swept a long diagonal to Hughes, who headed down for the advancing McClair. Barrett lunged in and took the ball before making contact with the forward. United fans howled for a penalty, but McClair's reaction was telling: he knew the tackle had been clean.

United continued the long-ball assault. Andy Holden dived

to head another punt clear, the ball finding Redfearn on the right. Oldham calmly worked the ball across the pitch, through Milligan, Henry and Barlow to Rick Holden on the left. He took on Phelan and beat him and then, under pressure from Ince, sent a cross low to the near post, where Pallister got in front of Ritchie to put the ball out for a corner. The frenetic, scrappy opening had yielded to a high-octane, end-to-end game.

Ten minutes before the break, Oldham won another corner on the right. As Rick Holden slung it in, Leighton shoved Ritchie before back-pedalling to palm the ball away for another corner. Worrall spoke to him, but opted not to give a penalty. That next corner found Andy Holden at the back post, but he couldn't guide his effort on target.

A long free-kick from Bruce was flicked on by Hughes. Andy Holden got in front of Webb and his header clear fell to Hughes, who played in McClair on the edge of the box. He laid it off again to Hughes moving infield. Andy Barlow got a touch and the ball squirted out to Ince on the right. As Rick Holden jostled him, he worked it back to Phelan. His cross was headed out by Barrett. Redfearn helped it on to Ritchie on the right on halfway. Bruce, who'd taken a whack on the collarbone from the forward a couple of minutes earlier, closed in but, having outmuscled him, he bafflingly nudged the ball back down the line, where Irwin, in space, ran onto it. He crossed but Marshall's header was blocked by Pallister for another corner. Redfearn took it. Leighton punched clear to the edge of the box, where Nicky Henry hit a low shot that beat the keeper but was cleared off the line by Ince.

Phelan scrapped hard to win the ball on halfway and knocked it to Hughes, who turned and played it right for McClair. His cross was dangerous, but Irwin, charging back, was able to block in front of Gibson. The ball rolled back for Robson, surging in from deep, but a combination of Irwin and Barrett were able to charge it down so the ball was deflected just wide. Webb drove it in and Hallworth, looking anxious, missed it.

Ritchie headed clear at the back post. United, suddenly, were in the ascendancy, their midfield starting to impose itself.

Ince came away with the ball from a midfield tangle and worked it through Robson to Gibson. He played it in for Hughes, who took it down on his chest and hit a dipping shot goalwards that Hallworth did well to hold low down. The keeper still looked uneasy with crosses, though, allowing a dangerous Webb cross from the right to bounce across his six-yard box. But at half-time it was still 1–1.

The second half began with a relative lull. There was vague Oldham pressure, their control highlighted by snappish fouls by Bruce on Ritchie and Ince on Milligan. United's sole attacking idea seemed to be balls hit over the top towards Hughes, but he was expertly marshalled by Barrett. Hughes committed a frustrated foul just inside the Oldham half. The free-kick was pumped long towards the United box, where Redfearn won the header down. Leighton, though, was alert to get to the ball before Marshall.

That seemed to spark the game into life again. An Irwin ball over the top set Marshall away against Pallister. He outpaced him and, bustling into the box, hit the bouncing ball ferociously. It was straight at Leighton but moving at such a pace that he could only palm it down in front of him; he was fortunate the rebound didn't fall to an Oldham player. Leighton was perhaps a better goalkeeper than the general memory of him acknowledges, but his spindly frame, the blobs of Vaseline on his eyebrows and his intense, jittery persona meant there was a sense that a mistake was never too far away.

Oldham were clearly on top at that stage, their directness troubling United. Ritchie collected a long clearance on the left flank and swept an arcing ball from deep across the top of the box. Leighton came out and Marshall stretched for it. Both missed the ball and clattered into each other, Martin mopping up. Both required treatment, although the damage done to Leighton seemed to be largely to his shorts, which he was forced to change in the middle of his penalty area.

United's threat was extremely limited at that stage, although they might have had a penalty on sixty-four minutes as Barlow nudged Webb in the back as he reached for a Martin ball in from the left. It would perhaps have been soft, but there was clear contact. A couple of minutes later, United got the benefit of a borderline decision on a push at the other end. An Irwin free-kick from deep on the right was headed out by McClair and when Holden hooked the ball back into the box, Henry was deemed to have committed a foul just before Redfearn slammed in a shot from just inside the box.

It was those balls from deep areas that seemed to be causing United the most concern and another Irwin delivery from just inside the United half almost picked out Ritchie in the box. Phelan, this time, got across to cover.

Slowly, the momentum began to shift. Andy Holden and Hughes jumped for a Leighton clearance and the ball fell for Webb. For once, he had time and he was able to turn and measure a smart angled pass in to Hughes on the edge of the box. Irwin, darting across from right-back, made an excellent tackle.

United, though, were in an unenviable position. The more they attacked, the greater the threat posed by the running of Ritchie and the aerial prowess of Marshall. Webb gathered an overhit cross from Gibson but his ball into the box was weak. Milligan came away with it and released Redfearn down the right. He could have played an early ball across the pitch, where Oldham had a two on one, but he tried to turn infield and lost control. Pallister made a challenge and the ball broke to Ritchie twenty yards from goal. He turned and scooped a shot goalwards, but the ball never sat comfortably for him and there was little power on the effort, which drifted wide anyway.

Robson had been far less of an influence on the second half than he had been on the first, the effects of his first game in three months perhaps catching up with him, and he was taken off for Danny Wallace with eighteen minutes to go.

Wallace went across to the right, with McClair moving into Robson's position in the centre. The substitute's first act was to win a throw off Barlow. Phelan took it to Wallace. He exchanged passes with Phelan and then, from the corner of the box, sent a cross deep beyond the back post. Gibson headed it back across goal. On the edge of the six-yard box, Hallworth and Andy Holden both jumped for it with Webb, who got to the ball and sent it looping gently into the empty net.

The advantage didn't last long. Oldham had been the better side for most of the half and falling behind simply provoked them into a renewed frenzy. Bruce got to a long ball ahead of Redfearn and put it out for a throw. Irwin took and got the ball back from Redfearn, then played it back to the midfielder on the right-hand side of the box. He got by Ince and crossed. The ball took a flick off Ritchie at the near post and came to an unmarked Marshall at the back. His mulleted curls bobbing, he jerked his right leg at the ball and, making contact with shin and boot, sent a low volley scudding into the net. United's lead had lasted only three minutes.

United came again. Ince almost played Hughes through but he trod on the ball. A clearance from Leighton was superbly controlled by Hughes just inside the Oldham half, allowing him to get away from Barrett. He played the ball out to Wallace, who found Webb's run with a clever angled ball. Webb's shot was beaten away by Hallworth to his right. It fell for Hughes but his follow-up was blocked by Barrett.

With six minutes to go, Oldham made their first substitution, bringing on the versatile Paul Warhurst to play in the centre of midfield in place of Henry. The biggest alteration in Oldham's dynamic, though, was the result of United's change. With McClair moved infield and Wallace lacking his defensive wherewithal, Rick Holden was becoming more involved on the left. As Barrett challenged Hughes, Milligan claimed the dropping ball and played it out to Holden on the left. He went down the line for Marshall. He took on Pallister and beat him. With Ritchie screaming for a ball rolled across goal, the forward shot, but was thwarted by a dreadful bobble, the ball hopping up so he shinned it well wide. Warhust, his pace and freshness evident, then surged through the centre, played a pass to Ritchie, took a return ball and spread the play to Marshall on the left. His cross towards Ritchie was headed out by Pallister as Oldham finished the ninety minutes in the ascendant.

The pattern seemed to be continuing into extra-time. Marshall got the better of Pallister, a recurring theme, and played the ball out to Rick Holden, who sent over a deep cross for Redfearn. He knocked it down and Marshall, in space in the middle of the box, controlled an awkwardly bouncing ball, turned and shot, Bruce blocking just in front of his goalkeeper.

Barrett played a ball out to Irwin, who went forward to Redfearn and ran on to take his lay-off. He played the ball to Ritchie and, under pressure from Bruce, he miscontrolled. McClair nipped in, turned away from Marshall and played a ball over the top for Wallace to run on to. He got between Andy Holden and Barrett and, as Hallworth advanced to meet him, pushed a neat left-foot finish just inside the right-hand post. United, somehow, had reclaimed the lead.

Royle played his final card, bringing on Roger Palmer, Oldham's all-time record scorer and a former Manchester City player, for Ritchie. The game for a while became scrappy, both sides seemingly weary. In quick succession Martin and Webb went down with cramp, which led to Gibson being redeployed at left-back with Martin struggling on in front of him. Marshall almost got on the end of a Barlow long ball, Leighton coming quickly off his line to thwart him. Then Ince, probably United's most effective player on the day, released Wallace down the right. A fit Martin might have got on the end of his low ball across goal but Barrett was able to intercept. That seemed to make Ferguson's mind up and, just before half-time in extra-time, he took off Martin for Mark Robins.

There was a sense that extra-time hadn't really got going, broken up by a series of stoppages. The second half began with another break as Pallister fouled Marshall, who seemed to catch him on the head with his knee as he fell. Pallister stayed down for several minutes but was able to head out Irwin's delivery soon after. Robins picked up the loose ball but his pass was intercepted by Milligan. As the defence pushed out, the Oldham captain slipped a ball through on the left for Marshall. He arced a ball across the box, between Leighton and Bruce, and Palmer arrived at the far post to finish. United had failed to close the game out. Ferguson was furious with Robins, blaming him for giving the ball away in the build-up to the equaliser and giving him what Martin described as 'a huge bollocking'.

'It epitomised us at the time that we kept getting equalisers,' said Ritchie. 'In that period, we felt that we could beat anyone and, individually, I thought I could score in every game. We had such an array of talent and such a great confidence in each other.'

For a time the game seemed to lapse into exhaustion, but there then came a flurry of United pressure. Wallace headed a ball back to Phelan, who launched an up-and-under forward. Hughes jumped with Barrett and the ball broke for Webb. He crossed and as Hughes and Robson closed in, Irwin made a remarkable lunging clearance. The ball trickled back towards the edge of the box where McClair was steaming in. His shot, though, flew perhaps four feet over the bar.

The goal-kick was won by Phelan who headed on for Webb. He whipped a first-time cross into the box and Robins, making a diagonal dart across the near post, got in front of Irwin and made good contact, but his header was straight at Hallworth who flopped gratefully on the ball. And that was that – an exhausting, thrilling game that was high in drama rather than quality and that ended for United in a sense that, although they'd allowed the lead to slip, they'd rather got away with it. Leighton, Ferguson concluded, 'might have done more to prevent two of Oldham's goals'.

The day had produced thirteen goals and an extraordinary

Martin Buchan jumps for a header with Alan Whittle against Crystal Palace in 1972.

Wyn 'the Leap' Davies, leaping but not winning at Selhurst Park.

Ron Atkinson completes the £1.5 million signing of Bryan Robson, a fee so shocking Matt Busby resigned from the board.

Bryan Robson puts United 1–0 up against Barcelona at Old Trafford in 1984.

Robson gets his second against Barça to level the aggregate scores.

Mark Hughes challenges the Oldham goalkeeper Jon Hallworth in the 1990 semi-final.

Two sides of Jim Leighton: making a brave save from Andy Ritchie in the
semi-final . . .

. . . and despairing after Gary O'Reilly gives Crystal Palace the lead in the
1990 FA Cup final.

Alex Ferguson arrives at Old Trafford, November 1986 . . .

. . . and says goodbye at the Hawthorns, May 2013.

Roy Keane heads United back into the 1999 Champions League semi-final against Juventus.

Dwight Yorke and Andy Cole break clear to put United 3–2 ahead in Turin.

Cristiano Ronaldo's header gives United the lead against Chelsea in the 2008 Champions League final in Moscow.

Edwin van der Sar celebrates after John Terry slips and misses his chance to win the Champions League for Chelsea.

Jesse Lingard runs away in delight after his brilliant winner in the 2016 FA Cup final.

level of drama. 'Palm Sunday has witnessed the rebirth of an English football season which was threatening to end up with the honours back in the familiar places, most of them called Anfield,' wrote Lacey in the *Guardian*. 'The season was in need of such a lift. For the past year memories of Hillsborough have hung over the English game like a shroud . . . Take a brilliantly sunny if chilly day, four sets of enthusiastic and well-behaved supporters, attacking football on all sides and one shock with maybe another to come, and all seems right with the world of football.'

It was also a hugely important day for United. They had battled through a game that could easily have gone against them to force a replay and while that was also a tense, difficult encounter – 'I've never felt such pressure,' said Ferguson, 'so much strain in one game' – United were never in as much danger as they had been in the first game.

Brian McClair put United ahead five minutes after half-time but with ten minutes to go, Andy Ritchie levelled to take the game into extra-time again. It was time for Robins again. 'In the second match, I remember Nick Henry had a volley that hit the underside of the bar,' he said. 'It looked like it was over [the line] but it wasn't given. It was a tough, tough game on a bobbly pitch, but it had bits of quality as well. When I came on, Archie Knox said, "Go out there and make a name for yourself," which was what I'd been doing throughout the Cup run.'

Robins had been on the field eleven minutes when, with nine minutes of the game remaining, he struck again. 'Mickey Phelan made a break and I got the ball from him,' he remembers. 'I took a touch, had another and steadied myself. The Oldham keeper, Jon Hallworth, had a habit of setting himself, so I dragged it across him and it bobbled in.'

The final was hardly less dramatic than the semis. Palace retained the back three they had adopted in the semi-final against Liverpool, with John Salako at left wing-back and John Pemberton on the right and set about physically imposing themselves. It very nearly worked again. Eighteen minutes in, Leighton came for Phil Barber's free-kick, didn't get there and the ball looped in off a combination of Garry O'Reilly and Pallister. Ferguson was irritated: before the game, he'd said, 'We decided that on free kicks in particular he [Leighton] should not come for the ball unless he was absolutely certain of taking it.' United then took control and levelled as Robson's header from a McClair cross flicked off Pemberton on its way past Nigel Martyn.

United went ahead just after the hour. Andy Thorn should have cleared Wallace's attempted cross but Webb blocked and the ball broke to Hughes, always a man for a final, and he cracked in a precise finish, high up just inside the far post. Seven minutes later, Ian Wright, barely recovered from a broken leg, came on for Phil Barber. Three minutes after that, he equalised. A long kick from Martyn bounced its way to Mark Bright, who, with his back to goal, flicked the ball behind him into the path of his strike partner. Wright accelerated ahead of Phelan, turned inside Pallister and slid his shot past Leighton.

'I felt I was born for this day,' Wright said afterwards, and it seemed even more like that two minutes into extra-time as Salako's deep cross drifted over Leighton allowing him to smash in a stretching volley. Palace got to within seven minutes of victory but then Wallace laid in Hughes – who else? – and he steered the ball past Martyn to level.

For the replay, Leighton, having been at fault for the first and third goals, was omitted as Ferguson demonstrated just how ruthless he could be. He had seen Leighton after the game, sitting with head bowed, looking 'like a broken man' and decided action had to be taken. Having missed out on the 1965 Scottish Cup final, Ferguson knew just how big a decision he was making. 'I had to discard poor old Jim,' Ferguson said. 'For the sake of Manchester United. I have never done anything like it before. And I don't want to do anything like it again – ever . . . He was absolutely sick – sick to the soles of his boots. The reality of missing out was bound to be like a knife thrust . . . But Jim hasn't got the rhino hide.'

Lee Martin described the decision as 'a bombshell'. No United player, he said, had felt Leighton had played especially badly. He only played one more game for United, in a League Cup tie against Halifax, then returned to Scotland. Les Sealey, who came in for him, only played fifty-five times for United over five years, but he became almost a talisman for Ferguson, appearing in four finals. 'Was he a better goalkeeper than Jim?' asked Ferguson. 'No, but he thought he was and that can sometimes be important in a Cup final.' The game was an anti-climax after what had gone before, but United hardly cared as Martin, bursting forward from left-back, chested down Webb's chip and rattled the ball into the roof of the net for the only goal of the game. It was one of only two he ever scored for United and, given the other had come as an Alvin Martin clearance bounced in off his knee during a game against West Ham, by far the best. Martin felt a twinge of cramp as soon as he struck the shot but laboured on to the end of the game.

Ferguson had his first trophy and his job was safe. 'There was a sense,' Martin said, 'that this victory was the first brick in the wall towards building a successful future.' But he played little part in that future. He damaged his back in a pre-season game that summer and, with Denis Irwin arriving from Oldham to play on the right and Clayton Blackmore having the best season of his career on the left, there was no place for him in the first team.

Atkinson had rarely had faith in youth – Ferguson described what he had inherited as 'a shower of shit' – and there was a sense that the club was turning back to the model that had served Busby so well. Robins, Martin and Russell Beardsmore had all made their mark, but the first really to impose himself on a wider audience was Lee Sharpe, a prodigiously quick left-winger who scored a hat-trick in a 6–2 victory over Arsenal in the League Cup in 1990–91 on 28 November, the day that Margaret Thatcher resigned as prime minister. Having beaten

Liverpool in the previous round, United reached the final but lost to Sheffield Wednesday, who were managed by Ron Atkinson. There was a feeling, still, that they hadn't quite moved on from the Atkinson problem of inconsistency, that United could beat anybody on their day but couldn't sustain their form over a full season to mount a serious title challenge.

Sharpe was an indication of what was to come in terms of youth products but his relationship with Ferguson was never straightforward. Three days after the Arsenal game, he scored the only goal in a victory at Everton and celebrated with the dance that became known as the 'Sharpey Shuffle'. Ferguson was furious. 'It's like he didn't want me to have a personality,' Sharpe told Andy Mitten in *Glory, Glory*. 'Something was lost between me and the manager that day.' Matters didn't improve after Ferguson caught sight of his tattoo after the 1994 FA Cup final. 'What the fuck do you call that?' he demanded.

The way Ferguson handled Sharpe was indicative of how he dealt with young players in general. When Sharpe was sixteen and playing for Torquay United, Ferguson went to the south coast himself to complete the deal and then picked Sharpe up at Piccadilly Station. Similarly he turned up at Ryan Giggs's house on his fourteenth birthday to persuade him to sign for United, even though he had been training with City.

Ferguson took a personal interest in their development, trying to ensure players avoided temptation. After a while in Manchester, Sharpe moved in with his girlfriend, but nine months later Ferguson ordered him back into digs and suggested he get rid of both his girlfriend and his dog. While many conformed to Ferguson's stern paternalism, Sharpe never quite did. Although he insists stories about his love of nightlife were exaggerated, he also acknowledges that he spent a lot of time in the Discotheque Royale where 'you could not move for girls trying to get close'.

Sharpe's career never attained the heights it looked like it might when he was named PFA Young Player of the Year in 1991, although he did start 193 league games for United.

While Ferguson blamed his lifestyle, it was illness and injury – first viral meningitis, then hernia and ankle problems – that undid him. By the time the Class of '92 came through, he was essentially a bit-part player and was sold to Leeds for £4.5 million in 1996.

Ferguson increasingly imposed himself, reasserting the reputation as a disciplinarian he had had at Aberdeen. In one game in which United trailed at half-time, Bruce's mobile phone went off as Ferguson was addressing the team. He explained he needed it on because his wife was in hospital with a bad back. 'I know four bad backs,' Ferguson roared, seizing the phone and smashing it against the ground.

United remained inconsistent in the League in 1990–91 and went out of the FA Cup in the fourth round, but the Cup-Winners' Cup showed further signs of progress. United's path to the final was relatively straightforward but in Rotterdam they faced Johan Cruyff's Barcelona. Robson produced what he believes was his best ever performance, better than at Old Trafford against the same opposition in 1984, despite having a hernia that meant he had only been able to use his right foot in training. With Phelan deployed in midfield as a more defensive alternative to Webb and McClair pushing tight on Ronald Koeman, United effectively negated Barça, who were troubled by the pace of Sharpe. As they doubled up on him, space was left elsewhere.

Midway through the second half, Hughes turned in a Bruce header from close range and then, with sixteen minutes remaining, Hughes ran on to a Robson through-ball, went past the goalkeeper Carles Busquets as he came careering out of his box and, from a narrowing angle, smashed an almightily powerful finish into the empty net. Koeman scored with a late free-kick – Robson suggested that had Sealey been fully fit rather than labouring with a gashed leg that had become infected he might have got there – and Blackmore cleared a Michael Laudrup effort off the line but Barça's charge was too late: United had their first European trophy since 1968.

Between the two finals, Edwards floated the club on the London Stock Exchange, looking to clear the personal mortgage he had taken out to support his father's rights issue and to redevelop Old Trafford. Ferguson was against the idea, openly asking whether Edwards was acting for his own or the club's benefit, and refusing to take up the shares to which he was entitled. Remarkably the flotation was undersubscribed, valuing the club at just £47 million.

A level of scepticism among fans was understandable, although for all those who asked whether United was a football club or a business proposition, there were others who liked the idea of being able to own a small part of the club they loved. In retrospect the flotation was indicative of two related issues: first, that United were approaching the commercial possibilities of football's new era with a more open mind than most, and secondly, that Edwards had decided that investment, both in personnel and infrastructure, was the economically sensible approach. The summer after the flotation, Ferguson signed Andrei Kanchelskis, Paul Parker and Peter Schmeichel.

To the FA Cup and the Cup-Winners' Cup, Ferguson added the League Cup in March 1992, with a 1–0 win over Nottingham Forest in the final. But it was the league that dominated Mancunian thoughts and the need to end a run of failure stretching back to 1967. United lost only one of their first twenty-one games of the 1991–92 season, but on New Year's Day they faced QPR at home. They stayed overnight at a hotel before the game, presumably to ensure a level of self-control, but were still 'oddly lethargic and tired', as Parker put it. Dennis Bailey scored a hat-trick, QPR won 4–1, and United became crippled by self-doubt.

Still, when they beat Southampton 1–0 on 16 April, only their sixth win in seventeen games, they were two points clear at the top of the table with five games to play, while Leeds United, the only team that could realistically catch them, had played a game more.

But United drew at Luton then lost to Forest, West Ham and

Liverpool in successive games. Leeds drew at Liverpool then beat Coventry and Sheffield United to lift the title with a game to spare. United had drawn twice with Leeds in the league and had beaten them in both cup competitions that season; they could, as Parker insisted, reasonably claim to have been the better side, but they finished behind them in the table.

Most gallingly of all for United fans, the league championship trophy was lifted by Gordon Strachan, the man Ferguson had offloaded, getting to the prize before him. United had suffered an almighty choke. They only lost six games all season, but half of them were in the last four matches. Two thirds of their goals came in the first half of the season; a failure to convert chances was responsible for a string of disappointing draws. Ferguson cursed his failure to sign Mick Harford from Luton, believing the striker's aerial prowess might have made the difference as the Old Trafford pitch deteriorated after Christmas. The press blamed Ferguson. Kanchelskis had got the winner against Southampton but was then left out against Luton. Hughes was omitted against Forest.

Ferguson, reasonably enough, blamed fixture congestion that had led to United playing four games in six days. Robson agreed: 'We would have been champions but for the backlog of fixtures and the injury toll with which we had to contend,' he said.

Less reasonably, Ferguson saw a conspiracy under which every team wanted to stop United winning the title. West Ham, he said, had made an 'obscene effort' against United. It was 'almost criminal', he said, that they should raise their game for that one match in a season in which they were relegated. Hughes and Bruce both deny Ferguson was nervous, but suggested that the players were, producing a string of anxious, uncoordinated performances at the worst possible time. Ferguson himself blamed the rutted condition of the Old Trafford pitch, saying it hindered their attacking football. 'Maybe we lost our collective bottle,' Parker told Andy Mitten. 'Maybe we didn't have the resolve or couldn't deal with the pressure of Manchester United or were just a bit naive. We didn't change tactics in key matches and lost games we might have drawn.'

The night United lost at Forest, Easter Monday, Giggs and Sharpe went clubbing in Blackpool. Ferguson was at a black-tie dinner in Morecambe the following Thursday when he found out. Furious, he left the event and drove to Sharpe's house, where he found a party in full swing. Sharpe and Giggs were there, as were three apprentices. Ferguson broke up the party, refusing to call the players by anything other than their shirt numbers. It was soon after that Sharpe was encouraged to move back into digs.

Aware of the psychological pressure, Ferguson had brought in a comedian to entertain his team before the match at Anfield. More significant in terms of the mentality of players was what happened afterwards. As they left the ground, Sharpe, Ince and Giggs signed autographs for a clutch of Liverpool fans who then ripped them up, laughingly asking why they'd want the signatures of losers. Ferguson told the players to remember that, and to enjoy knocking Liverpool off their perch.

Giggs was part of a wider phenomenon. Sharpe, Martin and Beardsmore, it turned out, had been just the start of the youth movement. In 1992, United won the FA Youth Cup for the first time since 1964. Although the term 'Class of '92' is now generally taken to refer to the core of Giggs, Paul Scholes, David Beckham, Nicky Butt and the Neville brothers, neither Scholes nor Phil Neville made the line-up until the 1993 final. Nonetheless, eleven of the fourteen players who played in the two legs of their victory over Crystal Palace went on to represent United's first team and seven became full internationals. This really was Ferguson reprising Busby's success.

Some of the new signings were proving their worth. 'His physique and football matured rapidly,' Ferguson said of Pallister, 'and, unusually blessed with balance and pace, he became the centre-half which I wouldn't have swapped for any in the world.' Ince, too, had begun to look indispensable.

The club was changing elsewhere. That May, Norman White-side was given his testimonial – only 7434 turned out for it – and a day later the Stretford End was demolished. According to Parker, the players still went out a couple of times a month but the heavy-drinking culture had been eradicated.

For all the desire to put right that squandered championship opportunity – as motivation, Ferguson pinned to the dressing-room wall a picture of the bench looking distraught as Bruce had missed a late headed chance against Forest – there was something missing. It was provided, serendipitously, by per-haps the most important telephone call in United's history. The Leeds chairman Bill Fotherby rang Edwards to ask if Denis Irwin might be available. Of course he wasn't, but Ferguson, who was sitting in his office, asked if there might be an oppor-tunity to sign Éric Cantona, who had been vital to Leeds's title success the previous season but whose relationship with the club's manager Howard Wilkinson was strained. There was. And for just £1 million – 'an absolute steal', as Ferguson put it. United had been responsible for Cantona coming to London in the first place: Leeds had only signed him because their regu-lar striker Lee Chapman had broken his wrist in an FA Cup tie against United.

Cantona was a tempestuous figure who had called the France manager Henri Michel 'a sack of shit' and had, at one of his many disciplinary hearings, walked up to each judge and called them an 'idiot' individually. His personality made him a risk – Wilkinson said he lived in fear of Cantona riding off on his Harley-Davidson with his watercolours strapped to his back, giving up football altogether and so costing the club its investment – but he proved arguably the most significant signing in United's history.

They not merely got a replacement for Dion Dublin, who had broken his leg a month after joining for £1 million, but also the man who, more than any other player, would bring the long drought to an end. That, at least, is the popularly held story: Edwards suggests that he was the first to broach the Cantona issue, having heard through the agent Dennis Roach that all was not well at Elland Road, and then rang Ferguson. Whatever the exact details of his arrival, his impact was undeniable. In the seventeen league games before Cantona's arrival, United scored eighteen goals; in the following twenty-five they scored forty-nine.

United had begun the 1992–93 season with back-to-back defeats and endured a run of seven games without a win, slipping to tenth in the table. Wins over Arsenal and Oldham had begun the revival, but it was after Cantona's debut against Manchester City on 5 December that their season took off. He scored four in his first six games. 'He infected the place,' said Ferguson. United lost only twice more all season, the widespread belief being that his self-confidence had helped counteract the anxiety that had undermined them the previous season.

There was a stutter in March as United went four games without a win, a run that made their Monday night game at Norwich, one of their two challengers, vital. Playing devastating counter-attacking football, United raced into a 3–0 lead inside twenty minutes with goals from Giggs, Kanchelskis and Cantona and won 3–1. Then came the famous Easter Saturday win over Sheffield Wednesday. United were nervous almost to the point of paralysis and when John Sheridan converted a penalty to put Wednesday ahead midway through the second half, it felt as though another title might have been slipping through their grasp. But with four minutes remaining, Bruce levelled with a looping header. Except there weren't just four minutes remaining. The referee Michael Peck had suffered an injury after an hour, and the time it had taken for him to receive treatment and then be replaced meant there were almost seven minutes to be added. Towards the end of it, Bruce added a second, turning in a Pallister cross that had taken a deflection off Nigel Worthington. The celebrations of Brian Kidd and Ferguson on the touchline – or in Kidd's case over it – suggested that was the moment at which they knew the title was theirs.

A further five straight wins to the end of the season meant they ended up winning the title by ten clear points. The championship was sealed on the penultimate weekend as Aston Villa faced Oldham, needing to win to maintain any hope of overhauling United. Rather than watching, Ferguson went to play golf with his son Mark at Mottram Hall. As the final whistle blew on a 1–0 win for Oldham, Ferguson was lining up a putt on the seventeenth green. He was interrupted by a man he'd never met before, Michael Lavender, who now runs a hotel in Poitiers. 'Excuse me, Mr Ferguson,' he said, 'you've just won the championship.'

Ferguson did a double-take, then, convinced the information was correct, in Lavender's words 'went absolutely berserk, jumping up and down'. He abandoned his round and, as he made his way up the eighteenth, he hugged a bewildered Japanese golfer wearing a cap bearing the logo of United's sponsors, Sharp, wrongly assuming him to be a United fan.

Parker watched the game at Bruce's house, where they were joined as the afternoon went on by Schmeichel and Ince. Within an hour of the final whistle the whole squad was there. Robson, a champion at last, spoke of a 'massive sense of relief'. United were playing Blackburn the following day but got extremely drunk anyway. Bruce recalls going to bed at 4 a.m. and waking at 7 to find Robson and his wife Denise doing the washing up in his kitchen. Still hung-over, they fell behind against Blackburn, but came back to win 3–1, Pallister, the only outfielder who hadn't scored that season, blasting in a late free-kick.

The drought was over and an extraordinary period of success was about to begin.

CHAPTER 8

Champions League semi-final second leg, Stadio delle Alpi, Turin,
21 April 1999

Juventus	**2–3**	**Manchester United**
Inzaghi 6, 11		*Keane 24*
		Yorke 34
		Cole 83

Angelo Peruzzi	Peter Schmeichel
Alessandro Birindelli	Gary Neville
(Paolo Montero 46)	
Mark Iuliano	Ronny Johnsen
(Nicola Amoruso 46)	
Ciro Ferrara	Jaap Stam
Angelo Di Livio	Denis Irwin
(Daniel Fonesca 80)	
Gianluca Pessotto	David Beckham
Didier Deschamps	Roy Keane
Edgar Davids	Nicky Butt
Zinedine Zidane	Jesper Blomqvist
	(Paul Scholes 68)
Alessandro Del Piero	Dwight Yorke
Filippo Inzaghi	Andy Cole

Ref: Urs Meier
Bkd: Davids; Keane, Scholes
Att: 60,806

AS THE FINAL WHISTLE BLEW at the Delle Alpi, Juventus fans rose to their feet and applauded. They knew they had witnessed a genuinely great performance and, quite possibly, something more than that. The age of Italian domination of European competition was, perhaps, coming to an end and with it the nature of the game was changing. Italian football was nowhere near as negative as the stereotype might have suggested, nothing like as cautious as it had been when *catenaccio* reigned in the sixties and early seventies, but it was still a highly tactical pursuit. United, in that sense, were a throwback to an earlier, rawer time, their game based on talent and an indomitable self-belief. 'There was nothing about them,' Alex Ferguson said, 'that I admired or valued more than their team spirit.' By the time they came from 2–0 down to record their first ever victory on Italian soil, to reach their first European Cup final for thirty-one years, it had reached the point when it felt as though they only started really to play when they fell behind.

Familiarity with the story has perhaps dulled just how extraordinary 1998–99 was. Winning the league in 1993 had scratched one itch but as the decade went on and United emerged as the pre-eminent side in the country, another grew up in its place. For Alex Ferguson to stand comparison with Matt Busby, for him properly to enter the pantheon of great managers, he had to win the Champions League. And that had proved frustratingly difficult.

That was a time when the European Cup still had the nature of a quest. In the modern age the competition can feel like a game of pass the parcel: the trophy circulating among the super-clubs until the music stops. But for Ferguson's United, the Champions League was a prize for which they had to fight for six years, for which they had to endure defeats both crushing and unfortunate.

When it finally came, it was in the most extraordinary manner possible. In 1983–84, Aberdeen had won the Double in Scotland but had lost to Porto in the semi-final of the Cup-Winners' Cup. Ferguson had sniffed a Treble before but had doubted how possible it really was. But 1998–99 was a season to end all seasons, a barely credible story of setbacks overcome, again and again and again. What happened in Turin was merely the centrepiece, an implausible comeback rooted not merely in great character but in a performance that Ferguson described as the best by any team under his management.

The long wait for a first post-Busby league title was achieved, but there could be no standing still. In the summer of 1993, United bought Roy Keane from Nottingham Forest for an English record fee of £3.75 million. After Cantona, it was probably the most important signing of Ferguson's time at the club. Cantona lit the flame, but it was Keane who kept it burning for more than a decade.

United knew better than most how satiation could set in after the achievement of a goal for which they'd been striving for so long, but not under Ferguson. Before the first game of the season, he wrote six names on a piece of paper, placed it in an envelope and locked it in a desk drawer, telling his squad that he'd listed the players he feared might disappoint him and he would check it at the end of the season. In fact, the only name he'd written down was his own, but the ploy – so derided when Brendan Rodgers later attempted it at Liverpool – seemed to work. United lost only one of their first twenty-nine league games of the season, a run that had them seven points clear with a game in hand by the end of February.

They were relentless, so much so that when United lost a 3–0 lead to draw at Liverpool, a furious Ferguson raged at Peter Schmeichel. As the argument grew heated, both exchanged personal insults and, two days later, the manager called the goalkeeper into his office and told him he had to fire him. Schmeichel apologised and went to apologise to his team-mates, precisely the response Ferguson had wanted. The threat of the sack quietly disappeared.

March 1994, though, saw a stutter. There was a defeat to Chelsea and then a run of four red cards in five games: Cantona collected two of them in the space of three days, in draws against Swindon and Arsenal, earning a five-game ban. He'd got away with a dreadful foul on Norwich's Jeremy Goss the previous December. Jimmy Hill described the incident as 'despicable and villainous', at which Ferguson called him 'a prat'. It was a typical response, determined never to criticise his players in public, always willing to build the sense that the world was conspiring against them. Yet in his autobiography, Ferguson himself used the word 'despicable' of Cantona's actions. In that, Ferguson was unapologetically hypocritical and there was perhaps a recurrence of the feeling that had grown up in the sixties of a sense of entitlement around United, as though the rules didn't quite apply to them.

In terms of the championship, it didn't matter: when Cantona returned, he scored three times in April as United went on to win the title by eight points from Blackburn, notching a record ninety-two points. Only a late equaliser from Mark Hughes saved United from defeat to Oldham in the FA Cup semi-final, but they won the replay and then hammered Chelsea 4–0 in the final to win the first Double in the club's history, an achievement that has been cheapened by the regularity with which it has been achieved since but which at the time felt hugely significant. Here was proof that United, an increasingly formidable commercial presence, were the dominant force in English football.

*

With Ryan Giggs injured for the trip to Turin, Jesper Blom-qvist started on the left with Paul Scholes omitted so Nicky Butt could partner Roy Keane in the centre-midfield. The Andy Cole–Dwight Yorke partnership was maintained up front, Ferguson eschewing the cautious option of leaving out one of them and fielding Scholes as a third central midfielder to match Juve shape-for-shape and try to combat the superiority they had had in the middle of the park at Old Trafford. 'They'll start at 100mph, you can be sure of that,' said Ferguson before kick-off. 'They'll try to finish us off, as they always do in the first thirty minutes of matches.' It seemed as if it hadn't taken anywhere near that long.

Not since 1973 had Juventus failed to score in the home leg of a European tie, and it never really looked as though that run would be broken. United had spells of possession early on and Mark Iuliano was fortunate not to be booked for an unpleasant foul on David Beckham, but Juve's threat on the counter was obvious. Twice in the first five minutes, United were almost undone by breaks initiated by Zinedine Zidane: first he slid a ball through for Antonio Conte, Denis Irwin un-easily shepherding the ball back to Schmeichel, and then he picked out Filippo Inzaghi's run off the shoulder of Jaap Stam. The forward chested it down, but Stam's pace allowed him to recover, putting the ball out for a corner.

It was Juve's second corner, after six minutes, that did the damage. Edgar Davids knocked a free-kick to Zidane then seemed to have done too much as the ball was played back to him. He went left, then right, then left again, Keane snapping at his heels before finally space opened up and he played a pass in behind Beckham for Gianluca Pessotto, overlapping from left-back. Beckham got back to slide the ball out of play. Zidane took the corner short to Angelo Di Livio, took the return and whipped a cross to the back post where Inzaghi stole in front of Gary Neville to nudge it over the line from no more than two yards: a classic Inzaghi goal, but, infuriatingly for United, a hugely sloppy one. 'We should be above conceding goals like that,' said Ferguson.

United responded immediately. After a Beckham cross had been cleared, Neville seized on the loose ball and lobbed a pass to Cole, whose overhead was cleverly conceived but straight at Peruzzi. The game fell into an ugly phase of midfield percussion and then, with their next attack, Juventus scored a second goal. Blomqvist was dispossessed by Didier Deschamps. He won the ball back but Keane couldn't retain possession and Di Livio advanced on the Juventus right. He played it forward to Davids, who touched it outside first time for Pessotto. The full-back hit an immediate angled pass for Inzaghi, who gathered it in the top corner of the box. Stam was tight against him, but as Inzaghi shaped to check back across goal, Stam followed the movement. That was just enough, as Inzaghi twisted onto his left foot, to create room for the shot. Stam stretched, but the ball deflected off his boot and looped over Schmeichel. In the eleventh minute, Juve led 2–0. Manchester United, Clive Tyldesley noted in commentary, 'need a minor miracle now'.

Ferguson had spoken of his previous visit to the Stadio delle Alpi, for a group game in 1997: 'I stood in the tunnel before kick-off and the Juventus players made ours look small.' The pattern seemed to be repeating. 'Physically,' Matt Dickinson wrote in *The Times* of that opening spell, 'the Juventus players looked stronger. Mentally, the team from Old Trafford looked as if they were in the grip of paralysing nerves.'

Had United been naive? Certainly Ron Atkinson, the co-commentator, seemed to think so, noting incredulously after United's next attack, as an Irwin shot was blocked at the edge of the box, that they were 'caught with four men upfield', describing that as 'much too cavalier'. As the television coverage dwelt on Ferguson, blankly chewing gum on the touchline, Atkinson continued, 'If he pulls this one out it will be the greatest achievement he's had since he's been at United.'

*

Just as important as progress on the pitch was progress off it. United seized the opportunities offered by the Premier League like no other club. Perhaps the location of Old Trafford, with space to expand, and the club's sense of glamour would always have given it an edge in the commercial boom of the early nineties, but Liverpool were slow to embrace the new era, understandably entering a period of introspection after Hillsborough.

When Sandy Busby's lease on the merchandising stall ran out, it was not renewed. Edwards appointed Tottenham's marketing manager Edward Freedman and he oversaw the construction of a megastore at the ground that was opened by Ferguson in December 1994. Freedman proposed putting names on replica shirts, set up a club magazine, oversaw the production of a video magazine and began wholesaling to stores around the UK and beyond. There were bars, restaurants and a museum: Old Trafford became a tourist attraction. The hooligan edge of the seventies had already melted away and in its place the stereotype grew up of the United fan from the stockbroker belt of Surrey, attracted by glamour and success rather than by any geographical or familial connection. At the same time, shares began to be bought up by larger investors, slowly stifling the (probably always over-romantic) dream of a club owned by its fans.

All that remained, it seemed, was for them to transfer that dominance to Europe. United were hampered, though, by the regulation that defined Scottish, Welsh and Irish players as foreign: they had to field seven English players in every Champions League game. In 1993–94, they went out on away goals to Galatasaray, following a brutal game in Istanbul after which players were attacked by police.

The following season, they were eliminated in the group stage. A 4–0 defeat to a Barcelona side inspired by Romário and Hristo Stoichkov offered an alarming indicator of how far English football had fallen behind the European elite during the years of the Heysel exile. 'It's the only time in my career,'

Pallister said, 'when I thought, "I couldn't get near the man I was supposed to be marking."'

There was a falling-back domestically as well. The 1994 FA Cup final team – Schmeichel; Parker, Bruce, Pallister, Irwin; Kanchelskis, Keane, Ince, Giggs; Cantona, Hughes – was regarded as one of the greatest of all United sides, yet it played together only twelve times, winning on each occasion and scoring twenty-eight goals to four conceded. But after the Cup final, that eleven never played together again.

Ferguson had begun to fall out with Ince, frustrated both by his attitude – as manifested in his insistence he should be nicknamed 'the Guvnor' – and his seeming desire to take on a more attacking role. 'The guvnor nonsense should have been left in the toy-box,' Ferguson said. At half-time in the defeat in the Camp Nou, he singled him out for criticism, calling him 'a bottler'; Ince didn't help his cause by getting sent off in the following Champions League game, away to IFK Gothenburg.

Fearing that Hughes, who had turned thirty in November 1993, was nearing the end of his useful playing career and desperate to bring in another Englishman, Ferguson tried to sign Stan Collymore from Nottingham Forest. When, after numerous inquires had been rebuffed, the Forest manager Frank Clarke was unable to take a call because of flu, Ferguson lost patience and signed Andy Cole from Newcastle for £6 million plus Keith Gillespie.

Twelve days later, Cantona was sent off for the fifth time in his United career in a draw at Crystal Palace in January 1995. As he left the pitch, he reacted to taunts from a Palace fan called Matthew Simmons by launching himself over the advertising hoardings and delivering a flying kick to the chest. United banned him until the end of the season; the FA decided he should be banned for eight months. A magistrates' court sentenced Cantona to two weeks in jail for actual bodily harm, although that was reduced to community service on appeal. At a press conference following his trial, he delivered a single gnomic sentence that would become notorious: 'When the seagulls follow the trawler it is because they think sardines will be thrown into the sea.'

The incident added to United's increasing reputation for thuggishness. Successful sides always stimulate a certain resentment and in United's case it was probably enhanced by their overtly commercial outlook. Ferguson fed off that, using it to build a siege mentality, but at times the fight was carried too far. When Keane was sent off for stamping on Gareth Southgate, the BBC commentator Alan Green called him 'a lout'. Ferguson tracked him down and pinned him to a wall while calling him far worse.

Would Cantona have made a difference in the title run-in? Perhaps. But in his absence, they took thirty-three points from fifteen games to go into the final day of the season two points behind the leaders Blackburn Rovers. But although Blackburn lost at Liverpool, United could only draw at West Ham, Cole being widely blamed for missing a number of chances. A Paul Rideout goal was enough to give Everton victory over United in the FA Cup final. From one point of view it had been a successful season: a point from winning the title and one game from winning the Cup, but Ferguson was desolate.

History has tended to paint what happened that summer as a cull, Ferguson ruthlessly offloading underperformers. It's true that in different circumstances he may have been less willing to let them go but each of the three had specific reasons for going. Hughes was offered a new deal but he was thirty-one and recognised he was unlikely to be a first choice, so left to play regularly at Chelsea; Ferguson in the end was shocked that he left, not realising that he hadn't signed a contract extension because of a concern over pension terms. Kanchelskis had been agitating for a move for some time and, after his agent had applied significant pressure, he went to Everton for £5 million. Had he known that was going to happen, Ferguson maintained, he would never have let Gillespie leave. Only Ince could really be said to have been forced out; he always claimed he'd fancied a move to Italy and had welcomed the transfer to Internazionale. Ferguson had asked the board to sell him four days before the Cup final and had had his doubts confirmed when a forward surge led to Ince losing the ball in the build-up to Everton's goal. And Ferguson may have acted very differently had he not been so convinced of the quality of the Class of '92.

There was no sign of United wilting. Perhaps Juve subconsciously thought the game was won. Perhaps United's task was made less complicated by having to chase. Perhaps it was simply the case that in the opening eleven minutes, although Juventus had scored twice, it hadn't been because they were particularly dominant. Two goals down, United began to take control. Yorke stepped over a low Irwin cross after nineteen minutes and, as Cole lofted the ball on to him, he took it on his chest only to slice wide. In that and a Yorke through-ball to Cole for which he was mystifyingly flagged offside, there were hints of the interplay that had devastated Barcelona in the group stage.

A Schmeichel clearance was flicked on by Butt. Cole ran on and bundled by Iuliano before being pulled back by Ciro Ferrara, who wouldn't have played had Paolo Montero been fit and was clearly nowhere near as mobile as he had been before the knee injury he had suffered the previous year. It was an obvious free-kick and a possible red card but the referee, Urs Meier, chose to wave play on as Peruzzi charged out to divert the ball away from Yorke. It fell for Beckham just outside the box, but his shot was blocked by Ferrara and Cole was – this time, correctly – called offside as the ball spun to him. United were, quite reasonably, frustrated not to get the decision but there was an ominous sense of them beginning to find their rhythm.

Yorke took a throw-in on the right to Neville, who looped it into the box. Pessotto headed clear to Ronny Johnsen, who knocked it back in to Cole, just outside the box with his back to goal. He flicked it to Beckham on the right, who went short to Yorke. He played it back to Neville, who worked it around to the other flank to start again: to Keane, to Stam, to Irwin, to Blomqvist, back to Irwin and then swiftly forward to Cole on the left flank. His cross was blocked by Ferrara and United had a corner. 'The next goal,' said Atkinson, sensing the moment, 'is the most massive goal of this season.'

Beckham whipped the corner to the near post. Keane made a diagonal run and leapt to guide the ball just inside the far post. 'It was as if his will had given the ball no choice but to land in the back of the net,' Ferguson said. There was no overt celebration. He just carried on his run and turned back to the centre-circle. The message was clear: there was still a job to be done and Keane, face set with intent, was going to do it. 'He got a thing in his head to carry the team,' said Butt. From the moment he scored, Keane dominated the game, although asked afterwards how he'd played, he replied merely 'all right'.

With sixty-eight minutes still to go, United were one goal from progress. Juventus had lost only once in twelve matches since Carlo Ancelotti had taken over, but suddenly another stat seemed more telling: it had been ten games since they'd kept a clean sheet. Juve were not the impenetrable force of legend; there was a vulnerability about them. It wouldn't be the last time an Ancelotti side lost a big lead in a European tie, but the three-goal leads he lost in the second leg of a quarter-final against Deportivo La Coruña in 2004 and in the second half of the final against Liverpool in 2005 had not at that stage sullied his reputation.

There followed a spell of midfield probing in which United were clearly the more dangerous. By the midpoint of the half, United had had 62 per cent possession. Yorke took down a ball from Irwin, played a one-two with Cole and dragged his shot from twenty-five yards wide. There was a persistent sense of menace, a feeling that United's front two, with their lively interplay, could open up Juve. Before that night, neither Yorke nor Cole had scored for a month, despite having banged in forty-seven between them that season. Ferguson had given both two games off, including the FA Cup semi-final replay, to restore some freshness, mental as well as physical.

Just as the game seemed to be settling into a pattern of United pressure and Juve resistance, the home side offered a reminder of just how dangerous they could be. Pessotto beat Beckham to a long pass from Johnsen, shook off the mid-fielder and played the ball forward to Di Livio, who passed it straight back to him. He played it inside to Deschamps, who swept a long ball out to the left flank, where Davids knocked it infield with his first touch. The ball was slightly behind Zidane but he checked, recovered it and turned, running at Gary Neville and creating just enough space to hook over a cross. Schmeichel came for it and didn't get there, the ball looping high off Conte's head and dropping goalwards when Stam got in front of Inzaghi to head the ball off the line, a vital intervention.

Undaunted, Schmeichel gathered a corner confidently three minutes later and, with a characteristic bowl out, got the ball swiftly to Yorke in the centre-circle just inside his own half. He played it to Blomqvist, who began to advance and then, forced inside, played a square pass towards Keane. It was slightly in front of him and Keane miscontrolled. Zidane nipped in and, as Keane tried to hook his foot around the ball, he tripped him. He'd got away with a late foul on Davids after eighteen minutes, but Meier would not be so lenient a second time. Keane was booked, and that meant he'd miss the final.

The comparison with Paul Gascoigne on the same ground in a World Cup semi-final nine years earlier was obvious, but there were no tears from Keane. Rather he adjusted his captain's armband, swore at somebody to his left and got on with it, producing perhaps his greatest performance in a United shirt. For weeks after the game, Keane moaned at Blomqvist, blaming his pass for the booking; the Swede always said it was Keane's touch that had been at fault. For Blomqvist, it was that sort of exchange that made United the team they were. He re-called another incident when Schmeichel tried to punch him following a challenge in training; Blomqvist refused to speak to him until he apologised, which he eventually did after two weeks. The capacity to keep coming from behind, he said, was another manifestation of a similar strength of will.

But United's character wasn't just a matter of hard work, argument and a relentless desire for self-improvement. There was also levity and a predictable diet of footballers' japery. David May had joined the club from Blackburn in 1994 and, after taking a year to settle, became the squad's practical joker. While there probably is some truth in his claims that he was essential to morale, his pranks don't seem to have been especially sophisticated, the highlights he lists being cutting the laces of Nicky Butt's trainers and putting Deep Heat in the kit man's shirt. Butt, meanwhile, claimed that he and Giggs were the 'jokers', although again the term is perhaps best understood loosely. Their greatest gags appear to have been filling Gary Neville's car with plastic cups and creeping up behind a naked Peter Schmeichel with a hot tea-urn, the goalkeeper being left with a blistered penis after he turned unexpectedly.

Paul Scholes, Nicky Butt, Gary and Phil Neville and Ryan Giggs all started against Aston Villa in the first game of the 1995–96 season. David Beckham and John O'Kane were on the bench. All seven were graduates of Eric Harrison's youth set-up. Also in the team were Keane, then twenty-four, and Andy Cole, then twenty-three. It was a return to the youth policy Busby had held so dear. United lost 3–1 to Aston Villa, adding to the misgivings of fans, and prompting Alan Hansen's remark on *Match of the Day*, that 'you can't win anything with kids'. It turned out that, in certain exceptional circumstances, you can, particularly when they are backed up by a core of experienced players.

There were a couple of other slip-ups: defeat to York City in the League Cup and an away goals exit to Rotor Volgograd in the Uefa Cup, but United soon found form. Ferguson had had to go to France to persuade Cantona not to join Inter, sneaking out of his hotel through the kitchen while wearing a motorcycle helmet to escape the press, but when the forward returned he was inspired. His first game back from his ban was against Liverpool at the beginning of October and he converted a penalty to equalise in a 2–2 draw. It was the first of thirteen equalisers or winners Cantona scored that season as United reeled in Newcastle, who at one point had headed the table by twelve points. The crunch came as United beat a dogged Leeds 1–0 and Ferguson, echoing comments he had previously made about West Ham, described Howard Wilkinson's side as 'cheating on their manager', pulling out performances only when it suited them. That, for reasons that are not entirely clear, riled Kevin Keegan into his 'I would love it' rant, which was widely interpreted as him having succumbed to a Ferguson mind-game, although Ferguson always insisted his intention had only been to support Wilkinson.

Whether that was the case or not, United wrapped up the title on the final day of the season with a 3–0 victory at Middlesbrough. They added the Cup with a 1–0 win over Liverpool, Cantona scoring the winner with a superb volley in a drab game otherwise memorable only for the (off-)white suits worn by Roy Evans's side. 'I cringed when I saw them,' said Nicky Butt. At the same time, Ferguson's contract negotiations were rumbling on, the board, in his opinion, taking advantage of the fact that he was emotionally committed to the club to deny him what he was rightfully owed. At one point, he was earning a third of Cantona's salary, meaning he wasn't even among the top three best-paid managers in the Premier League.

That summer, United failed to sign Alan Shearer, either because he preferred to join Newcastle United, the club he had supported as a boy or, if Martin Edwards is to be believed, because Blackburn's owner Jack Walker wouldn't sell to United. The end of the three-foreigners rule in European competition meant that was less of a blow than it might have been as United signed Jordi Cruyff, Karel Poborský, Ronny Johnsen, Ole Gunnar Solskjær and Raimond van der Gouw.

The 1996–97 season began with Beckham's chip from the halfway line against Wimbledon, the goal that propelled him into the national consciousness, and, despite a 6–3 defeat to Southampton and a 5–0 defeat at Newcastle in successive games, ended with a fourth league title in five seasons. Europe, though, by then the prime focus, was again a disappointment. United struggled to get through their group in the Champions League, losing their unbeaten home record against Fenerbahçe. A majestic 4–0 demolition of Porto in the home leg of the quarter-final – Ferguson called it a 'peak of excellence' – raised hopes but United fell in the semi-final with what Ferguson described as 'an earthquake of disappointment'.

United had looked to be holding out in the first leg away to Borussia Dortmund, and Butt hit the post, but they conceded a seventy-sixth-minute goal to René Tretschok. Cantona, Ferguson said, had been 'low-key and marginal'. United lost Peter Schmeichel and David May before the second leg, something that, May said, 'spread unease'. They fell behind to a Lars Ricken goal after seven minutes and, despite a string of chances, never quite seemed at their sharpest. 'Some sinister magic,' Ferguson said, 'seemed to be at work.' Cantona, especially, seemed oddly uninspired as United, needing three goals to go through, failed to score any. Ferguson spoke of the Frenchman's 'sluggishness'.

The next day Cantona, whom Ferguson had thought 'subdued' all season, wondering if he were putting on weight, went to see his manager, telling him he was planning to retire. At the end of the season, aged only thirty-one, he confirmed his decision. 'I didn't want to play any more,' he said. 'I'd lost the passion.' He blamed the commercialism at United. 'I didn't play football for business,' he said, saying the club had treated him 'like a pair of socks, like a shirt, like a shit'. Remarkably, he hadn't even been booked since his return from the eight-month ban but, as Wilkinson had feared, once the mood took him, he abruptly packed up and left.

*

With thirty-four minutes gone in Turin, Neville launched a long forward pass to Yorke. Iuliano was close to him, though, and won the ball, clipping it out to Di Livio on the left. Neville waited his moment then inserted his body between Di Livio and the ball, brushing him off and giving himself time to turn. This time his forward pass was aimed at Beckham, who nodded it back for Cole. He lobbed a cross into the box where Yorke, having pulled off the back of Ferrara, beat Peruzzi with a lunging header. For the first time in the tie, United, with the extra away goal, had the advantage. 'The early goals maybe gave the players the impression that it was too easy and from then on they lacked the necessary aggression,' said Ancelotti. 'After we let in the first goal we just could not keep the ball and we could not control the game. We did not have the mentality to carry on with the same style.'

For another side, having an away-goals lead might have been the time to close the game down, but not United. The five minutes after the equaliser were ridiculous, an end-to-end free-for-all that would have seemed more appropriate for the dying seconds as one team sought a goal that would keep them in the tie. Another low cross from Irwin found Cole on the edge of the box. He turned sharply and hit his shot crisply, but it was close enough to Peruzzi that he could make a comfortable save.

A minute later, Di Livio played a ball in from the left for Inzaghi. He had his back to goal and Stam was tight to him, but a key part of the forward's arsenal was his ability to create shooting opportunities. He wriggled to his right and unleashed a shot that struck the advancing Schmeichel in the chest, then, as the rebound came back to him, he couldn't quite direct his effort goalwards.

But it was United who still had the upper hand, playing on a wave of euphoria as though they felt they couldn't lose. Keane's pressure won the ball in midfield and it broke to Beckham. He played it to Neville, took it back, played it to Cole who knocked it to Keane then back to Neville, to Beckham and back to Neville again. The full-back was always looking for a direct pass towards one of the strikers and he played another one, towards Cole. Iuliano got there first but his clearance fell to Yorke who jinked by Pessotto and struck an angled shot from the edge of the box. It zipped across the damp turf and, with Peruzzi beaten, bounced back off the post, just evading Blomqvist as he closed in on the rebound.

United retained their advantage until half-time, thanks in part to two incorrect offside calls that stifled Juve attacks, although it was the away side who still looked the more likely to score. Blomqvist, chasing back, made a superb sliding challenge on Alessandro Birindelli, in at right-back for the suspended Zoran Mirković, gathering the ball and turning in one movement before charging forwards. Yorke had been playing noticeably deeper than he had in the first leg, supporting the midfield and, as he did in this instance, helping create different angles of attack. A quick one-two gave Blomqvist the opportunity to cross, but Ferrara – just – beat Cole to the bouncing ball.

Teddy Sheringham, already thirty-one, was signed from Tottenham for £3.5 million to replace Cantona but, for all his ability, he didn't energise the club as Cantona had. 'He was a good finisher,' said Ferguson, 'especially in the air, and had the tactical perception and passing skills to release other attackers into scoring positions.' It didn't help that Sheringham and Cole didn't get on, supposedly for no better reason than that Cole had replaced Sheringham when making his England debut.

In 1997–98, as Arsène Wenger turned Arsenal into a relentless winning machine, United won nothing. They finished second in the league, went out of the FA Cup to Barnsley and, most gallingly of all, stumbled again in the Champions League. Five wins in their first five games had carried them through their Champions League group to a quarter-final against Monaco and a goalless draw away in the first leg seemed to bode well. But five minutes in, possession was squandered cheaply and David Trezeguet smashed in a vital away goal. Sol-skjær levelled eight minutes into the second half, but it wasn't enough. 'Oh, Teddy, Teddy,' Spurs fans chanted. 'He went to Man United and he won fuck all.' He would soon prove them wrong.

The similarities to the Dortmund game were obvious and, as after the defeat to Partizan in 1966, it began to feel as though United would never win the Champions League. 'Europe had become a personal crusade,' Ferguson acknowledged. 'I knew I would never be judged a great manager until I won the European Cup.'

At least this time, though, United didn't have to win the league again to gain readmittance to the tournament, non-champions having been admitted to the Champions League from 1997–98. Ferguson responded to the disappointment by bringing in Jaap Stam, Jesper Blomqvist and Dwight Yorke for a combined fee of £28 million. The Tobagan's ebullience was a remarkable contrast to the introverted Cole, who was so self-conscious that he once bought a Porsche and couldn't take it out in public for two months, but they nonetheless struck up a formidable partnership.

At last, United were ready for a second European title. It was a season when it seemed United could do no wrong: there were probable victories as well as improbable ones, on and off the pitch.

In September 1998, for instance, Rupert Murdoch's BskyB offered £2.40 per share to buy the club valuing it at £623.4 million. Edwards and most of the board were apparently keen to accept but fans were troubled by the prospect. Andy Walsh of the Independent Manchester United Supporters Association and Michael Crick of Shareholders Utd led a clever campaign against the takeover. The following month, Peter Mandelson, the Trade and Industry Secretary, referred the takeover to the Monopolies and Mergers Commission. The following April, Stephen Byers, who had succeeded Mandelson, announced that the takeover could not go ahead.

Again and again, United staged late recoveries. No game, it seemed, was ever lost. Most dramatic, at least until the very end of the season, was the FA Cup fourth-round tie against Liverpool. United fell behind to a third-minute Michael Owen header. For eighty-six minutes, United trailed. Twice they hit the post. But finally, with two minutes remaining, Beckham shaped a free-kick to the back post where Andy Cole headed down for Yorke to score from close range. A replay? It should have been, but in injury-time, Scholes took down a long ball in the box, Solskjær nicked it off his toes and finished with a crisp low shot. At the time it seemed merely a remarkable comeback, but it would turn out to be a blueprint.

United's start in the league had been little more than adequate: there were too many draws, too many defeats. By Christmas, after failing to win any of their first four games in December, they lay third in the table. There were draws in Europe too, but they were magnificent, memorable ones that hinted at greatness. After beating ŁKS Łódź in the preliminary round, United were drawn in a tough group with Barcelona, Bayern and Brøndby.

'It is the nature of our club always to do it the hard way,' Ferguson said after the semi-final. 'We have done it in the most difficult way possible. We conceded two goals but they composed themselves well and started to express themselves. Everyone showed the courage to play and the ability to do it. The first goal gave us options and hope and from that moment on, Juventus were nervous at the back.'

It was no great surprise that two defenders were replaced before the second half began. Iuliano went off for Montero, while Birindelli was replaced by Nicola Amoruso, with Di Livio dropping in to right-back as the shape shifted to a lopsided 4-3-1-2 with Conte playing far wider on the right than Davids did on the left.

United, though, continued to have more of the ball, playing with an easy swagger. Ferguson had urged his side at the break to 'concentrate and keep going for that third goal', while complaining about the 'two sloppy goals' they'd conceded. However dangerous United looked going forward, that defensive laxity meant they could never be entirely secure. In the fifth minute of the second half there came a warning as Zidane lifted a cross into the box from the left. Stam was caught between the two strikers with Johnsen too far forward to make a difference. The ball floated just over Amoruso, though, and Stam, falling backwards, was able to scuff the ball away as Inzaghi lurked behind him.

They had more good fortune a couple of minutes later as Zidane slipped a pass through for Inzaghi. Schmeichel was out quickly to smother but perhaps made contact with Inzaghi before the ball – largely, it should be said, because the forward made sure he did; Meier didn't have a decision to take, the flag having already, incorrectly, gone up. The lesson still wasn't learned. Not a minute had passed when Pessotto played a familiar angled ball into the box, finding Inzaghi as he made a diagonal run between the centre-backs. This time he got a clean shot away, but Schmeichel saved with his feet.

That Inzaghi run had been a persistent threat and there seemed a deliberate policy on the part of Juve to attack down their left, the United right, despite having the midfielder Di Livio at right-back. Amoruso touched on a Pessotto ball for Zidane, who, with space on the left, sent over a cross that Stam cut out at the near post. United, by then, seemed to have slipped into a position in which they were never entirely comfortable, protecting what they had rather than chasing another goal. Just after the hour, Irwin swept a ball down the left for Cole – that long pass from the full-back into the channel was a clear tactic. The forward nodded it back for Yorke, floating again in that deep-lying position. He moved it infield but no United player seemed willing to take a shot as the ball was worked square. Eventually Beckham hooked it into the box, where the presence of Keane was enough to persuade Ferrara to concede a corner. Beckham took it, but Peruzzi had only to take a hop to his right to save Yorke's header.

Juventus, though, without reaching the heights they had in the first half of the first leg, were enjoying their best period of the game. Johnsen was penalised as he jumped with Zidane just inside the United half. Deschamps took the free-kick quickly to Conte who played it to Zidane and back to Deschamps and then out to Di Livio wide on the right. His cross was headed out by Stam, but, on the edge of the box, Blomqvist was beaten to it by Conte. The ball fell for Deschamps twelve yards out to the right of goal, but he slipped as he shot and although his mishit effort beat Schmeichel it was drifting wide when Inzaghi knocked it in. He ran away, arms outstretched in celebration, but the linesman's flag was correctly raised.

United had grown wary and it seemed indicative of their reduced ambitions that when Beckham won a free-kick on the right a couple of minutes later, luring Montero into the sort of block for which he was notorious, only Cole and Yorke were in the box as United's number 7 arced his delivery across goal. Soon after that Cole won possession about ten yards inside the Juve half. He shifted it right to Butt, who slipped it to Yorke cutting in from the right. With nobody in the box, though, he attempted an ambitious chip and skewed the ball way over the bar. The point was less the attempt than that he'd been forced into it: United had simply stopped getting men forward.

Zidane, at last, began to exert real influence. Deschamps carried the ball forward and gave it to his compatriot just inside the United half. Zidane surged forwards with that characteristic stooped, muscular gait, gliding away from Keane and then sending Butt to ground with a dragback. Conte hurtled outside him and Zidane pushed the ball into his path. Another touch and Amoruso had it on the edge of the box, but Stam was there to shrug the forward aside. After his early struggles with the movement of Inzaghi, the Dutchman had become an increasingly commanding figure and he headed out a Pessotto cross soon after.

United, though, were shaking. Ferguson responded by withdrawing Blomqvist for Scholes, with Butt moving out to the left. Seconds after he had made the change, though, a long punt from Ferrara dropped over Johnsen. Inzaghi had stolen between him and Neville but the bounce of the ball was high enough for Johnsen to recover.

United had begun their Champions League campaign against Louis van Gaal's Barcelona at Old Trafford, a game of stunning quality. Giggs headed in a sweeping Beckham cross to give United the lead. Another Beckham cross set up a second, Scholes following in after Yorke's brilliant overhead had been saved. But in the second half Barça came back first through Sonny Anderson, then a Giovanni penalty. A thirty-yard Beckham free-kick restored United's advantage, but Nicky Butt was then sent off after handling a goal-bound shot, Luís Enrique converting another penalty for a 3–3 draw.

A 2–2 draw in Munich followed, before a pair of convincing victories over Brøndby took United top of the group. Barcelona, after twice losing to Bayern, had to beat United at the Camp Nou to have a chance of progressing. It was another breathtaking game. Anderson struck after forty-nine seconds to give Barça the lead, but Yorke cancelled that out after twenty-five minutes, running on to a Blomqvist pass and finishing crisply from the edge of the box.

Eight minutes into the second half, United took the lead. Yorke stepped over a Beckham pass to allow it to run to Cole, then took his pass and returned it to give his strike partner a relatively simple finish. Their partnership was devastating, a wholly natural connection, Yorke said, something that barely had to be worked on in training. A Rivaldo free-kick levelled the scores four minutes later, but Yorke headed in a Beckham cross to put United 3–2 up. Rivaldo equalised with an overhead kick, but the draw was enough to put Barça out. A draw at Old Trafford against Bayern, though, meant United went through only as one of the two best runners-up. Where Bayern got a relatively simple tie against Kaiserslautern, one they won 6–0 over the two legs, United faced Internazionale.

The opener at Old Trafford came after six minutes, Beckham's cross being diverted past Gianluca Pagliuca by a diving Yorke. Another Beckham cross and another Yorke header made it 2–0 just before half-time, a lead they took to the San Siro. There, United survived a sustained assault until Nicola Ventola, running on to a scooped pass from Benoît Cauet, gave Inter the lead after sixty-three minutes. But United sealed the tie with two minutes remaining, Cole heading a Gary Neville cross down for Scholes to finish calmly.

By the beginning of April, United were in the semi-finals of both the FA Cup and the Champions League, while a run of nine wins in ten league games had taken them top of the table. The chance was there for a Treble unprecedented in English football history.

The month began poorly. United drew at Wimbledon and struggled against Juventus in the home leg, falling behind midway through the first half as Davids slipped in Conte to score with a smart shot across Schmeichel. 'In those first forty-five minutes, we might have lost three goals,' Ferguson acknowledged. But this was a season when everything United did best had involved them falling behind. Beckham played a little narrower in the second half and helped cut off the supply to the Juve forwards. The match became a constant wave of United pressure. Sheringham had a goal ruled out for a marginal offside. Peruzzi made a string of saves. And then at last, deep into injury-time – because that season it was always at last, deep into injury-time – Beckham hooked a ball across goal, it was headed on twice and Giggs at the back post lashed the ball into the roof of the net. United had a draw to take to Turin.

Before that, there was an FA Cup semi-final to be played against Arsenal, who had emerged as United's main domestic rivals. The first game finished goalless; the replay three days later was yet another scarcely credible game in a season packed with them. Sheringham created space with an abrupt turn that drew three defenders for Beckham, who whipped a shot just inside the post from twenty-five yards to give United a first-half lead. Bergkamp levelled from similar range midway through the second half and the game seemed to lurch decisively Arsenal's way as Keane was sent off for a second bookable offence. In the final minute of normal time, Arsenal were handed the chance to win it when Phil Neville tripped Ray Parlour just inside the box. Schmeichel, though, saved Bergkamp's penalty and with eleven minutes to go in extra-time came one of the Cup's most famous goals. A wayward Patrick Vieira pass gifted Giggs possession just inside his own half and he set off on a forward charge that took him by Vieira and Lee Dixon, then between Dixon and Fredrik Ljungberg. From the angle of the six-yard box, he thrashed a shot over David Seaman and United were in the final.

However nervous they were in their away-goals lead, United remained dangerous. Butt flicked on a Schmeichel kick for Cole, who knocked it back to him. He played it to Yorke, who sent it right to Keane. He spread it wide for Beckham, who went back to Keane. He played it to Neville, who played that familiar long ball down the channel, this time for Yorke. Forced wide and with two men on him, Yorke squeezed it back to Beckham. He nudged it to Keane, who measured a pass down the line through the smallest of gaps for Yorke. He went back and inside for Scholes, about thirty-five yards out in the centre of the pitch, and he worked it left for Irwin. Juve seemed strangely to pause and as they waited to see to whom he would pass, Irwin set off on a run. He went outside Conte and inside Di Livio and, from the edge of the box struck a firm low shot that beat Peruzzi but came back off the inside of the post. The ball flew almost directly back at him but he couldn't control the rebound and his second attempt drifted into the side-netting at the near post.

Twice Cole almost got onto long balls played in behind the

Juve defence, the first time slipping as he turned, the second being beaten to Beckham's pass by Peruzzi. There was, perhaps, the slightest contact between Cole and the goalkeeper as they ran past each other, enough for Ferrara to react furiously, pushing his palm into Cole's face. If Cole hadn't looked so bemused, if he'd gone down, the defender could easily have been sent off.

As Juve's need became more urgent they became ever more direct. Increasingly, patient build-up was eschewed for direct balls into the box. An Inzaghi knock-on almost found Conte, but Beckham, covering diligently, swept up. Conte smashed a cross far too long. But with fourteen minutes to play and just as United seemed to be locking the game down there came a major blow. Scholes, as he was always prone to do, lunged in needlessly on Deschamps. Deschamps's foot was arguably high, but Scholes's challenge was two-footed and he was booked, meaning that, like Keane, he would miss the final through suspension. He looked appalled and threw his hands down but, like Keane, seemed immediately to settle to the more immediate task, a neat sidestep and jink allowing him to feed the ball wide to Beckham.

United calmly maintained possession and won a corner as a Beckham cross was blocked. Keane, making a similar run to the one that had brought his first-half goal, just failed to reach Beckham's delivery but the ball came to Johnsen, whose header was blocked. United recycled, running down more valuable seconds before another Beckham cross was deflected behind.

Ancelotti made his final change, bringing off Di Livio for the Uruguayan centre-forward Daniel Fonseca. He was involved immediately, thrusting his left thigh in the way of Yorke's header from Beckham's cross to divert it behind for another corner. This time Beckham played it short to Scholes. It was rolled back to him but, for once, his delivery was poor and Peruzzi gathered at his near post.

The game had become stretched, a dozen or more players

chasing Peruzzi's clearance in a loose gaggle. Inzaghi, the referee decided, had been fouled in the midst of it. The free-kick was worked wide to Fonseca on the right. He crossed left-footed towards Amoruso, but Johnsen got in a clearing header to concede a corner. Fonseca slung it in but Schmeichel, two-handed, fisted it clear. Yorke jumped for the loose ball with Davids, who had been far quieter than at Old Trafford. The ball broke for Beckham, who gave it back to Yorke and began a sprint upfield. Yorke miscontrolled but had time to gather himself, turn and send a pass into the path of the tireless Keane. He knocked it by Montero and seemed to be fouled by him, but Meier allowed play to continue. 'Roy,' said Cole, 'was mind-boggling.'

There were nine minutes plus injury-time to go. Zidane took a throw on the left, got the ball back and played that same diagonal pass into the box that had been troubling United all night. This time the recipient was Fonseca, who was forced wide. He cut the ball back and Inzaghi couldn't quite stretch to meet it.

Scholes intercepted a Montero pass midway inside the United half. He knocked it right for Beckham. There was an acute consciousness at that point that every pass took United closer to the final. Beckham advanced then went inside for Keane. He laid it off first time for Neville, who looked up but, for once, decided against the long pass down the channel. He clipped it awkwardly into the centre-circle for Scholes, who turned and played it to Butt. He helped the ball left to the advancing Irwin. He went forward to Yorke, who strolled at Fonseca, threatening a trick that never came. As Zidane moved over to close him down, Yorke checked back and rolled the ball to Butt. The midfielder advanced, stopped, and went back to Scholes, who prodded it to Keane back in the centre-circle. He twisted back with the outside of his right foot and gave it to Neville who made a startled sprint forward as though excited by the space in front of him, then slowed and rolled the ball square inside for Scholes. He took a touch and played it back out to Beckham, a model of nonchalance. With his left foot Beckham scooped it forward for Neville who had continued his run. He cut it back for Yorke on the edge of the box, and he ran at Ferrara, jinking once then twice before teeing up Cole, whose shot was hit with no great power and was comfortably saved by Peruzzi. Butt, who had been unmarked to Cole's left, was furious the ball hadn't been helped on another stage to him. The whole move had taken fifty seconds, vital time in which Juve could feel the game slipping away from them.

A long ball from Davids landed in Schmeichel's arms. Six minutes and forty-five seconds, plus injury-time, remained. Schmeichel went long, his kick dropping perhaps eight yards outside the Juventus box. Ferrara, back-pedalling awkwardly, miscued, the ball bouncing of his shin as he tried to volley clear and falling for Yorke. With just two off-balance defenders between him and the goal he charged, jinking between them. Suddenly it was Yorke against Peruzzi. He checked then prodded the ball to his right. Peruzzi lunged clumsily and pulled him down. It was an obvious penalty and a red card – but it didn't matter. The ball rolled on to Cole and, from a narrow angle, he tapped in his finish. United led 3–2 and Juventus needed to score twice.

Beckham almost volleyed a fourth after an Irwin run down the left, but even without that, Juventus were done. 'Juventus are a proper football club,' said Cole. 'They had great players like Zidane and we'd just smashed them everywhere, physically and tactically.' For the first time in seven seasons there was no Italian side in the final: United had had to beat two of them to get there. They'd won in Italy for the first time, at the eighth attempt, and had done so deservedly, having had fourteen attempts on goal to Juve's five, having scored three and hit the post twice. 'The maturing of Manchester United,' Matt Dickinson wrote in *The Times*, 'is complete.'

The only blight on a brilliant evening was the suspensions to Scholes and Keane. 'Inside I am hurting and feeling the disappointment,' Keane said, 'but Manchester United is always bigger than any individual. The most important thing now is that we go on to win the final. I knew as soon as I made the tackle that I would miss it, but now we all just have to look forward and hope we can win this competition.'

For the final eight games of the league season, United alternated draws and wins. Arsenal's defeat to Leeds in their second-last game of the season gave United an edge, but they failed to take advantage the following night, being held to a goalless draw by Blackburn. That meant they went into the final match, at home to Tottenham, a point clear. Arsenal did what they could by beating Aston Villa but United, having – of course – fallen behind, won 2–1 to regain the title. The following weekend they beat Newcastle 2–0 in an anticlimactic Cup final to complete a third Double in five years. All that was left was to win the trophy they'd been chasing for thirty-one years.

For much of the Champions League final against Bayern, that didn't seem likely. With Keane and Scholes suspended, United began with Beckham and Butt in the middle, Ryan Giggs switched to the right and Blomqvist on the left. Ferguson had considered playing Giggs through the middle but had decided his pace would trouble Michael Tarnat, the Bayern left-back. The new system didn't work, although Ferguson claimed in his autobiography that Beckham was 'the most effective midfielder on the pitch' and that Giggs's running and the need for Bayern to help Tarnat had worn them out.

It was as though it was all too much, that the toll of reaching the final after a decade of struggle had worn the players down; and nobody was unaware of the symbolism of the game falling on what would have been Matt Busby's ninetieth birthday. Bayern dominated the centre of the pitch and the majority of the game. They took a sixth-minute lead as Markus Babbel blocked off Butt on the end of the wall, creating space for Mario Basler's low free-kick to zip low past an unsighted Schmeichel.

As Martin Thorpe wrote in the *Guardian*, United were 'riding their luck' to get to half-time just one goal down. It was then that Ferguson gave a team-talk that would enter legend. 'You will be six feet away from the European Cup,' he said, 'but you won't be able to touch it. I want you to think about the fact that you'll have been so close to it and for many of you it will be the closest you ever get. And you will hate that thought for the rest of your lives. So just make sure you don't lose. Don't you dare come back in here without giving your all.'

Yet however vaunted that speech has become, the truth is that United didn't particularly improve after half-time and Bayern very nearly added a second in the seventy-ninth minute as Mehmet Scholl's chip hit the bar. 'I didn't turn round because I knew that was 2–0,' said Schmeichel. 'When it came straight back to me I knew we would win.' Four minutes later Carsten Jancker headed a corner against the woodwork.

A frustrated George Best left the stadium to find a bar. As the fourth official held up the board indicating there'd be three minutes of injury-time, the Uefa president Lennart Johansson left his seat in the executive box to go down to the pitch to present the trophy. Stefan Effenberg blocked a Gary Neville cross to concede a corner. Beckham, pushing back against a crowd of photographers, swung it in. Schmeichel, having gone forward in one last desperate bid to salvage the game, jumped for the header and got a touch that sent the ball beyond the backpost where Yorke, back-pedalling, miscontrolled. Thorsten Fink jabbed at the bouncing ball and sent it out of the box to Giggs. He hit a first-time shot. It was scuffed, but six yards out Sheringham, who had come on as a sixty-seventh-minute substitute for Blomqvist, pivoted and hooked the ball over the line. Johansson reached the side of the pitch, saw the celebrations, and turned back to watch extra-time from the executive box. He never got there.

Solskjær, an eighty-first-minute substitute for Cole, forced a corner off Sammy Kuffour's shins. Beckham took it. Sheringham, running across the near post, won the header, but didn't get quite enough purchase on it. It flashed across goal and seemed to be heading wide when Solskjær, from no more than three yards, stabbed it over the line. Johansson turned back for the pitch, having missed the most preposterous finish to any major final in history.

As the players paraded on an open-top bus through Manchester, Yorke contemplated retiring there and then: what, he wondered, could ever match up to this?

CHAPTER 9

Champions League final, Luzhniki Stadium, Moscow, 21 May 2008

Manchester United   **1–1**   **Chelsea**

Ronaldo 26　　　　　　　　　　*Lampard 45*

(Manchester United won 6–5 on penalties)

Tévez (scored)	*Ballack (scored)*
Carrick (scored)	*Belletti (scored)*
Ronaldo (missed)	*Lampard (scored)*
Hargreaves (scored)	*A Cole (scored)*
Nani (scored)	*Terry (missed)*
Anderson (scored)	*Kalou (scored)*
Giggs (scored)	*Anelka (missed)*

Edwin van der Sar	Petr Čech
Wes Brown (Anderson 120)	Michael Essien
Rio Ferdinand	Ricardo Carvalho
Nemanja Vidić	John Terry
Patrice Evra	Ashley Cole
Owen Hargreaves	Claude Makelele (Juliano Belletti 120)
Paul Scholes (Ryan Giggs 87)	Michael Ballack
Michael Carrick	Frank Lampard
Cristiano Ronaldo	Joe Cole (Nicolas Anelka 99)
Wayne Rooney (Nani 101)	Florent Malouda (Salomon Kalou 92)
Carlos Tévez	Didier Drogba
Alex Ferguson	Avram Grant

Ref: Ľuboš Micheľ

Bkd: Scholes, Ferdinand, Vidić, Tévez; Makelele, Carvalho, Ballack, Essien

Sent off: Drogba

Att: 67,310

THE PROBLEM AFTER A GREAT TRIUMPH, as United had found before, is where you go next: 1998–99 was a season that couldn't be repeated. Perhaps there could be another Treble season, but it surely wouldn't come with quite so many ridiculous comebacks, with quite so many brilliant games. United, anyway, ensured there wouldn't be another Treble the following year, bowing to FA pressure to withdraw from the FA Cup to play in the inaugural Club World Cup, something that, it was believed, would help England's chances of winning the right to host the 2006 World Cup.

It proved a dreadful decision, both for the FA Cup and for United – and it did nothing at all to help England combat the machinations of the German bid or the emotional pull of South Africa. The FA Cup was devalued, England's bid looked naive and for United the trip to Brazil for the Club World Cup was a shambles. A late Dwight Yorke equaliser salvaged a point against the Mexican side Necaxa after Beckham had been sent off, then Romário tormented them again as Vasco da Gama put them out of the tournament with a 3–1 win.

But even before Brazil, there was a sense that things weren't quite as they had been, that an intensity had been lost. In the summer of 1999, United toured Australia. The players, it's fair to say, didn't take things entirely seriously. At one training session at the Olympic Stadium in Sydney, Yorke fell asleep while stretching; the rest of the players went for a run, leaving him dozing in a sitting position.

Domestically at least United didn't need to be fully focused. They won the league comfortably, amassing ninety-one points, a record for a thirty-eight-game season, but there were troubling signs of decline. 'We got to the stage where we didn't really enjoy winning in the league,' Nicky Butt said, 'because it was the norm.'

Peter Schmeichel, at thirty-five, had left for Sporting in the summer, going out at the summit, and neither Mark Bosnich nor Massimo Taibi really convinced as replacements. Beckham married but rather than seeing that as a sign he was settling down, Ferguson was concerned by the influence of his wife, Victoria, and the lure of a celebrity lifestyle. When Beckham skipped training to look after his ill son and Victoria was that night photographed at a London Fashion Week event, Ferguson was furious, fining him two weeks' wages and suspending him from the following game, a 1–0 win against Leeds.

Yorke too had dalliances with a showbiz world of which Ferguson emphatically disapproved, and the decision to sign Ruud van Nistelrooy was in part provoked by that. A £19 million fee was agreed with PSV but the medical showed up problems and a few days later the striker collapsed in training in Eindhoven with a serious knee injury. The deal eventually went through in spring 2001.

Yet the game that really raised questions was never as bad as it was made out to be, as Rob Smyth outlines in Issue One of *The Blizzard*. United had passed comfortably enough through the two group stages of the Champions League to reach a quarter-final against Real Madrid. A 0–0 draw at the Bernabéu seemed to have given them the edge but was seen by some as a missed opportunity against a Madrid side having an awful domestic season. 'In the first game,' said the substitute goalkeeper Raimond van der Gouw, 'we had too much respect for the name Real Madrid.'

Did that stem from Ferguson? Perhaps. Neither Denis Irwin nor Gary Neville played with much adventure that night, but was that tactical or psychological? Ferguson, wrote his main press-box confidant Hugh McIlvanney the following Sunday, 'was sincerely dismayed by the drop in standards we had witnessed: the mental and physical sluggishness that allowed Real long periods of comfortable possession, the basic flaws in ball control and passing, the failure to match the fluency of the opposition's movement. But his hard words are better understood in the context of his pre-match feelings. "I was looking forward to the meeting with Real Madrid and wanted to use it as a platform to let everybody know Manchester United are the best in the game," he told me later in the week. "Real are the team with the greatest record in the European Cup and we were facing them on their own midden. I was disappointed, and so were the players, that we didn't take the opportunity to show our true worth."'

The second leg is widely misremembered now, goals leading the narrative. Real Madrid got three in the first fifty-two minutes and then, with the game as good as lost, United scored twice. This was not, though, a case of their being outplayed, being taught a lesson by continental sophisticates. Ferguson castigated himself for not reacting to Madrid's unexpected 3-3-2-2 formation by switching to a 4-3-3, but United still created chance after chance. Yes, they were too open. Yes, they never controlled the game. Yes, their cavalier approach opened the door to misfortune. But the fact remains that they lost largely because luck, after a lengthy spell on their side, deserted them.

Roy Keane diverted a Michel Salgado cross into his own net after twenty minutes and, as so often, reacted to adversity thrillingly. With Keane at their heart, United created six clear chances before half-time. But Iker Casillas was brilliant in goal and when he was beaten by a Cole header Aitor Karanka pushed the ball over the bar with his hand – and got away with it. Had the penalty been awarded, had the defender been shown a red card, the outcome might have been very different.

Five minutes into the second half, Madrid cleared a United free-kick. A three-on-two break opened up. Steve McManaman and Raúl worked the opportunity perfectly, the latter getting the goal. Within seconds of the restart, Keane had fired over the bar with Casillas out of the picture and only Roberto Carlos on the line to beat and then, 138 seconds after his first goal, Raúl added his second, tapping in after Fernando Redondo had devastated Henning Berg with a backheel nutmeg. David Beckham pulled one back and Paul Scholes converted a penalty three minutes from time but even for this United, who had come from behind to draw or win thirty-one times since the beginning of the 1998–99 season, the deficit was too much, the time remaining too short.

Narrow and unfortunate though the defeat had been – Ferguson said that if the match had been played ten times, United would have won seven – its impact was profound. 'One of the forceful reminders delivered by that defeat was that consistent success in Europe would be more readily achieved if we improved our capacity to defend against the counter-attack,' Ferguson said. No longer would United base their approach on trying to outscore the opposition. Defeats away to PSV and Anderlecht in autumn 2000 confirmed the lesson: United had been vulnerable to the counter-attack in both games, losing 3–1 and 2–1. No longer would there be a sense that any setback could be overcome. Previously Ferguson's reasoning had seemed to be that if you had fifteen chances and the opposition five, you would win more often than not; after Madrid the theory seemed to run that if you had five chances and the opposition none, you couldn't lose. Madrid confirmed the lessons of Monaco and Dortmund. 'Manchester are a very good side,' the great former AC Milan coach Arrigo Sacchi said after the quarter-final. 'But their win last season was exceptional. Madrid, I believe, are more likely to win the Champions League on a regular basis. Their style of play, alone, means they are better equipped to dominate Europe.'

The shift of approach would prove traumatic, as Roy Keane predicted at the time. 'You can't keep giving yourselves mountains to climb, especially against the top teams,' he said. 'But it is the way we play and I think it will be hard for us to change.'

Ostensibly the pattern seemed to be repeated in 2000–01

as Fabian Barthez arrived to take over in goal. With their few rivals woefully inconsistent, United surged to a league title with such ease that it was hard to regard it as much of an achievement. It was their seventh title in nine years and included a 6–1 win over the side who finished second, Arsenal. Europe, though, was a different matter. Again they reached the quarter-final, and this time they lost 3–1 over two legs to Bayern. 'Maybe this is the end of the road for this team,' said Keane. 'Maybe it is time to move on. We've given our all and we're just not good enough.' Part of the problem was that at home they were rather too good; as many teams have found, domination of a domestic league can leave a side without the necessary hardness to fight against more evenly matched opponents.

That wasn't Keane's only outburst that season. In the November, troubled by the flat atmosphere in a 1–0 home win over Dynamo Kyiv, he railed against the Old Trafford crowd, accusing them of being more interested in their prawn sandwiches than the match. Many older fans agreed with him; the nature of United's support had changed. Commercialism had won; corporate support had diluted the raucousness of old. The protestations of United's commercial manager that there were no prawn sandwiches on offer at Old Trafford did little to deflect the barb; it hardly invalidated Keane's complaint that the menu was far more sophisticated than that.

Whatever the reason, the admission was damning. In March 2000, a month before the defeat to Real Madrid, Ferguson's assistant Steve McClaren had made an attempt to define greatness in a football team, effectively setting out what United, the reigning European champions, hoped to achieve. 'While you are top of the pile it is very, very important to continue winning and then you will become one of the legendary sides,' he said. 'That means winning the European Cup two, three, four out of five years. The players want to do that. They are a great team, but I believe they can be so much better and become one of the all-time legendary teams.'

Alex Ferguson turned sixty on 31 December 2001. Intimations of mortality had begun to trouble him; he was haunted by the memory of Jock Stein, then sixty-two, collapsing next to him on the touchline at Ninian Park in 1985. Ferguson had made United the third club in English history to win three successive league titles, but he knew that it was winning a second Champions League that would elevate him into the ranks of indisputable international greatness. The 2002 Champions League final was at Hampden Park, where he had watched in awe as Real Madrid beat Eintracht Frankfurt 7–3 in the 1960 European Cup final. In his home city, it would be the perfect stage, he decided, to bid farewell. Ferguson announced he would like to retire. Initially he planned a clean break with the club but then committed to a roving ambassadorial role worth £1 million a year. Privately, Martin Edwards was irritated, knowing the damage Busby's lingering presence had done, but, having stood down as chairman in 2000 to be replaced by the former Umbro executive Peter Kenyon, he lacked the authority to do anything about it.

There were significant differences between Edwards and Kenyon. Edwards had always been cautious with the finances to the point of irritating Ferguson, who had been baffled since the mid-nineties that George Graham at Arsenal should earn twice as much as him. Kenyon was far more prone to spending. He upped Ferguson's salary for what was supposed to be his final season at the club to £3 million a year, and released funds for the £18.5 million signing of Ruud van Nistelrooy and of Juan Sebastián Verón for £28 million. Verón was on £80,000 a week, shattering the traditional tight wage structure at the club. There was also a significant departure in 2001, with Jaap Stam sold to Lazio in the September. Ferguson claimed that he'd slowed after an injury, but it was widely believed he was offloaded for comments he'd made about other players in his autobiography. Laurent Blanc, then thirty-five, was brought in as a replacement.

By early December 2001, United had the second-worst

defensive record in the league. By Christmas, they had suffered six league defeats. Barthez was error-prone, the ageing Blanc was not as commanding as Stam and Verón looked bewildered by the pace of the Premier League. There were tactical issues: the decision to break up the Beckham-Keane-Scholes-Giggs midfield by bringing in Verón and using Scholes behind Van Nistelrooy affected United's rhythm, however reasonable the decision to add an extra body in central midfield in European competition may have been. Ferguson became increasingly frustrated by Verón. Although he defended him vehemently at the time – 'He's a fucking great player and youse are all fucking idiots,' he once shouted at journalists after one question too many about the Argentinian – he later admitted his lack of positional discipline had been a major problem: 'He just played everywhere. He went where he liked. If I managed him for a hundred years I wouldn't know where to play him.'

But the factor most widely blamed was Ferguson's decision to retire, which rendered even somebody of his authority and ferocity a lame duck. Then, in February, Ferguson announced that he had changed his mind. The trigger was unclear. Gary Neville said he persuaded Ferguson to stay by pointing out he only had twelve games left. Perhaps he simply wanted to leave on a high. Ferguson himself has always said that it was his wife, Cathy, who made him realise his mistake, asking him what on earth he was going to do with himself.

United, after a remarkable surge that saw them win eleven of twelve league games, came third in the league, but the dream of a Champions League success at Hampden remained alive until the semi-final, in which United were beaten on away goals by Klaus Toppmöller's Bayer Leverkusen. Keane, furious at what he saw as United's sloppiness, raged that they had lost their hunger.

There was perhaps an issue, too, with the coaching. Steve McClaren had replaced Brian Kidd when the former United striker took the Blackburn job in 1998 but had departed two years later to take charge of Middlesbrough. He was succeeded by Jim Ryan but players spoke of finding his sessions unin-spiring. Ferguson responded in 2002 by bringing in the Portuguese former South Africa manager Carlos Queiroz. His influence, coupled with the frustration of the regular near misses in Europe, led to United becoming far cagier.

Adaptation takes time and United's start to 2002–03 was in-different, five defeats in the first twenty games leaving them third on Boxing Day. The new signing Rio Ferdinand, bought from Leeds for £29.3 million, struggled with injury, as did Beckham and Keane; the latter was also dealing with the fall-out of his departure from the Ireland squad at the previous summer's World Cup. United lost 3–1 to City in the last derby at Maine Road, prompting such a tirade from Ferguson that Gary Neville said he'd never seen his manager so angry.

Everywhere, it seemed, there were distractions. In Febru-ary 2003, the Irish businessman and racehorse owner John Magnier told Ferguson that he did not in fact own a stake in the stud rights in Rock of Gibraltar, a hugely successful horse that ran out of Magnier's Coolmore stables in Ferguson's red colours. Ferguson was always listed as the owner at race meet-ings and he believed there was a verbal agreement giving him a half-share despite there being no formal documentation. The stud fees were estimated as being worth £3 million a year over ten years.

The following day, United hosted Arsenal in the fifth round of the FA Cup and lost 2–0. Ferguson, angered at the way Beck-ham had failed to track back in the build-up to the second goal, lost his temper in the dressing room and kicked out at a boot. It flew up and caught Beckham just above the eye, leav-ing him with a small gash that was soon covered by a neatly heroic plaster. Ferguson had already begun to be frustrated by Beckham's courting of celebrity – most notoriously when he announced he was to reveal a new haircut at a game and wore a beanie for a day beforehand to disguise the fact he'd had his head shaved – but 'the main issue,' Ferguson wrote in his most recent autobiography, 'was that his application level had dropped from its traditionally stratospheric level.' From then on, Beckham's departure felt inevitable and he moved to Real Madrid in the summer. 'The minute a Manchester United player thought he was bigger than the manager, he had to go.'

Yet, despite the chaos, United took fifty-one points from their final nineteen games of the season to surge past Arsenal and claim the title. That success took Ferguson past Bob Paisley's record of seven league titles and meant he had won more trophies than all other United managers combined.

The Champions League, though, brought familiar disappointment. United won 3–0 at Juventus in the second group stage, but lost 3–1 away to Real Madrid in the first leg of the quarter-final and although Beckham, coming off the bench to score twice and claim the limelight, ensured they won 4–3 at home, Ronaldo's hat-trick had already meant the tie was beyond them. The lasting significance of the game, in fact, had little directly to do with United; it was watching the seven goals at Old Trafford that supposedly persuaded the Russian oligarch Roman Abramovich to find a football club in which to invest.

Chelsea wasn't the only club whose ownership came under discussion that summer. John de Mol, the Dutch television executive behind *Big Brother*, bought 2.9 per cent of United's shares. Dermot Desmond, the owner of Celtic, bought a further 2 per cent, as did the owner of Tampa Bay Buccaneers, Malcolm Glazer. But the biggest investors were Cubic, the Magnier–McManus horse-racing group.

That autumn, Ferguson sued Magnier for his share of Rock of Gibraltar. Magnier and Cubic stepped up their assault on Old Trafford. By November they had bought Rupert Murdoch's stake, leaving them with 21 per cent of the club. They began asking awkward questions about Ferguson's salary and about exactly who had acted as agent in certain players' deals after it had been revealed in Michael Crick's biography of Ferguson that there was a close relationship between the club and the agency run by Ferguson's son, Jason. David Gill, in a defensive move, began to encourage the other new investors to increase their stakes. By November, Glazer had 14 per cent. In early March, Ferguson reached a private settlement with Magnier thought to be worth £2.5 million. That at least headed off the prospect of a Cubic takeover, but on the pitch the season was already set on a frustrating course.

Ferguson had offloaded Verón to Chelsea in the summer, but the three signings he made were of distinctly mixed quality. 'We rushed down the path of buying in proven players,' Ferguson acknowledged. On the debit side, there were Kleberson and Eric Djemba-Djemba, two midfielders who never looked remotely equipped to thrive in the Premier League; on the profit side was Cristiano Ronaldo, young and raw but ready to fulfil Ferguson's promise that 'he is going to be the best player in the world'.

Adding to the general sense of disharmony, Rio Ferdinand missed a routine drugs test that September and was banned for nine months. United ended up finishing third, behind not only Arsenal, who went through the season unbeaten, but also Chelsea. That summer, Abramovich sacked Claudio Ranieri and replaced him with José Mourinho, who had led Porto to the Champions League after announcing himself to the English public at Old Trafford. United had swept through the group stage, winning five out of six games but once again had fallen down at the first knockout stage. After a 2–1 defeat in Portugal, United went a goal up through Paul Scholes, who had another effort wrongly ruled out for offside, and looked to be going through on away goals when Costinha struck in the final minute. Mourinho reacted by sprinting down the touchline and sliding on his knees. A year after United's Champions League exit had persuaded Abramovich to buy Chelsea, another Champions League exit provided Chelsea with their manager.

As Arsenal's Invincibles won the league in 2003–04, the only comfort for United came in the FA Cup, as they beat Arsenal in the semi-final and went on to crush Millwall in the final. But that was a trophy that had come to be seen as a consolation. United, it seemed, were in retreat and, with Abramovich's billions elevating Chelsea, English football was moving into a new age.

Wayne Rooney, still only eighteen, was signed from Everton after dazzling at Euro 2004. 'A remarkable raw talent,' said Ferguson. 'Plus natural courage and energy . . . [but] he was not the quickest learner.' After recovering from a fractured metatarsal sustained in the quarter-final of the Euros, he marked his debut with a hat-trick against Fenerbahçe in the Champions League. On his nineteenth birthday, he was instrumental in helping United end an Arsenal unbeaten run that stretched back forty-nine games. Rooney fell over Sol Campbell's leg to win a penalty that Ruud van Nistelrooy converted and then added the second in a 2–0 win. The game had been undercut with rancour from the start and tempers bubbled over after the final whistle as players hurled food at each other in what became known as the Battle of the Buffet, the low (or high, depending how you look at it) point of the rivalry that had developed between the sides.

That win aside, 2004–05 was largely forgettable on the pitch for United. They again finished third in the league, went out of the League Cup to Chelsea in the semi-final, lost on penalties in the FA Cup final to Arsenal and, yet again, were eliminated in the Champions League as soon as they reached the knockout phase, this time by AC Milan.

Everything was overshadowed by what was happening in the boardroom. Steadily, Glazer upped his bid. Fans, slowly coming to terms with what a leveraged buy-out might mean, tried to oppose his takeover. Keith Harris, who had advised Sky on their abortive takeover attempt, tried to put together a rival consortium. Had Ferguson come out in support of it, the Glazer bid would probably have collapsed. He didn't and, in May 2005, Cubic and Magnier sold their stake to Glazer for a £30 million profit. By 16 May, the Glazer family owned 75 per cent of the club and so was able to delist from the stock exchange. The club was valued at £800 million but the Glazers put up no more than a quarter of that; the rest all came from loans, most using the club as collateral. This meant that, right from the start, a squeeze was placed on finances.

Nothing much improved in 2005–06 as Ferguson reached his lowest ebb since 1999. Had, perhaps, the decision not to retire been a mistake? Even Hugh McIlvanney in his *Sunday Times* column noted that 'eventually there comes a moment when the best and bravest of fighters shouldn't answer the bell'. It was noted by an uneasy press that Glazer had forced out a long-serving and popular coach shortly after taking over Tampa Bay Buccaneers in 1995. Old certainties weren't so certain any more. It wasn't even clear that Ferguson remained popular; there was a substantial section of United's support who felt he should have done more to resist the Glazers. And it slowly became apparent that Keane, Ferguson's furious enforcer for so long, was not the fixed point he had been. There'd been a bust-up on a pre-season gathering at Vale do Lobo in Portugal after Keane complained to Queiroz about training arrangements. A hip injury meant he played only infrequently.

United started the season indifferently against a constant backdrop of tension. Before the Champions League qualifier against the Hungarian side Debrecen there was a march of 3000 fans demonstrating against the takeover. United were sixth after ten games but, although they'd won half of those, their form was scratchy. Fans wondered why Ferguson had abandoned 4-4-2 for 4-5-1. There were chants of 'Four-four-two! Four-four-two!' and the issue became so sensitive that when the MUTV presenter Paul Anthony questioned the move away from a formation that had served United so well, Ferguson boycotted the club's in-house television channel, a remarkable move akin to Brezhnev boycotting *Pravda*. Before the home game against Lille, he used his programme notes to explain the move to 4-5-1. 'When Roy was at his peak and worked from box-to-box,' he said, 'we needed only two players in the engine room.'

Keane himself, still injured, was in Dubai, from where he watched in horror as United were dismantled 4–1 by Middlesbrough at the end of October to slip thirteen points behind Chelsea. Ferguson described it as 'a shocking performance' and told the players afterwards that they weren't 'fit to wear the shirts'. On MUTV's *Play the Pundit* programme, Keane called it far worse, slaughtering a number of United players, most notably Kieran Richardson. The episode was never aired. Ferguson made Keane show it to the squad at the training ground, then went berserk at him. Queiroz called for loyalty to which Keane responded that he'd been quick enough to leave when Real Madrid came calling, only to return when it didn't work out. As United lost at Lille in the Champions League, fans chanted Keane's name; they, it seemed, agreed with Keane's criticisms.

That November, Keane was told to leave and departed for Celtic. Whatever other doubts there may have been about Ferguson by then, he remained as ruthless as ever.

This time United didn't even make the knockout stage of the Champions League, eliminated by an away defeat at Benfica. Since winning the tournament in 1999, they'd won only one knockout tie in the competition; dreams of a side that could dominate Europe as Liverpool had in the late seventies and early eighties evaporated almost as soon as they'd been articulated.

United went out of the Cup in a toxic atmosphere at Liverpool and, as Chelsea retained their league title, were forced to form a guard of honour for them at Stamford Bridge; it's perhaps as well that Keane was long gone by then. If there was hope, it came in a run of ten straight league wins from February and victory in the League Cup. Even then, though, nothing was straightforward. Van Nistelrooy was left out of the starting line-up for the final, in which United beat Wigan 4–0. Disaffected, he attacked Queiroz and Ronaldo so vehemently that he essentially made his departure inevitable. After five seasons in which he'd scored 150 league goals in 219 games, he joined Real Madrid that summer.

The mood round Old Trafford was mutinous. In the *Guardian*, Rob Smyth, a United fan, denounced Ferguson in typically eloquent fashion, calling him 'a manager who shreds his legacy at every turn'. The squad he denounced as 'a baggy mess of has-beens, never-will-bes and Liam Miller'. 'United,' Smyth went on, 'are making exactly the same mistakes that Liverpool did: lack of pheromones in the transfer market; laughable, fall-back signings at suspicious and ridiculous prices; deluded ramblings ("we are as good as Chelsea, no question") – and, worst of all, a dressing room where playing the field seems as important as playing the game.' It's a column that came to be held up as an example of the fickleness of the media, but the truth is that Smyth was simply more forthright, his phrasing more memorable than most. There were plenty of fans, journalists and others, who were thinking much the same.

Everything seemed to be going wrong for United. Even the World Cup brought no respite and Cristiano Ronaldo was caught winking after Wayne Rooney had been sent off in England's penalty shoot-out defeat to Portugal in the quarter-final. How could they ever play together again?

Quite easily, it turned out, and supremely well. As Chelsea had signed Andriy Shevchenko and Michael Ballack that summer, United had picked up Michael Carrick and Tomasz Kuszczak. Fans were alarmed United were being left behind and chanted Van Nistelrooy's name in pre-season. Once the league campaign got under way, though, it turned out that team-building was more important than simply gathering big names. Rooney said that Ronaldo returned after the World Cup 'all muscly and buffed up, like he'd been on the weights all summer'. His attitude had changed as well. He'd become more pragmatic. As Rooney put it, he'd cut out 'all the fancy tricks and flicks' and had begun 'finding an end product to his mazy runs down the park'.

United scored four in the first nineteen minutes of the season as they thrashed Fulham 5–1 and never looked back. United's football became thrilling again, never more so than when they thrashed Roma 7–1 in the Champions League quarter-final. After a 3–2 home victory over Milan in the first leg of the semi-final, though, they were well beaten 3–0 in the San Siro – 'They blew us away,' said Rooney. 'Kaká was unplayable.' Chelsea overcame them in the FA Cup final, the first at the new Wembley, but in the league United were unstoppable, collecting eighty-nine points.

That summer, United signed Anderson, Nani, Owen Hargreaves and, perhaps most significantly, Carlos Tévez. Whatever the misgivings about the Glazer ownership, both morally and in terms of the long-term direction of the club, that season United's squad was exceptional. Rooney, Ronaldo and Tévez created a constant whirl of movement at the head of a system often described as strikerless, with Giggs offering a steadying presence on the left.

Arsenal surged into an early lead in the title race, going unbeaten for fifteen games, but they ended up drawing too often as injures and suspensions weakened them. Chelsea lost only three times all season and yet were top for only a week at the end of August but United, after dropping seven points in their opening three games, were remorseless. They sealed the title on the final day with a 2–0 win over Wigan Athletic.

Portsmouth beat them in the sixth round of the FA Cup, but of far greater significance was what happened in Europe. The progress of the previous season was built upon. United dropped only two points in making it through their group to set up a last-sixteen tie against Lyon. Karim Benzema put the French champions ahead after fifty-four minutes with a crisp shot from just outside the box, the last goal United would concede until the final. United's approach had changed, but they could still conjure late goals when they needed them. With three minutes remaining, a Nani corner came to Michael Carrick at the back of the box. His shot was blocked but found its way back to Nani who crossed again. As Ronaldo closed in, the ball struck the Lyon substitute Fred and bounced back across goal for Tévez to slam in.

At Old Trafford, Ronaldo was inspired, although the only goal of the game was, for all the quality of the finish, again slightly scruffy in the build-up. A half-cleared Nani cross fell to Anderson and, when his shot was blocked, Ronaldo reacted first to work space for a shot and tuck his finish just inside the post.

A close-range finish from Rooney and a powerful header from Ronaldo gave United a 2–0 win away to Roma in the first leg of the quarter-final, Tévez's second-half goal making absolutely certain of progress in the home leg.

This was a different United. The cavalier days of old were gone. The forward line was capable of stunning football, but United's progress was predicated on solidity. In that, perhaps, there was evidence not merely of Ferguson's recognition of the dangers of all-out attack but also of the influence of Queiroz, a coach whose style was to hold the ball in midfield, to maintain possession, to allow the opposition nothing. Perhaps it wasn't as much fun as nine years previously, but it was undeniably effective.

There were three Premier League teams in the semi-finals of the Champions League; United got the other one, Barcelona. They were in their last weeks under Frank Rijkaard and nothing like the team that had beaten Arsenal in the 2006 Champions League final, but United, having come so close so often, were never going to take a risk. In the Nou Camp, with Park Ji-Sung, Michael Carrick and Scholes forming a solid central midfield, they stifled Barcelona. The result might have been very different had Ronaldo not missed a third-minute penalty, but it finished goalless. The second leg was tense but tipped United's way after fourteen minutes as Gianluca Zambrotta's clearance came to Paul Scholes twenty-five yards out. His shot, he later acknowledged, was a slight mishit, but the slice on the ball took it past Víctor Valdés. Barça dominated possession and had chance after chance but United held out for their first final since 1999.

In Moscow, they faced Chelsea, who had finished two points

behind them in the league despite the dismissal of José Mourinho following a 1–1 home draw against Rosenborg in their opening Champions League group game. Under Avram Grant they had gone unbeaten in the league since 16 December and had reached the final of the League Cup, losing to Tottenham. That enhanced the reputation Grant had developed in Israel as a coach who couldn't win finals.

It was the first ever meeting of two English sides in Europe's major final and only the third of two teams from the same country, but there was a sense of two worlds colliding: Ferguson, a manager from the heartlands of the Scottish game who stood in the lineage of Busby, Stein and Shankly, a believer in youth development augmented by self-generated wealth (despite the Glazer takeover), against the oligarchal funds of Roman Abramovich, the icon of football's new money.

Away against Chelsea in the April of that year, Ferguson had fielded a 4-3-3 with Darren Fletcher and Anderson flanking Michael Carrick in midfield and had lost 2–1. United, in fact, had won only two of their previous fourteen meetings with Chelsea. For the final, Paul Scholes and Owen Hargreaves were recalled as Ferguson, to widespread surprise, adopted a 4-4-2. That meant Rooney and Tévez paired up front with Ronaldo on the left and Hargreaves on the right, presumably to try to counter the attacking threat from left-back of Ashley Cole.

United's hopes at Stamford Bridge had been hit when Nemanja Vidić was forced off early on after taking a knee in the head from Didier Drogba and it soon became apparent that their personal battle would once again be critical. Just seven minutes in, Drogba was left bleeding from his lip after catching an arm in the face from Vidić as the two jumped for a high ball.

There'd been much discussion before the game about the pitch at the Luzhniki Stadium, the grass having been laid a matter of weeks before the final to replace the artificial surface on which England had lost a Euro 2008 away tie to Russia the previous October. It was wet after hours of heavy rain that day and the result was a slick surface and a game that in its early stages was rapid to the point of being frantic. The game kicked off at 10.45 Moscow time, something that a number of players admitted unnerved them. Rooney spoke of 'going mad' in the middle of the afternoon as he realised there were still seven hours until kick-off. The pace of those early minutes suggested he wasn't the only one to have been straining at the leash.

United's back four dealt comfortably with some early Chelsea crosses and then Ronaldo, dropping deep and moving central, initiated a move that led to Hargreaves slinging over a dangerous cross from the right. John Terry, who was playing despite having dislocated his elbow a couple of weeks earlier, got there just in front of Rooney but the avenue of attack was clear.

Although both Hargreaves and Ronaldo cut infield repeatedly, United's intention was to attack Chelsea wide. An Evra pass isolated Essien against Ronaldo and he skipped by him before sending over a cross that was just too high for Hargreaves. Joe Cole was forced deep on the Chelsea right to help protect Essien, whose defensive shortcomings against Ronaldo were obvious. Paulo Ferreira, who had played at right-back in the April league game, wasn't even on the bench, although Juliano Belletti was, suggesting Grant thought the best way to deal with Ronaldo was to try to force him to defend against an attack-minded full-back.

But it wasn't just on their left that United were prospering. A simple move began with the goalkeeper Edwin van der Sar, whose signing had ended the search for a replacement for Peter Schmeichel, was worked through Ferdinand to Brown, who chipped the ball over the top to release Hargreaves. Terry came across to block at the expense of a corner. Hargreaves's delivery flicked off Drogba and went out for a throw on the United left. It was taken quickly and Drogba fouled Ronaldo sixteen yards from the goal-line. Chelsea, it seemed, couldn't get out. Frank Lampard, who had been linked with a move to Internazionale on the eve of the final, headed Hargreaves's free-kick clear and, as the ball broke, Scholes jumped clumsily into Makélélé. Mystifyingly, both were booked when Scholes was the obvious aggressor. Chelsea were furious, surrounding the referee – as they had when Rooney had prevented Makélélé taking a quick free-kick a little earlier – suggesting he had led with the arm. The challenge was reckless, but it was Scholes who came off worse from it, being forced off for treatment as blood dripped from his nose.

A man down, United's pressure eased and when Tévez was caught in possession in his own half, a Lampard cross caused a moment's panic, Vidić needlessly heading behind for a corner. Terry, though, was penalised for a push on Brown as Lampard's cross came over.

Scholes, cotton wool shoved up his nostrils and a tissue in his hand, returned to the field and United returned to the ascendant. Hargreaves won a throw off Ashley Cole deep on the United right. Brown took it to Scholes, who played back to Brown. They exchanged passes again to work a crossing opportunity around Lampard and Malouda, and when Brown shaped the ball in to the back post, Essien got caught under the ball leaving Ronaldo, neck muscles thrusting like those of a traditional number 9, to power a header just inside the far post and give United a twenty-sixth-minute lead. It was his forty-second goal of the season and his eighth in eleven Champions League games. 'We really should be out of sight already,' Rooney said, reflecting back on the game in his second autobiography. 'We've dominated but we haven't taken our chances.'

Chelsea responded immediately and Ballack drove over the bar from just outside the box, but United's wide men still posed the greatest danger. Ronaldo got to another Brown cross and headed down, but this time Carvalho was able to hack clear as Hargreaves closed in. After a slightly scrappy opening, the game had settled into a pattern of United dominating, controlling possession and looking persistently threatening.

When Drogba went down clutching his shoulder after a

challenge from Ferdinand, the assumption was he was trying to break the flow of the game and find a way of disrupting United's rhythm. But then, thirty-three minutes in, came a warning. A Rooney ball forward towards Tévez was intercepted by Carvalho, who played the ball left to Ashley Cole. The ball was worked across field to Ballack, who swept a long pass back out to Cole. He slipped the ball forward to Florent Malouda, who was challenged by Brown, the ball coming to Terry inside his own half on the left. He advanced and played it forward to Malouda. He played it left for Cole, who knocked it back for Lampard in space. The midfielder swept a cross beyond the back post, where Drogba headed across goal and, as Ferdinand and Ballack challenged for it six yards out, it was the defender who made contact, sending the ball goalwards. Van der Sar, who had perhaps been a little hesitant, batted the ball away and Scholes put it behind for a corner. Chelsea's menace may have been hidden, but it was there.

The corner, though, almost brought a brilliant United second. The ball was cleared to Carvalho on the Chelsea left, but he was tackled by Rooney, who advanced and then hit a superb long cross-field ball into the path of Ronaldo charging down the United left. He took one touch then crossed first time for Tévez, but his first-time effort was scrambled away by Petr Čech. Terry hacked clear and as the ball fell for Carrick just outside the box, he had a clear shot. He opted for a sidefoot but placed his effort too central and Čech made a fine save with an outstretched right hand.

Ronaldo then headed a Hargreaves cross just wide and Tévez couldn't quite stretch to meet a Rooney cross after a break initiated by Hargreaves. United looked sharper and more aggressive, but shortly before half-time came an unexpected Chelsea rally. First Ferdinand was booked for a block on Lampard twenty yards out, Ballack firing the free-kick over and then, from almost nowhere, came an equaliser. Drogba, on the Chelsea left, held off Brown to chest an Ashley Cole pass down for Malouda. He cut infield but was tackled by Ferdinand.

Lampard won the header on halfway but there seemed little danger as it spun right for Essien, surging forward from full-back. From thirty-five yards he hit a speculative shot that hit first Vidić, then Ferdinand to present Lampard with the simplest of finishes as Van der Sar slipped. It was the first goal United had conceded in six Champions League games.

The half ended with another minor outbreak of tetchiness, players surrounding the referee L'uboš Michel' and squaring up to each other after Carvalho had been booked for a shin-high foul on Ronaldo. Chelsea couldn't realistically have been aggrieved; they must have been delighted to go in level after a first half in which they'd been largely outplayed.

There was a stop-start opening to the second half, both sides struggling to settle into any kind of rhythm, but it gradually became apparent that it was Chelsea who were on top. 'By getting closer to Ronaldo after the restart,' David Pleat wrote in the *Guardian*, 'Essien was able to deter the supply line to the winger. He was not able to do this alone, however, and there was considerable assistance from the centre of the Chelsea midfield as well as from Florent Malouda and Joe Cole, who worked assiduously to deny United space and room to manoeuvre the ball.'

Carrick and Scholes exerted nothing like the same control over the game, a snappish foul by Joe Cole on Carrick five minutes in suggesting their determination to get closer to United's two pivots. 'I could feel the game slipping away from us,' Rooney said. 'It did my head in.'

Ronaldo still had the beating of Essien, and a lovely pass inside the full-back created a crossing opportunity for Evra nine minutes in, only for his delivery to drift slightly too deep for Hargreaves as he came in off the right flank. But after his part in the equaliser, Essien seemed energised, far more prepared to take on Ronaldo and surge forward, knowing the winger almost certainly wasn't going to track him. He very nearly put Chelsea ahead after fifty-five minutes, running on to a Malouda pass and dragging his shot just wide from the edge of the box as Van der Sar slipped again – almost any shot on target would have gone in.

United, abruptly, looked rattled. Lampard released Joe Cole and only a fine header from Vidić prevented his cross from reaching Drogba, who then got to Lampard's corner but headed over. Ballack surged away from Scholes and drove an effort from thirty yards just wide. A Malouda free-kick – harshly awarded after a slight tug by Vidić on Drogba – was superbly cleared by Carrick, stretching back towards his own goal as opponents closed in. Terry then headed over with Van der Sar flapping.

Perhaps if there'd been more flow to the game, Chelsea could have taken advantage, but the bittiness continued. Hargreaves went down after catching an arm in the face from Makélélé and then Ferdinand required lengthy treatment after pulling up with what appeared to be cramp in his calf. As Lampard also had medics look at his calf, it seemed that the fears about the pitch were being borne out, but both were able to continue.

The break in play did United good. A long Van der Sar clearance after seventy-one minutes found Rooney on the left. He played the ball square along the top of the box to Tévez, who laid it off for Carrick. He had time and space but his shot hit Ballack and was deflected to safety. Ronaldo, having won another corner with a shot that spun wide off Joe Cole from a narrow angle, then couldn't quite climb high enough to meet Hargreaves's delivery after finding space at the back post.

The tide against United, it seemed, had been at least partially stemmed, but Ferguson still wasn't happy and switched Rooney to the right, pulling Hargreaves inside to make a 4-5-1, matching Chelsea three against three in the centre of midfield.

The sense of niggle continued. Makélélé was wrestled to the ground by Tévez as they waited for a cross and stayed down, having apparently taken a clout on the jaw. Malouda, after pulling down a high ball, stumbled under the challenge from

Ferdinand, who, after an anxious glance to make sure the referee hadn't given a penalty, berated him for diving, although in this instance it seemed he had simply lost his footing. Joe Cole and Evra then clashed as they waited for a throw, the full-back catching him with an arm.

When the throw was eventually taken, Cole held off Evra. Scholes made a tackle but only knocked the ball to Drogba, who turned away from Vidić and advanced, first to the left and then more directly at goal. As Hargreaves challenged, Drogba slipped but, from a prone position, still managed to force the ball wide to Malouda. He played it back to Drogba, who, with very little backlift, arced a shot goalwards from twenty-five yards. With Van der Sar beaten, the ball cannoned back off the face of the post.

Chelsea were back on top. Rooney, in his new position wide on the right, mishit a pass under pressure from Joe Cole, pushing the ball behind Ronaldo. Lampard gathered and helped it on to Malouda on the left. As Ferdinand slipped, he crossed low towards Drogba but, under pressure from Vidić, he sent his first-time effort wide. Twice more in the five minutes that followed, Drogba got to crosses but couldn't get his shots on target, and Chelsea might have had a penalty when Ferdinand, trying to bring down a high ball, clipped the top of Joe Cole's head with the underside of his thigh. The linesman flagged but didn't signal for a penalty and then seemed to think better of it.

With three minutes to go, Ryan Giggs was brought on to replace Scholes, who was struggling with his bloodied nose; the Welshman was making his 759th appearance for United and so taking the record for most games for United previously held by Bobby Charlton. There was a moment when it seemed space had opened for him to round the game off with the most fairy-tale of finishes, but the ball ran away from him. The final whistle blew at 1–1, Chelsea having been so dominant in the second half that they'd probably had the better of the game overall.

Salomon Kalou came on for Malouda early in extra-time, his pace an obvious threat, but for the most part the additional half-hour was uneven and fragmented, the surface having taken a severe toll on just about everybody. Chelsea, though, did come close to taking the lead a minute after Kalou's entrance. The substitute won a throw on the left off Brown and then received the ball from Ashley Cole. He went past Hargreaves into the left side of the box, and pulled the ball back to Ballack eighteen yards out. He laid it off for Lampard, who, not quite set for the shot, let it run across his body, turning away from Hargreaves to create space for a left-footed strike. The ball was a fraction behind him and there was a slight scooping motion to Lampard's hooked shot, but it beat Van der Sar and pinged back off the crossbar. The ball dropped for Joe Cole, but the bounce was awkward and he couldn't get over his follow-up attempt, seeming to injure himself in the process. There was a long pause while he received treatment and he was replaced by Nicolas Anelka after ninety-nine minutes.

That perhaps disrupted Chelsea's policy of doubling up on Ronaldo, Anelka offering Essien nothing like the protection Cole had. Anelka had been on the field only a minute when a long diagonal pass from Rooney on the halfway line released Ronaldo. Essien headed his cross away, but Evra got to the loose ball before Anelka, burst into the box and, as Čech left his goal to close him down, cut a cross back. The ball didn't quite fall into Giggs's stride but he stabbed it goalwards with the outside of his left foot and was denied only by a brilliant twisting headed clearance from the backtracking Terry. Two feet either side of him and it would have been a goal.

That pass was Rooney's last act as, struggling with a hip injury, he was withdrawn for Nani, and that chance was the last meaningful one of the game, although Tévez fired a speculative shot straight at Čech and Drogba fired a free-kick wide after Vidić had been booked for a foul on Anelka.

There had been an undercurrent of spite throughout the game and it spilled over with six minutes remaining. Carvalho went down with cramp and the ball was put out by Chelsea so he could receive treatment. Ashley Cole, Terry, Ferdinand and Carrick all went down at the same time. When the game was finally restarted, Nani threw it to Tévez, who knocked it out for a Chelsea throw. Mystifyingly Chelsea were enraged – twice earlier in the game in similar circumstances they'd returned the ball to United in far less advantageous positions; here it wasn't even clear what they expected Tévez to do. Terry, Lampard and Ballack all squared up to Tévez and in the melee that followed, Drogba slapped Vidić. Enraged, he momentarily made for revenge but was held back by Ballack. Michel' booked Ballack and Tévez (although he had apparently done nothing but stand looking confused), and sent off Drogba. As the game sputtered to its conclusion, the significance of that slowly sank in: United didn't really threaten in the final minutes, but Chelsea were left without one of their key penalty-takers, the man, in fact, who would score the winning penalty in the final against Bayern Munich four years later.

Before the game, as Simon Kuper and Stefan Szymanski revealed in *Why England Lose*, a mutual friend had put Avram Grant in touch with the economist Ignacio Palacios-Huerta, who was one of the first people to take the study of penalties seriously. In 1995, when he was still a graduate student at the University of Chicago, he had started recording how penalties were taken and, in 2003, had published a paper on the theme. Huerta sent Grant a report about how United took penalties that made four key points.

It's easier for a right-footed penalty-taker to hit the ball hard to his left, the goalkeeper's right, and for a left-footer to hit the ball hard to his right, the goalkeeper's left – what Palacios-Huerta calls his 'natural' side. Van der Sar, he had observed, had a marked tendency to dive to the striker's natural side. The recommendation, then, was clear: penalty-takers should at least consider putting the ball the other way. Palacios-Huerta also pointed out that 'the vast majority of the penalties that Van der Sar stops are those kicked to a mid-height (say, between 1 and 1.5m) and hence penalties against him should be kicked just on the ground or high up'.

That was about how to beat Van der Sar, but Palacios-Huerta also had recommendations for thwarting Cristiano Ronaldo. The forward, he said, was adept at waiting for a goalkeeper to commit one way or the other and then putting the ball to the other side. That meant that Petr Čech, against Ronaldo, should stand up as long as possible. Furthermore, if Ronaldo did check his run, 85 per cent of the time he ended up putting the ball to the right.

The final piece of advice was more general. Sixty per cent of all penalty shoot-outs are won by the side going first, presumably because of the pressure if a player knows he has to score to stay in the game. Therefore, if John Terry won the toss, he was advised to kick first. It's impossible to know to what extent Huerta's advice was followed, but what is clear is that he was broadly correct.

It was Ferdinand, though, who won the toss. He turned to his bench to ask whether he should go first or second, at which Terry offered to go first. Ferdinand ignored him and United took the first kick. Tévez scored as did Michael Ballack, going to his unnatural side, although Van der Sar went the right way. Carrick made it 2–1 and then Belletti, also striking to Van der Sar's left, levelled.

Then came Ronaldo. Čech remained motionless as Ronaldo approached the ball. He checked and then, as Palacios-Huerta had predicted, went to his right. Čech saved and Chelsea had the advantage. Lampard, right-footed, sidefooted to his right, the unnatural side again, and although Van der Sar got a hand to it, scored: 3–2 to Chelsea. Owen Hargreaves scored with a magnificent strike into the top corner. Then came Ashley Cole. Left-footed, he went to his right, the natural side. This time Van der Sar went the right way but couldn't keep the shot out. Nani converted. John Terry had a penalty to win the Champions League. He went to his right, the unnatural side. Van der Sar dived the other way. But Terry had slipped as he struck the ball, pushing it slightly wider than intended. His shot hit the outside of the post and bounced away. After five penalties each, it was 4–4.

Anderson scored, thumping his penalty down the middle, over Čech's dive. The right-footed Salomon Kalou went to his right, the unnatural side, and scored. Four times out of six, Van der Sar had gone to the natural side, just as his track record had suggested he would. Ryan Giggs on his record-breaking night, casually stroked the ball in as Čech went the wrong way.

Nicolas Anelka had to score. At that point, every Chelsea penalty had gone to Van der Sar's left – the five right-footers striking to their unnatural side and Cole to his natural side. As the right-footed Anelka stepped up, Van der Sar pointed to his left. Did that put doubt in the substitute's mind? Had he planned to take Huerta's advice? Was it even wise to keep taking the advice without occasionally breaking the pattern? Anelka went left. It was a poor penalty, at mid-height, in precisely the spot Huerta had warned about. Van der Sar saved, Ferguson had only his second ever win in a penalty shoot-out and at 01:34 Moscow time, United, for the third time, were European champions.

Terry wept; but for Drogba's dismissal, he wouldn't have taken a penalty. 'You can see what it means to John,' said Frank Lampard. 'He's Mr Chelsea. He's Chelsea through and through. He wanted this more than anyone at the club. I just want to say not many centre-halves would have stood up and taken the fifth penalty, a penalty of that importance. He's a man's man. No one at Chelsea will criticise him at all.'

As in 1999, there was ultimately an element of fortune to United's victory. They had not been at their best in the final. But as in 1999, they had produced some stunning football earlier in the campaign. 'There is a weakness in the European trophies we've won and I hope we can make that better,' said Ferguson. 'Winning is important but skill is what we do.' Given how much ill fortune they'd had at various times under Ferguson in Europe, no United fan was much minded to wonder what might have happened if John Terry hadn't slipped on the wet Luzhniki pitch. 'We deserved it,' said Ferguson afterwards, hair plastered to his head by the rain, shoes ruined so that he had to attend the post-match banquet in trainers. 'With the history of this club we deserved to get this trophy tonight. We should have been three or four up by half-time.'

The only negative was Ronaldo's reaction. As his team-mates celebrated the win in front of the United fans, to the left of the goal where the penalties had been taken, he sat alone on the halfway line, weeping. This was the first real glimpse of how deep his solipsism ran: his goal hadn't been the winner and in the shoot-out he'd almost lost it for his team, so he didn't join the celebrations. His supporters have suggested this was evidence of the tremendous desire for self-improvement that drove his rise, and perhaps it is. But it also gave a fairly clear indication that his first loyalty was not to United and that he might not be at the club for the long term, even if he did announce after the game that he intended to stay.

Fifty years on from Munich, Bobby Charlton presented Nemanja Vidić with the Cup. He had referred to the disaster in his team-talk. 'I said that we wouldn't let down the memory of the Busby Babes,' he said. 'We had a cause and that was very important because people with causes are very difficult for people to barter against. I have to say I thought it was over when Cristiano missed his penalty. But that slip by John Terry gave us an opening. Maybe it was fate, him missing his kick like that. I really think fate has played its hand.'

Ferguson became the sixth manager in European history to win the competition twice. Nobody else had done it twice with the same club as long as nine years apart. His legacy, which had seemed so flimsy two years earlier, was secure.

CHAPTER 10

FA Cup final, Wembley, London, 21 May 2016

Crystal Palace	**1–2**	**Manchester United**
Puncheon 78		*Mata 81*
		Lingard 110

Wayne Hennessey	David de Gea
Joel Ward	Luís Antonio Valencia
Scott Dann	Chris Smalling
(Adrian Mariappa 90+)	
Damien Delaney	Daley Blind
Pape Souaré	Marcos Rojo
	(Matteo Darmian 66)
Mile Jedinak	Michael Carrick
James McArthur	Marouane Fellaini
Wilfried Zaha	Wayne Rooney
Yohan Cabaye	Juan Mata
(Jason Puncheon 72)	(Jesse Lingard 90)
Yannick Bolasie	Anthony Martial
Connor Wickham	Marcus Rashford
(Dwight Gayle 86)	(Ashley Young 72)
Alan Pardew	Louis van Gaal

Ref: Mark Clattenburg
Bkd: Dann, Delaney, McArthur; Smalling, Rojo, Mata, Rooney, Fellaini
Sent off: Smalling
Att: 88,619

IT REMAINS UNCLEAR AT PRECISELY what moment Louis van Gaal realised that he would be replaced by José Mourinho – could it really be true, as was rumoured, that the first he'd known of it was when his wife Truus texted him having seen the news on television shortly after the final whistle? – but the rest of the world knew at some point between the end of the FA Cup final and Van Gaal's subsequent press conference. That morning the Spanish newspaper *AS* had reported Mourinho's appointment was imminent. It should have been the perfect way for him to bid farewell, ensuring that he had won a trophy at every club he had managed in a career stretching back a quarter of a century, but instead the mood was awkward. 'I hope I'll see you next season,' he said pointedly, but everybody knew he wouldn't.

Van Gaal had failed just as David Moyes had failed, the task of replacing Alex Ferguson beginning to seem just as difficult as the task of succeeding Matt Busby had four decades earlier. The contrast with 1990 was obvious: back then, beating Crystal Palace in an FA Cup final had been the beginning of Alex Ferguson's reign of remorseless success, coming at the end of his fourth season at the club. Twenty-six years later, beating Crystal Palace in an FA Cup final at the end of his second season as manager merely softened the blow of Van Gaal's departure. United had changed, of course, starting from a much higher base, and football had changed, the rigid stratifications caused by the distribution of revenues within the sport making it a far less patient game. And there were other, far more profound, changes within United.

Even on the morning of the game, *The Times* was citing a source within the dressing room describing the 'bafflement' players regularly felt at Van Gaal's approach: 'Sometimes the players turn up and think, what the fuck are we doing this for?' Van Gaal had been booed during a 3–1 league win over Bournemouth the previous Tuesday (a game delayed for forty-eight hours after a bomb scare caused by a package taped to a pipe in the toilet that turned out to have been left over from a training exercise) while banners had called for his removal.

Yet the mood when Ferguson retired had been optimistic. 'It was important to me to leave an organisation in the strongest possible shape and I believe I have done so,' Ferguson said when he left in May 2013. 'The quality of this league-winning squad, and the balance of ages within it, bodes well for continued success at the highest level, whilst the structure of the youth set-up will ensure that the long-term future of the club remains a bright one.' Of course it was only to be expected that he would insist he was bequeathing a healthy situation but there were few at the time who disagreed. The mess into which the club descended in the three years that followed was remarkable.

The next step after winning the Champions League is to win it again, a point Alex Ferguson made at the celebratory banquet in Moscow. 'The manager gets up for another speech,' said Rooney. 'He's just watched us win the Premier League and the Champions League, but now he's talking about next season, how we have to do it again.' In part, of course, that was simply Ferguson's relentlessness speaking, his hunger to add silverware to silverware, but there were also specific reasons. No side had retained the European title in the Champions League era: this was United's chance really to make their mark, to establish the sort of dynasty that had once characterised the best sides in European competition. For a club of United's stature, it seems remiss that it has won the European title on only three occasions. But there must also have been a personal ambition: at that point only Bob Paisley had won it three times. And with the pace, power and mutual understanding of that forward line, plus a central defensive partnership at least as good as any other in Europe, there was no obvious reason why United should not go on to greater success.

Perhaps they would have done but for one event that, even if they had foreseen it, they could hardly have prevented: the rise of Barcelona under Pep Guardiola, who was chosen ahead of Mourinho to replace Frank Rijkaard that summer.

When United lost 2–1 at Arsenal in November 2008 to slip to fourth, there were some voices of concern. But they then kept a club-record fourteen consecutive clean sheets in the league and lost just twice more as, for the second time under Ferguson's leadership, they won a third successive league title. At one point Liverpool led by seven points, although United had two games in hand, but they seemed to lose their way after Rafa Benítez's notorious 'facts' press conference at which he listed all the ways in which football was weighted in favour of United. Wayne Rooney remembered seeing the footage and thinking, 'The manager has got under Rafa's skin.' There were plenty who thought the talk of mind-games and Ferguson's psychological warfare was overstated, but at the very least Benítez's litany of complaints seemed an error of judgement.

The eighteen-year-old forward Federico Macheda emerged as a surprise hero, coming off the bench to score late winners against Aston Villa and Sunderland in April. Everton put them out of the FA Cup on penalties, but United beat Tottenham in a shoot-out in the League Cup final. It wouldn't have taken much for United to have won a quadruple. Or at least, that was how it felt as they lined up against Barcelona in the Champions League final in Rome.

United had drawn four of their six group games without ever looking as though they weren't going to make it through. They'd beaten Inter in the last sixteen with a classic example of Ferguson's revised approach in Europe, drawing the first leg 0–0 at San Siro before goals from Vidić and Ronaldo completed a 2–0 triumph at home. Porto posed greater problems in the quarter-final, Aly Cissokho's surges forward from full-back unnerving United as they draw 2–2 in the away leg. At home, Ferguson switched Rooney to the flank to pen in the full-back and shifted Ronaldo to centre-forward, a decision vindicated as Ronaldo scored the only goal of the game with a forty-yard drive, a strike that became the inaugural winner of Fifa's Puskás Award for the best goal scored that season. After a 1–0 win over Arsenal in the home leg of the semi-final, United were devastating on the break at the Emirates, Park Ji-Sung getting one and Ronaldo two in a 3–1 win. Darren Fletcher, though, was sent off with quarter of an hour remaining, ruling him out of the final in Rome. Would he have made any difference? Probably not. Ferguson admitted United's planning had been 'poor' and that they'd chosen 'a bad hotel', but that probably didn't matter either. Barcelona were brilliant. United could realistically claim to have been the better side when Samuel Eto'o put Barça ahead after ten minutes, but thereafter they could barely get a kick. Lionel Messi, operating as a false nine, was superb and added the second with a seventieth-minute header, but it was the collective that did for United, Barça pressing in a swarm when out of possession and then, having regained the ball, passing in sharp filigrees as their opponents lumbered in their wake. 'We can't get into the match,' Rooney wrote in his autobiography. 'It's tiring, too. We're chasing shadows, tracking players, putting in challenges without getting a grip on the contest.' The thought after Barça's slightly fortunate semi-final win over Chelsea was that United would dominate them physically, but they never got near enough to make any advantage tell. Ferguson felt United could have won, suggesting that if his side had played more defensively, as they had in the semi-final the previous year, they might have stopped Barça settling. He accused Tévez and Ronaldo of becoming hypnotised by Barça's passing, 'spectating' rather than looking for space to counter.

But even Ferguson accepted that they 'were beaten by a great team'.

There was some surprise about Van Gaal's team selection for the FA Cup final, with Juan Mata preferred on the right to Jesse Lingard, who by the end of the season had come as close to being a regular as anybody in Van Gaal's United could ever be said to be. 'You have to compare in the moment,' Van Gaal explained. 'And in this moment we think the way we play against Crystal Palace, Mata is more the man than Lingard.' The thinking was presumably that with Palace likely to sit deep, it would be more valuable to have a player whose passing could exploit narrow gaps than somebody rapid who was perhaps more effective against a defence that leaves spaces behind it.

There was less surprise that the increasingly overblown pre-match ceremonials overran, leaving soldiers – an oddly insistent presence at recent football matches at Wembley – scurrying over the pitch to remove the coverings. The sense of farce was inflated when the singer Karen Harding missed her cue for the national anthem, belatedly joining in on the second verse. As a metaphor for United's standard performance that season – barely apparent in the first half before making their presence felt in the second – it could hardly have been bettered.

After a slightly frenetic opening, Connor Wickham pressuring Chris Smalling and forcing him to hoof into touch within seconds of the kick-off, the game settled into a familiar pattern of United possession. Smalling and Daley Blind exchanged passes, then Marouane Fellaini swept the ball out to Mata on the right. He moved forward and took a return pass and the ball was worked inside through Luís Antonio Valencia and Michael Carrick to Rooney, whose attempt to release Valencia behind the defence was slightly too strong. He would find his range soon enough.

Wickham's height and presence had caused Watford

significant problems in the semi-final and the expectation was that set-plays might be a way for Palace to unsettle United. Four minutes in, they got their first chance to test the theory as Yannick Bolasie won a corner after his cross was deflected behind by Valencia. Yohan Cabaye swung it in to the near post, where David de Gea claimed it above a group of players with almost dismissive ease.

In those early stages, Palace seemed to be making a concerted effort to press United, which led to a lot of scrappiness around halfway. Carrick was dispossessed by Cabaye but the ball was won back by Valencia, who played it out to the eighteen-year-old Marcus Rashford on the right. He was beaten by Pape Souaré. The ball came to Carrick, who was chopped down by Cabaye. Rooney, for all the criticism he would subsequently receive for his efforts in a midfield role, particularly during the Euros, soon emerged as the game's controlling figure. José Mourinho would comment before the start of the following season that it's easy to play good passes when you're not under pressure, and it's perhaps true that as the game went on and Palace dropped deeper, Rooney was afforded time, but it was still his passing that seemed likeliest to unlock Palace. Five minutes in, he released Marcos Rojo down the right. He came inside the full-back Joel Ward, but Wilfried Zaha got back to concede a corner.

Blind took it short to Mata, received the ball back and floated a cross to the back post for Fellaini. Mile Jedinak, whose battle with Fellaini would be one of the features of the first half, got there in front of the Belgian and headed the ball into the air where Wayne Hennessey made the catch.

A minute later it was Rooney again puncturing the Palace back line to set Rashford through. He took on Damien Delaney, who, stretching into the challenge, got just enough on the ball to put it out for a corner. Again Blind took it short to Mata, who played it back to Anthony Martial. He exchanged passes with Blind, then won another corner as James McArthur intercepted. This time, Blind swung it to the back post. It went over Smalling and came through to Rooney wide on the right. He beat Bolasie and then crossed deep to the left side of the box where Mata took it down and crossed towards Fellaini. Hennessey claimed, but the aerial threat posed by Fellaini was clear.

Events are always there to interfere with the best-laid plans. If Barcelona's rise had been unforeseen, Ronaldo's departure had been extremely predictable. The Champions League final turned out to be his final game for the club before a world-record £80 million move to Real Madrid. Carlos Tévez also left before the start of 2008–09, although with rather less good will. Because of the complicated rules surrounding third-party ownership, he had initially been signed on a two-year loan but attempts to make that permanent fell through, and he ended up being signed by Manchester City who, after the arrival of Sheikh Mansour to replace the hapless Thaksin Shinawatra the previous summer, had emerged as a serious force. That left United weakened, but they had at least signed Dimitar Berbatov a year earlier and that summer brought in an ageing Michael Owen to add attacking depth.

United traded blows with Carlo Ancelotti's Chelsea all season but in the end defeats home and away against them proved decisive and United finished second, a point behind the champions. They did, though, win the League Cup and thrashed AC Milan 7–2 on aggregate to reach the Champions League quarter-final. There they faced Louis van Gaal's Bayern Munich. Rooney, in the form of his life, scored his eighteenth goal in thirteen games to put United ahead after two minutes, but a deflected Franck Ribéry free-kick levelled the scores with thirteen minutes to go and then, two minutes into injury-time, Ivica Olić gave Bayern a 2–1 win. Worse, in the build-up, Rooney damaged ankle ligaments. He has arguably never been the same since.

There was widespread surprise when, for the second leg at Old Trafford, Ferguson selected Rooney despite concerns over

his ankle; this was fairly clear evidence of United's depend-
ence upon him since the departures of Ronaldo and Tévez.
Still, the decision seemed vindicated as United raced into a
two-goal lead within seven minutes with goals from Darron
Gibson and Nani. Nani added a third four minutes before half-
time and even when Olić pulled one back two minutes later,
United seemed in control.

But the game had had a spiteful edge. Bayern from the start
of the first leg had set out to dive, feign injury and spoil. In
the second, it seemed fairly apparent they were targeting
Rooney's ankle. 'I think that's obvious,' Ferguson said. 'I don't
think there was anything serious, but there were a couple of
challenges. We expected that, and the referee should have
handled it.'

With a 4–3 aggregate lead, it was a time for cool heads.
Rafael, the nineteen-year-old Brazilian full-back, was found
wanting. He'd been booked in the first half for a stray kick at
Mark van Bommel; five minutes after half-time he pulled back
Ribéry and collected a second booking. 'They got him sent off,'
raged Ferguson. 'There's no doubt about that and they would
have never won if we had eleven men. He [Rafael] is a young
boy, inexperienced and there's a bit of immaturity about what
happened but they got him sent off. Typical Germans. That
sending off changed the game.'

Rooney, hobbling badly, was substituted five minutes later.
An Arjen Robben volley sixteen minutes from time put Bayern
ahead on away goals and United were out.

Owen, his pace largely gone, hadn't really worked out as a
signing and Ferguson's only significant summer transfer was
to sign the rapid Mexican forward Javier Hernández to en-
hance his attacking options and take some of the pressure off
Rooney. So unhappy was Rooney with United's transfer activity, in fact, that in October 2010 he announced his intention
to leave the club. An improved contract persuaded him to stay.

It was one of the forwards already at the club who was the key
figure as United regained the league title in 2010–11, Dimitar

Berbatov finishing as the league's joint top-scorer with twenty. That he tied with Tévez suggested how the landscape of the Premier League was changing: United, with a surprisingly low eighty points, won the league with ease, finishing nine points clear of not only Chelsea but also Manchester City, who beat United in the FA Cup semi-final.

The Champions League brought another final as United, having dropped just four points in the group stage, eased by Marseille, Chelsea and Schalke 04 to face Barcelona again, this time at Wembley. The outcome was little different. Rooney briefly raised hopes when he cancelled out Pedro's opening after thirty-four minutes, but United again spent much of the game grasping at shadows as Barcelona, slicker, quicker and faster, passed their way around them. Goals from Messi and Xavi completed a 3–1 win. The Barça of 2011, Ferguson said, was even better than the Barça of 2009, 'the best team ever to line up against my Manchester United sides'. Three finals in four years was a mighty achievement, but a Barcelona team widely recognised as one of the greatest of all time, had out-classed United in two of them.

Rivals were also rising on the domestic front. The threat City had hinted at crystallised in 2011–12. As they signed Sergio Agüero, Samir Nasri and Gaël Clichy, United's captures of David de Gea, Phil Jones and Ashley Young seemed nota-bly unglamorous. Ferguson had dismissed City as the 'noisy neighbours', but this was the season when they went beyond that. United beat City in the third round of the FA Cup as Paul Scholes came out of retirement, but three games from the end of the league season, City, having won 6–1 at Old Trafford earlier in the season, beat United 1–0 at the Etihad to go above them on goal difference. On the final day, United won 1–0 at Sunderland and seemed to have the title sewn up only for City to score twice in injury-time to beat QPR 3–2 and claim their first title since 1968.

That capped a frustrating season for United. Liverpool had beaten them in the fourth round of the FA Cup, Palace in the fifth round of the League Cup and they'd been eliminated from the Champions League in the group stage. They survived one knockout round of the Europa League before being obliterated by Marcelo Bielsa's Athletic Bilbao.

United, settling into their rhythm as the first half went on, gained possession deep as a throw was taken to Blind, he came left to Rojo, then back to Blind and on to Rooney, deep in his own half. He chipped the ball square to Smalling, who exchanged passes with Fellaini and gave it to Rooney. He advanced, checked past Wickham onto his right foot then swept a pass wide for Valencia, who headed down to Blind. He played it inside to Rashford, who went back to Valencia and inside again to Carrick. He passed square to Rooney, who helped it on to Martial and out to Rojo, who played it back to Rooney. This was typical of United under Van Gaal, the long, slow probing build-up, almost devoid of risk, almost certain to maintain possession. Then, abruptly, an injection of pace as Rooney played it forward to Rashford, who played a quick one-two with Mata and, from just inside the box, his shot was deflected over off Souaré.

Blind took the corner low. It was perhaps a mishit, but it confused Palace, and Mata might have done better when taking a swing in front of the near post. He missed and the ball bounced behind off Souaré. This time Blind's corner was taken to the centre of the box, where Fellaini and Jedinak went for it. Fellaini got in front of the Australian but his stooping header was wide.

Rooney may have been the dominant figure of the half, but he was far from perfect. An attempt to slice a pass out to Mata on the right was intercepted by Bolasie, who surged forward. A rapid turnover and a counter using the pace of Bolasie or Zaha always looked Palace's likeliest source of a goal from open play, but Blind got a touch on a pass to Wickham and the ball ran through to De Gea.

The pattern of United pressure, of long skeins of passes,

working the ball back and forth across the pitch, became more pronounced, with Rooney always the man who seemed most likely to break from the calm flow and try something to penetrate Palace. A thirty-yard drive took a slight deflection and, skidding awkwardly, forced Hennessey to scramble to retrieve the ball after fumbling the initial effort. A Rooney ball behind Joel Ward found Rojo in space, only for the Argentinian to slice his cross.

But then came the sort of break to which United had always looked vulnerable. Cabaye, coming in from behind and slightly to the side, poked the ball away from Rooney. McArthur played it to Delaney, who hit a first-time left-footed ball down the line for Wickham. He chased it with Smalling, shoulder-to-shoulder, and both went down. There was a pause as the ball trickled on, then Wickham was up and in pursuit of it, cutting into the box and whipping a shot into the net. The whistle, though, had long since gone for a Palace free-kick. Smalling was booked and Pardew was furious, arguing afterwards that the advantage should have been played. Perhaps it should, although it was far from clear who had fouled whom and the free-kick could easily have gone the other way. The idea that Wickham would have scored had play continued, though, is fanciful: the whistle had clearly gone and everybody bar Wickham had stopped.

Cabaye took the free-kick, Bolasie rose highest and flicked the ball goalwards, but De Gea tipped over comfortably. United were rattled, something most evident in the play of Carrick. Usually so calm, he seemed to have an unfortunate habit of nervousness in major games, something particularly apparent in the Champions League in 2009, when he wilted in the face of Barcelona's pressing. Ferguson acknowledged that he 'lacked bravado'. Here he played a poor backpass under pressure to concede a corner needlessly. A few minutes later, after De Gea had saved a long-range effort from Bolasie, Carrick squandered possession, giving Wickham a run on goal. He created space for himself, but dragged his shot wide.

United settled themselves with another extended spell of pressure that ended with Valencia playing a pass with the outside of his right foot inside Souaré for Mata. He was half-challenged, the ball bouncing back off the full-back to present him with a shooting chance. Hennessey, diving to his right, pushed the ball away. It was cleared, returned to the box and hacked out again at which Cabaye bundled over Carrick. Rooney's ambitious attempt from the free-kick was wide and high, but at the mid-point of the first half United had had 75 per cent of the possession and seven chances to Palace's one.

That link-up down the right between Valencia and Mata seemed United's most likely source of a breakthrough, perhaps vindicating Van Gaal's decision to play Mata over Lingard. A one-two between the pair yielded another corner as a cross bounced behind off the face of Souaré. Fellaini got to Blind's delivery first but didn't make clean contact, the ball glancing off Jedinak, in attendance as ever, and behind for another corner. Fellaini was again the target, deep beyond the back post this time, but as he tried to chest it down, Bolasie got a foot in and Jedinak completed the clearance.

United were on top, but they'd begun to stutter. Pardew had suggested the previous day that United often faded in games, despite their record in second halves, and here they did seem to lose focus as half-time approached. Or perhaps Palace simply became sharper in the tackle. In that, of course, lies one of football's great paradoxes. The more encouraged Palace were to chase the ball high up the pitch, the more vulnerable they became to a United counter. Rooney, picking the ball up twenty-five yards from his own goal, tiptoed deftly away from a flail of limbs and spread the ball right to Valencia, who had space to advance a few yards and then play a pass down the line to Rashford. Palace, suddenly, were stretched and, having isolated Delaney, Rashford skipped by him, accelerating into the right side of the box. Mata was the most advanced supporting United player, drawing defenders with him, so Rashford drove the ball behind him to Martial at the back post. Ward blocked, but given how far he was from his man, there was more than a little fortune in his challenge.

That move demonstrated the positive of Rooney playing in that deep role but the attendant danger was soon exposed. His awkward pass back to Blind led to the Dutchman being caught in possession by Zaha, who drove into the box. Rooney charged back to make amends and, in as much as the attack was thwarted, did so. He was lucky, though – his tackle made no contact on the ball and, while he couldn't be said to have chopped Zaha down, there was enough clumsiness in his challenge that a penalty justifiably could have been given.

United sought to calm themselves once again with possession and a typically languorous move led to a shooting chance for Mata from just inside the box. Souaré made a fine block. But still United seemed jittery. Rojo was booked for tugging back Ward as he threatened to get behind him on the Palace right – and was perhaps grateful that Clattenburg again chose not to play the advantage – and Mata was then booked just before half-time for treading on Souaré's ankle.

It was around 10.15 in the evening of Wednesday, 8 May 2013 that news broke that Ferguson was to retire, although he was retained as a club ambassador, being paid the equivalent of £108,000 a day if he did the minimum required twenty days a year. That immediately prompted concern. Hadn't Ferguson himself stated that a 'clean break' would be desirable? Would his presence, glowering down from the executive seating, not be a hindrance to the new manager? 'He'll know when he should be involving himself and when he should not be involving himself,' said the chief executive David Gill, but nobody was entirely convinced. Gill also left the club that summer, being replaced by Ed Woodward, an investment banker who had advised the Glazers on their takeover of the club.

On the face of things, United seemed in a strong position. Robin van Persie had been signed the previous summer and with twenty-six goals had finished as the Premier League's top-scorer as United had swept to the title, Ferguson's thirteenth in charge of United, eleven points clear of City. Chelsea had beaten them in a replay in the sixth round of the Cup, but the only real disappointment had come in the Champions League as United were eliminated in the last sixteen by Mourinho's Real Madrid.

United had looked in control after a 1–1 draw at the Bernabéu, Cristiano Ronaldo cancelling out Danny Welbeck's opener. A Sergio Ramos own goal just after half-time gave United the advantage at Old Trafford, but then Nani was controversially sent off by the Turkish referee Cüneyt Çakır for a high foot on Álvaro Arbeloa. As against Bayern three years earlier, down to ten men, United couldn't hold out. Goals from Luka Modrić and Ronaldo turned the tie to Madrid. Ferguson was so distressed, perhaps having already decided this would be his final European tie, that he didn't attend the post-match press conference, instead sending his assistant, Mike Phelan.

At the time, the exit that was being talked about was not Ferguson's but Rooney's. He had – pointedly, it seemed – been left out of the starting line-up and was only introduced with seventeen minutes remaining as United chased the game. That night, after the game, he sat in a restaurant in subdued conversation with Gary Neville and Ryan Giggs, for whom the game was his 1000th for United. Diego Maradona, sitting at another table, took off his tie and sent it over to Rooney as a gift. It was a strange gesture but it had been a strange day for Rooney, the contrast with three years earlier clear. Then, barely half-fit, he'd been forced into action by Ferguson; here, fully fit, he wasn't trusted.

That wrangle, certainly in retrospect, seemed Ferguson's last great act. He had prepared the way for Rooney's departure, had made him droppable. 'I took Wayne off because Villa were a very fast, young side, full of running and their substitute was running past him,' Ferguson said after the 3–0 home win over Aston Villa that sealed the title with four games of the season remaining. Given his general adherence to Scott

Symon's rule of never criticising players in public whatever you might say behind closed doors, it was almost always significant when Ferguson did so. That suggestion that Rooney was too slow was his hint to those who would take over the management reins to move Rooney on. None of them, though, chose to do so.

David Moyes, having been recommended by Ferguson, was soon named as his successor, reward for years of punching above his weight with Everton. He had 'all the skills needed to build on United's phenomenal legacy', said Ed Woodward. In retrospect, changing manager and CEO at the same time was probably an error.

The appointment of Moyes wasn't universally welcomed. Some fans felt a little underwhelmed and, it was pointed out, he had very limited experience of European football and none at all of managing a club of United's stature.

Nobody, perhaps, was as disappointed as José Mourinho. On 7 May 2013, Mourinho arrived alone at the Sheraton Madrid Mirasierra to prepare his Real Madrid side for a league game against Málaga, having refused to travel with his players after accusing them of disloyalty. A contingent of the Ultras Sur, who saw themselves as Madrid's most devoted fans, were waiting for him with a banner that proclaimed their love for him. By then, there was effectively a state of open warfare between Mourinho and the club captain Iker Casillas. That Mourinho's fractious time at the club was coming to an end wasn't in any real doubt. That night, the story broke that United were going to appoint Moyes. According to Diego Torres in his biography of Mourinho, the Madrid manager was appalled. He'd believed he had a special relationship with Ferguson, but the outgoing United manager hadn't even called him to let him know of the decision. That night Mourinho was restless, fretful, constantly checking the news to see if there might have been some mistake. The following morning he called his agent Jorge Mendes to see if it might be possible to derail the deal and reinsert himself into the picture.

It wasn't. His previous behaviour, most notably poking the Barcelona assistant coach Tito Vilanova in the eye during the Spanish Super Cup, had counted against him. As when he was turned down for the Barcelona job, there was a sense that he just didn't fit. 'A United manager,' Bobby Charlton told the *Guardian* in December 2012, 'would not do what he did to Tito Vilanova . . . Mourinho is a really good coach, but that's as far as I'd go.' His behaviour at Madrid had raised other doubts. According to Torres, one United executive had told Gestifute, Mendes's agency, that 'The problem is when things do not go well for Mou, he does not follow the club's line. He follows José's line.'

By the following day, Mourinho was insisting that his intention had always been to go back to Chelsea, that his wife wanted to live in London.

That weekend, Ferguson said goodbye to Old Trafford after a 2–1 victory over Swansea City. Alongside the nostalgia and the gratitude, there was also an instruction to the fans that would become increasingly significant as the following season went on. 'When we had bad times,' Ferguson said, 'the club stood by me, all my staff stood by me, the players stood by me. Your job now is to stand by our new manager.'

The second half of the Cup final began scruffily. Scott Dann was booked for tugging back Rashford, then Palace caused United discomfort with a couple of throw-ins down the right, both taken long by Wickham. The second fell for Bolasie at the back of the box but he slipped as he hit his shot and it went harmlessly wide.

But gradually the pattern of the first half began to re-emerge: United holding possession, often ponderous in the build-up, Palace more dynamic, always looking for breakaways and set-plays. Valencia took a throw high up on the right, sending it back to Mata. He played it inside to Rooney, who advanced three or four paces and returned it to Valencia. An injection of urgency: a firm ball square to Rashford just outside the box, who flicked it between his legs for Fellaini. He hit his shot hard and high to Hennessey's near post and the ball thudded off the woodwork. Again Rashford had been the catalyst, a moment of imagination adding energy to the whole attack.

There was a sense of United building. A deep ball from Rooney found Valencia and Ward hacked away his awkward low cross. But Palace's threat was always there. A handball by Smalling gave Palace a free-kick on their right. Cabaye's delivery was headed out by Smalling as far as Jedinak, but he couldn't control his shot. A minute later, a Blind foul on Bolasie gave Palace another free-kick in almost exactly the same place. This time the free-kick was poor and easily claimed by De Gea.

United returned to the ascendancy and the game came increasingly to be played in Palace's half. Delaney was forced to clear behind as Fellaini closed in on a Rojo cross. Blind took the corner deep for Fellaini, who headed back towards Rojo only for Delaney to clear again. Souaré stopped a Martial run to give United an eleventh corner of the game.

Palace were being forced deeper and deeper. Another Souaré clearance fell to Valencia, who slipped it outside for Mata in a little space on the right. He knocked it back to Valencia, who shaped a cross for Martial. He made good contact and directed his header beyond Hennessey, but the ball came back off the post.

Delaney, surging forward into United's half, lost control and, reaching for the ball, made a wild challenge on Rojo for which he was booked, although Clattenburg must have considered a red card. Rojo himself was clearly in trouble: he struggled on and played the wall in a one-two with Martial that led to the forward having a shot that was half-blocked and bobbled through to Hennessey, but after sixty-six minutes was taken off for Matteo Darmian.

Rooney, his frustration at United's failure to convert their chances perhaps showing, fouled Cabaye on the Palace right. Given a third opportunity to cross from a similar position, his ball in was better. Dann flicked it on, Smalling headed out and, from the edge of the box, Delaney hooked a speculative shot over the bar. Cabaye made just one more contribution, treading on Rashford's knee after the forward had fallen in front of him following a tackle. Both were substituted within a minute, Cabaye for Jason Puncheon and Rashford for Ashley Young.

There was a lull, in which the only issue of note was the realisation that Young was playing through the middle with Martial on the left. It wasn't the first time Van Gaal had played Young, a player who had arrived at the club as a winger, as a centre-forward but that didn't stop it being surprising he should do so here. His reasoning was presumably that Young's movement could disrupt Palace, but given he had Martial and Rooney, both more natural central strikers, on the pitch, it seemed a curious decision.

Valencia bundled over Wickham on the Palace left, just inside the United half. Delaney floated the ball into the box, where Jedinak rose and flicked the ball on. United cleared through Smalling. Ward, out by the touchline, made a lunging header to keep the ball in play, helping it on to Zaha. He floated his cross towards Dann but Smalling again won the header, putting the ball out for a corner. Puncheon took it and Fellaini headed out as far as Ward. The full-back crossed long to Puncheon, who took the ball down and, from a narrow angle, lashed it in at De Gea's near post. On the touchline Pardew danced: with twelve minutes to go, Palace led 1–0.

The lead didn't last long, Pardew's jig soon reduced to an embarrassing internet meme, a celebration too early from a man who had twice before had Cup final victories snatched from his grasp in the final minutes. Darmian battled with Zaha on the United left. Rooney nipped in with a decisive challenge and knocked the ball infield to Blind, who hit a slightly awkward pass forward to Mata. He controlled the ball and turned it on for Carrick, who slipped it forward to Rooney, left of centre, perhaps forty-five yards from goal. He set off on a diagonal run across the pitch. He beat McArthur, then went between Jedinak and Puncheon and past Delaney. Souaré at last stopped his surge, by which time Rooney was to the right of the box. He still had the ball, though, and chipped it to the back post. Fellaini, having been such a threat in the air all afternoon, chested the ball down and might have been about to strike at goal himself, but Mata was better placed and hammered a low volley goalwards. Ward again tried to block, but this time he paid for not being tight enough to the ball-striker, the shot ricocheting between his legs and over the line. Palace's lead had lasted two minutes.

After the long periods of probing, there was an air of frenzy about the final minutes. Ward lost out to Martial, who advanced down the left and played the ball in to Young. Dann blocked but the ball fell for Valencia, who surged into the box and hammered a low drive across goal. Young almost got to the rebound but the ball was hacked clear.

Wickham, having worked ferociously hard as a lone striker, was withdrawn for Dwight Gayle after eighty-six minutes. Rooney, after a wild challenge on Zaha, was booked and then Zaha, having been picked out by a Souaré cross, missed his volley, although he still forced a corner. Smalling beat Dann to the delivery but headed behind again. Dann got to the next ball in but couldn't guide his effort on target. The centre-back, it turned out, was struggling with an ankle problem and, despite Bolasie looking exhausted, went off in injury-time for Adrian Mariappa. More consequentially, as it turned out, Jesse Lingard came on for Mata who had barely sat down when he checked with the other subs whether he really had seen Pardew doing his little dance. Still there was time for Palace to give Pardew something else to dance about as Zaha, chasing a high ball, got in behind Smalling but dragged his shot wide.

It's easy to say in hindsight, of course, but even at the time it was evident that Moyes was struggling from the off, the magnitude of the job seeming to intimidate him. It was, of course, a huge step up from Everton, but he might have been better advised not to have confided the fact. 'Sitting in the chair for the first time felt odd,' he said a few weeks after taking over Ferguson's office. 'I did it myself with nobody looking. I thought I would have to see how it feels in case anybody thought I looked stupid.'

His opening press conference was full of the use of 'hope' and 'hopefully'. It's a minor thing and would have been soon forgotten had results been better, but his choice of words hinted at his lack of confidence. Then there was his decision to bring in his own staff from Everton, dispensing with Mike Phelan, Eric Steele and René Meulensteen. A later admission that he'd felt the need to assert himself only seemed to confirm the suspicion that he was out of his depth.

Moyes saw out his contract at Everton, taking charge of United only on 1 July, something that immediately ate into the time available to assess the squad, identify transfer targets and complete negotiations. There are those who blamed Moyes's dithering for missing out on Thiago Alcántara from Barcelona, which is perhaps a little unfair given the player's evident desire to link up with Pep Guardiola again at Bayern Munich, but Moyes was certainly culpable for United's failure to sign Leighton Baines from his former club. He insisted on a joint bid for Baines and Marouane Fellaini, believing that would lower the price, but Everton refused to budge. The consequent delay meant that United ended up missing the deadline to trigger a release clause in Fellaini's contract and so paid £4 million more than they needed to. Fellaini turned out to be the only transfer of the summer as efforts to sign Cesc Fàbregas came to nothing. The suspicion was that the midfielder had been using United to pressure Barcelona as he negotiated a new contract; United ended up looking a little foolish, Woodward's inexperience exposed.

The issue of Wayne Rooney continued to haunt the club. He had been left out of the final two games of the season. Doubts about his future at Old Trafford were only amplified when he withdrew from the pre-season tour of Australia with a hamstring injury. His relationship with Moyes was uneasy anyway, after the manager had successfully sued Rooney over a claim in his autobiography that he'd leaked a private conversation with the player to the press during their time together at Everton. Moyes only made matters worse when he clumsily suggested he saw Rooney as back-up for Robin van Persie; what he'd meant was that Rooney was an option as a central striker as well as being a deeper-lying player, but the forward let it be known that he was left 'confused and angry' by the comment. Chelsea made a bid to sign him.

Then there was the fixture list, which saw United face Chelsea, Liverpool and Manchester City in their first five games. Of course an easier start would have been preferable, would have allowed Moyes to begin to understand his players and impose his methods, but equally the schedule could be seen as an opportunity: win a couple of those games and a lot of the scepticism about his capacity to do the job would have disappeared. 'I've never seen Manchester United get a tougher start in any season,' Moyes said. Perhaps it was an attempt to hint at a conspiracy against him and United, an attempt to generate a siege mentality, but it just sounded like getting his excuses in early.

The season began well enough, with a 4–1 win at Swansea. United were uninspired in a 0–0 draw at home against a defensive Chelsea side using André Schürrle as a false nine, but the result was reasonable enough. Transfer deadline day brought further farce as a deal to sign the midfielder Ander Herrera from Athletic Bilbao that had seemed dead looked to have been resurrected, only for it to emerge that United knew nothing of the three Spanish lawyers who claimed to be acting on their behalf. Rooney remained at the club.

United lost to Liverpool, beat Palace and then were thrashed 4–1 by City. It got worse. They lost at home to West Brom and then, after a brief flurry of improved results, to Everton and Newcastle. United's dressing room, once the most secure in the country, began to leak. Players were unhappy, it was suggested, with training, finding Moyes's methods dull. Rio Ferdinand openly questioned the effectiveness of Moyes's preference for revealing the team only a few hours before kick-off. 'It's hard to do that mentally,' he said, 'because you spend a lot of nervous energy thinking, "Am I playing?" or "Am I not playing?" and you're just going round in circles in your head.' Come the end of the season, Ferdinand would say that he and Nemanja Vidić had lost faith in Moyes when, after the defeat to City, he'd shown them videos of Phil Jagielka at Everton and encouraged them to follow his example (Moyes, it should be said, denies having done so).

There was a strange spat with Danny Welbeck, whom Moyes seemed to imply wasn't training hard enough, wasn't staying back after sessions to work on his finishing as Rooney did. Welbeck replied that he had always done that but injuries were restricting his time on the training pitch. As a detail it was almost nothing, but there was a constant drip of similar stories, which, at the very least, suggested Moyes's hamfistedness with the media was undermining relations with the players.

January 2014 brought only one addition – Juan Mata, unwanted by Chelsea, signed for £37 million. Still Rooney didn't leave and, on 21 February, he signed a new five-and-a-half-year contract worth £85 million. Four days later came probably United's worst performance of the season as they lost 2–0 away to Olympiacos in the first leg of their Champions League last-sixteen tie. Van Persie complained afterwards about other players occupying the spaces he wanted, which might have been true but was a striking breach of protocol. On ITV, Roy Keane was apoplectic about the display and then, after Moyes had given a measured interview, was apoplectic about that as well. Flatness, he suggested, bred flatness.

United beat Palace and West Brom, leaving them sixth before a home game against Liverpool. 'Their league position suggests they're ahead of us,' Moyes said. 'They possibly do come here as favourites.' It was another occasion when his honesty let him down. United fans were furious at his negativity, all the more so after a 3–0 defeat. 'Nobody wants to lose,' said Rooney, 'especially in this way.'

Olympiacos offered some relief as United, for the first time since the win over Barcelona in 1984, came from a two-goal first-leg deficit to win a European tie. Forced to attack, some of the old verve returned. But it was a victory that came at a cost, as Van Persie was injured, ending his season. Those glimpses of something brighter never coalesced into anything greater. A 3–0 defeat at home to City, Edin Džeko opening the scoring after forty-three seconds, made the end all but inevitable. Fans at Old Trafford had been broadly supportive of their new manager, but that night Ferguson was abused in the stand for having essentially selected Moyes as his successor, while the banner at the Stretford End that hailed Moyes as 'the chosen one' had to be defended by stewards.

'It just brought it home to United fans how far they have fallen in the ten months since Fergie had retired,' David Anderson wrote in the *Mirror* in September 2016 as part of a more general piece asking when the lowest point of the post-Ferguson era had been. Three of the five fans and writers whose opinions were canvassed named that week in March 2014 as the nadir. 'If this embarrassment were not enough,' Anderson went on, 'Manchester City rubbed it in United's noses again nine days later when they completely outplayed them to win 3–0 . . . The club had visibly shrunk and the fear factor, which left many teams beaten before they had even emerged from the tunnel at Old Trafford, had gone.'

All that could have saved Moyes was an improbable victory against Bayern Munich in the quarter-final of the Champions League. For a time, it seemed possible. Bayern at times looked defensively vulnerable in the first leg at Old Trafford. Vidić put United ahead only for Bastian Schweinsteiger to equalise. Welbeck wasted a one-on-one, a miss that had profound consequences for him. The forwards had all been told that in such a situation against Manuel Neuer they should shoot low because the keeper was supposedly suspect around his feet, but Welbeck tried to dink it over him and his shot was saved; it was that failure to follow instructions, it was later suggested, that persuaded United's coaches he would never quite be good enough at the very highest level; he was sold the following August, with Van Gaal describing him as a reserve player. In Munich, United took a second-half lead with a ferocious drive from Evra, but Mario Mandžukić equalised within twenty-two seconds of the game restarting and Bayern went on to win 3–1. Moyes, recognising the significance of the result, turned on his squad for the first time, frustrated by the way United had conceded their advantage. 'I've got a team of experienced players,' he said, 'and it's the sort of thing you learn as a schoolboy.'

A 2–0 defeat at Everton on Easter Sunday came as the final straw. News broke the following day that his six-year contract was to be terminated. Moyes met with Ed Woodward at Carrington at 8 a.m. the following day for confirmation, having never quite seemed to believe he was big enough for the job. There would be no such problem with his successor.

As the players gathered by the side of the pitch before extra-time, it was Van Gaal who appeared the more animated manager. As Pardew smiled and cajoled, Van Gaal strode around, fist clenched. Darmian was given specific instructions by a member of the coaching staff. As the players went to line up for kick-off, Van Gaal shouted, 'Zero–one behind.' What did he mean? That he wanted United to play as they had after conceding, that he wanted them to have the urgency of a team chasing a goal? But if that was the case, why had his sides at United so often played in such a ponderous and self-consciously controlled manner?

Young switched to the left for extra-time, with Martial moving into the middle, but at first it was Palace's attacking players on top. Puncheon initiated a Palace break with a ball to Zaha, who sent it right to Bolasie. First time, he hooked it over his shoulder for Zaha to run on to and for a moment it seemed he might be clean through. Blind, though, got back to make a tackle that was – just about – precise enough.

United reacted to being put under pressure as they had done all game, by holding possession – which raised further questions as to what Van Gaal's final words had meant. There was a spell of not much happening. Young wasted a crossing opportunity. Rooney sent an unconvincing curler wide. Lingard, though, fresh as others wearied in the humidity, posed a threat, running on to a Martial pass only for his cross towards Fellaini to be blocked.

There was a general sense of tetchiness. Rooney, misjudging a dropping ball, caught Puncheon late, and while he had seemed to be trying to withdraw from the challenge as he became aware of the Palace player, there was a moment when it seemed Clattenburg might show him a second yellow. Fellaini was booked for a clumsy aerial challenge on Jedinak. The free-kick was pumped forward by Delaney. Blind headed it clear but only as far as Bolasie twenty-five yards out. He hit a first-time shot on the volley but De Gea, diving low to his right, was able to push the ball wide.

Palace had been much the more threatening side in extra-time and for United the first half got even worse. As Palace broke on the stroke of half-time, Bolasie turned Smalling, who grabbed his leg to prevent him getting away. It was as clear a yellow card as it's possible to imagine and, having already been booked, Smalling was sent off, the fourth man to suffer the indignity in an FA Cup final.

If Moyes had seemed a little overawed by the job, the impression Louis van Gaal gave was that he felt the club should be overawed by him. At his unveiling, he was clearly keen to make a point about the overall management of the club. After a fairly routine question about fulfilling expectations, his answer was unexpectedly spicy. 'I think I can,' he said. 'But it is difficult because the greatness of this club is more than other clubs. And this club is guided in a commercial way and it is not always possible to meet commercial and football expectations. That is my big challenge after two days.' There was no suggestion of meekly fitting in, of surreptitiously practising in the manager's chair: right from the off, Van Gaal was offering advice to the directors, making an overt effort to ensure footballing concerns were never subjugated to the drive to increase revenue. That argument would take on more specific form on the pre-season tour to the US, when Van Gaal was clearly unhappy about the schedule and ended up moving the players into a hotel nearer the training ground than the one that had originally been arranged.

That summer brought the signings of Daley Blind, Marcos Rojo, Ángel Di Maria and, on deadline day, Radamel Falcao. Pre-season went well and the mood was generally positive. United again began against Swansea, this time at home. And this time they lost. 'You have to believe in the philosophy that we make again a big club but it needs time and it's not an overnight job,' Van Gaal said. References to his 'philosophy' or 'process' would become a familiar part of his dealings with the media.

United drew 1–1 at Sunderland. There was a clear lack of drive from midfield. Van Gaal said it would take three months for his philosophy to take effect – as it had at Bayern Munich. There, he'd had a difficult start in 2009–10 before everything clicked in a 4–1 win away to Juventus in the December. Bayern didn't lose until the following March and went on to win the league and cup while getting to the Champions League final. The patterns of play he demanded, Van Gaal said, needed to be internalised and that would take time.

Which was reasonable enough, but whatever stage of a process a Premier League club is at, losing 4–0 in the League Cup away to Milton Keynes Dons of League One is a humiliation. 'For the fans,' Van Gaal said, 'it's very difficult to still believe in the philosophy of Louis van Gaal but you have to do that because I am here and I am here to build a new team and a new team is not built in one month, it takes time.'

But how much time? United drew 0–0 at Burnley, recorded their first win by dismissing QPR 4–0 at home and then lost 5–3 at Leicester. They beat West Ham at home, but the sense of a squad ill at ease with itself seemed to be confirmed by Rooney's red card for chopping down Stewart Downing. When United lost 1–0 to Manchester City at the Etihad after Chris Smalling had been sent off in the first half, it meant United had thirteen points from ten games, half the total of the league leaders Chelsea and their worst start since 1986–87 when Ron Atkinson was sacked. Even Moyes had picked up four more points than that. Van Gaal began to point out his contract was for three years, suggesting that the process of reconstructing the squad he had inherited would take rather longer than the three months he'd initially promised; the assertions Ferguson had made about the strength of what he'd left behind had come to seem far less convincing.

Gradually, though, United did begin to improve, something that unexpectedly was down to the improved form of Marouane Fellaini, used by Van Gaal almost as a target-man coming from deep positions. United won six in a row in the league, although without a definitive performance to match Bayern's in Turin. But then they faltered again: a run of one win in five. Welbeck – of course – scored the winner for Arsenal in an FA Cup quarter-final at Old Trafford.

And then there did seem to come that moment of clicking. United hammered Tottenham 3–0 at home and followed it up by winning 2–1 away to Liverpool and beating Aston Villa and Manchester City at home: four games, three against top sides, all won with a level of comfort. But Michael Carrick limped off late in the derby and that, it turned out, was critical. United lost away at Chelsea and lost their next two as well. They at least finished fourth, and so qualified for the Champions League, but the season had been distinctly mixed.

Van Gaal's second season wasn't much better. Di María, who

after a promising start had faded, unsettled apparently by a burglary at the family home, was sold to Paris St-Germain. An option on Falcao, who had never looked fit, wasn't taken up. But a raft of signings did arrive: Bastian Schweinsteiger, who had been such a key part of Van Gaal's Bayern side, Morgan Schneiderlin, Matteo Darmian, Sergio Romero, Memphis Depay and Anthony Martial. This was United flexing their financial muscle.

But results and the style of football barely improved. The promise of two early wins sputtered out. There was a struggle for goals, particularly in the first half of games. By the turn of the year, United had drawn 0–0 seven times in all competitions and scored just nine goals before half-time in nineteen league games. They went out of the Champions League with a 3–2 defeat to Wolfsburg and out of the League Cup on penalties against Middlesbrough. Successive defeats in December against Bournemouth, Norwich and Stoke felt like they might bring the end for Van Gaal, particularly with Mourinho available following his dismissal from Chelsea, but the Dutchman struggled on.

United, though, never won three successive league games after that and finished fifth. They lost away to Midtjylland in the Europa League and, although they turned that around at home thanks to two goals from Marcus Rashford, an unheralded eighteen-year-old debutant, they were outplayed by Liverpool in the first leg of the second knockout round. Only the FA Cup – and Rashford, who also scored twice on his league debut, against Arsenal – offered succour. A late Rooney penalty saw United edge past Sheffield United and Derby County were then beaten 3–1. Shrewsbury away, coming immediately after the Midtjylland defeat, could have been awkward, but United were comfortable 3–0 winners.

Then came West Ham at Old Trafford. Dimitri Payet put West Ham ahead midway through the second half with a brilliant free-kick, but Martial squeezed in an equaliser with seven minutes to go, as Schweinsteiger seemed to foul the

West Ham keeper Adrián. Goals from Rashford and Fellaini helped United to a 2–1 win in the replay. Fellaini converted a Martial pull-back to give United the lead against Everton in the semi-final, but Everton rallied and had much the better of the second half. David de Gea brilliantly saved a Romelu Lukaku penalty but a Chris Smalling own goal levelled matters with sixteen minutes to go. In the final minute, Martial seized on a weak Phil Jagielka pass, surged into the box and finished calmly; from nothing, United were in the final.

United reorganised at half-time in extra-time. Young went to left-back, with Darmian moving into the centre alongside Blind. It felt vaguely typical of Van Gaal and his propensity for playing players in unfamiliar positions that his final back four featured two converted full-backs playing in the centre and two converted wingers playing at full-back, one of whom had come onto the pitch to play at centre-forward.

Palace, recognising the advantage was theirs, poured forward. Delaney played the ball forward to McArthur, who swept it right to Bolasie. He headed down for Zaha, who came inside Young and poked the ball through for Gayle. With just De Gea to beat, though, he jabbed his shot into the goalkeeper's left foot. The ball broke for Bolasie, who muscled his way into the box before Young finally forced the ball behind for a corner. The look on Gayle's face said everything: he knew he had missed a chance that might have won the Cup.

Yet United, who might have been expected to sit back and play for penalties, found new life. Carrick rolled a pass to Lingard, who played a one-two with Martial and burst into the box. A little jink created space against Mariappa to cross and when he did, Carrick's header was just wide of the far post.

United came again. Valencia surged down the right and beat Puncheon then sent in a low cross that was blocked by Delaney. The ball bounced up to Lingard, just inside the box and the substitute cracked a first-time shot from thigh height into the top corner – a stunning finish to win the game. As

Lingard swirled his shirt above his head and earned a book-ing, Van Gaal leapt from the bench and trotted forward, both hands raised, before engaging in a desperately awkward hug with Ryan Giggs.

With ten minutes remaining, there was still time for Palace to find an equaliser, but the life had gone from them. Jedi-nak sidefooted an effort just wide from twenty yards, De Gea smothered at the feet of Zaha as he chased a through-ball from Ward and then Zaha, having beaten Young and Carrick, put a long-range shot over but, having gone ahead, United rarely looked like letting the game slip.

And so Van Gaal went out with a trophy, meaning he had won the Cup in every country where he had worked. Although it hardly felt like it in the immediacy of the fractious press conference in which he, understandably, wanted to revel in his victory and journalists, equally understandably, wanted to find out exactly whether or not he was being replaced by Mourinho, there was dignity in his departure, silverware at the end of a two-year period in which he had never quite seemed to burn with the same energy or fury as he had in his heyday. He might not even have gone to Bayern in 2009 had he not lost millions in Bernie Madoff's Ponzi scheme; seven years later, he could retire and take the rest he seemed to need.

Mourinho's appointment seemed welcome with fans. After the game Wembley Way and the tubes into London rang with chants of his name from United fans. It seemed welcome too with players, who were only too quick to brief against Van Gaal over that weekend. Van Gaal's 'evaluation sessions' the day after each match were especially unpopular: so caustic could Van Gaal be that Rooney and Carrick were deputed to ask their manager to tone down his criticism. He began send-ing players emails outlining mistakes he felt they had made with attached video clips; when he began to suspect players were ignoring them, he embedded trackers to record whether the emails were opened and, if they were, for how long. There were plenty of complaints too about the rigidity and cautiousness of the tactics: strikers told not to hit the ball first time – Lingard happily ignored that instruction – and wingers told to wait for support from the full-back rather than taking on their marker.

But for United there was the question of why Mourinho was the right man then, when he hadn't been three years earlier. Needs, perhaps, must. But there was also a sense that the power of the old-school board members, the likes of Bobby Charlton, had been diminished as a newer, brasher, even more commercially oriented mood took hold. To listen to the crowd outside Old Trafford now is to hear not just the flat vowels of Salford but also voices from Scandinavia, the US, Japan and Korea. United are one of a handful of truly global super-clubs. There was a spell in Van Gaal's time as manager when barely a week seemed to go by without United announcing some new commercial deal – a noodle partner here, an official timekeeper there. By January 2016 they had the third-highest revenue of any football club in the world according to the Deloitte report, which expected them to overtake Barcelona and Real Madrid in the near future. Increasing wealth brought a change of ethos. It wasn't merely that the restrictions against which Ferguson railed in the late nineties were no longer there, it was that the club's traditional emphasis on youth, established as a core principle under James Gibson, came to seem largely irrelevant. Celebrity players, after all, have a commercial value of their own.

The appointment of Pep Guardiola at Manchester City forced United's hand. There was a need to react. There couldn't be another season of drift, of waiting for the process. Just as Mourinho had been seen as the antidote to Guardiola by the Real Madrid president Florentino Pérez, so he was by the United board. And so the shift in United's outlook was laid bare. For eighty years they had prioritised youth development. If their approach had resembled that of a Spanish club, it was Barcelona. But something had changed. After Di María, Martial and Schweinsteiger came Paul Pogba, Zlatan Ibrahimović and

Henrikh Mkhitaryan. United, like Real Madrid, had begun signing *galácticos*. Appointing a former Real Madrid manager to take on a former Barcelona manager was the confirmation of that process.

United, historically, have not dealt well with the transition from a great manager to his successor. It remains an extraordinary fact that although United have won the league on twenty occasions, that is the work of just three managers. It took forty-one years from the first wave of success to the second and twenty-six from the second to the third. The way modern football's finances are structured means it's unlikely to be anything like as long before a fourth, but United have rarely before undergone such a profound change of self-image.

In domestic terms, United are the most successful side in English history. In European terms their history is both tragic and glorious. They remain the wealthiest club in England and perhaps soon the world. But the lessons of the past are clear: when a great manager goes, there will be turbulence. The question in 2017, after an indifferent first season under José Mourinho, was for how long that would endure.

BIBLIOGRAPHY

Atkinson, Ron, *Big Ron* (Andre Deutsch, 1999)
  The Manager (De Coubertin, 2016)
Auclair, Philippe, *Cantona* (Pan, 2010)
Balagué, Guillem, *Cristiano Ronaldo* (Orion, 2015)
Blundell, Justin, *Back from the Brink* (Empire, 2007)
Best, George, *Blessed* (Ebury, 2002)
Burns, Jimmy, *Barça* (Bloomsbury, 1999)
Busby, Matt, *Soccer at the Top* (Weidenfeld & Nicholson, 1973)
Charlton, Bobby, *My Manchester United Years* (Headline, 2008)
Clarke, Alf, *Manchester United* (Newservice, 1948)
Connor, Jeff, *The Lost Babes* (Element, 2007)
Crerand, Pat, *Never Turn the Other Cheek* (HarperSport, 2007)
Crick, Michael, *The Boss* (Pocket, 2003)
Docherty, Tommy, *The Doc* (Headline, 2006)
Dunphy, Eamon, *A Strange Kind of Glory* (Heinemann, 1991)
Ferguson, Alex, *Managing My Life* (Hodder & Stoughton, 1999)
  My Autobiography (Hodder & Stoughton, 2013)
Gibson, Alfred and William Pickford, *Association Football and the Men who Made It* (Caxton, 1905)
Green, Geoffrey, *There's Only One United* (Hodder & Stoughton, 1978)
Hall, David, *Manchester's Finest* (Corgi, 2009)
Hamilton, Duncan, *Immortal* (Windmill, 2014)
Haslam, Dave, *Manchester, England* (Fourth Estate, 2000)
Jackson, Jamie, *A Season in the Red* (Aurum, 2015)
Keane, Roy, *Keane* (Michael Joseph, 2002)
Leighton, James, *Duncan Edwards* (Simon & Schuster, 2013)
Lovejoy, Joe, *Giggs* (Penguin, 2011)

Lowe, Sid, 'The Brain in Spain' in *The Blizzard*, Issue One (June 2011)

Malam, Colin, *The Boy Wonders* (Highdown, 2006)

McCartney, Iain, *Building the Dynasty* (Pitch, 2015)

   Rising from the Wreckage (Amberley, 2013)

McGuinness, Wilf, *Man and Babe* (Know the Score, 2008)

Mitten, Andy, *Glory, Glory* (Vision, 2009)

   United, United (Vision, 2011)

   We're the Famous Man United (Vision, 2011)

Neville, Gary, *Red* (Bantam, 2011)

O'Farrell, Frank, *All Change at Old Trafford* (Backpass, 2011)

Ponting, Ivan, *Match of My Life: Manchester United* (Pitch, 2012)

Robson, Bryan, *Robbo* (Hodder & Stoughton, 2006)

Rooney, Wayne, *My Decade in the Premier League* (HarperSport, 2013)

Schmeichel, Peter, *Schmeichel* (Virgin, 1999)

Scholes, Paul, *My Story* (Simon & Schuster, 2011)

Smyth, Rob, 'Manchester United 2 Real Madrid 3' in *The Blizard*, Issue One (June 2011)

Stiles, Nobby, *After the Ball* (Hodder & Stoughton, 2003)

Sutcliffe, C. E. and F. Hargreaves, *History of the Lancashire Football Association* (George Toulmin, 1928)

Taylor, Daniel, *This is the One* (Aurum, 2008)

White, Jim, *Manchester United: the Biography* (Sphere, 2009)

Whiteside, Norman, *Determined* (Headline, 2007)

Wilson, Jonathan, *Angels with Dirty Faces* (Orion, 2016)

   Inverting the Pyramid (Orion, 2008)

Young, Percy, *Manchester United* (Sportsmans Book Club, 1962)

NEWSPAPERS

Athletic News
Belfast Telegraph
Birmingham Daily Gazette

The Daily Mail
Diário de Noticias
Football Chronicle
The Guardian
The Independent
The Independent on Sunday
Leeds Mercury
Lincolnshire Echo
London Daily News
Manchester Evening News
The Mirror
The News of the World
The Observer
Politika
Sunday Post
Sunday Telegraph
Sunday Times
The Telegraph
The Times
Today

INDEX